# Thebes, Its Tombs and Their Tenants, Ancient and Present: Including a Record of Excavations in the Necropolis

Alexander Henry Rhind

**Nabu Public Domain Reprints:**

You are holding a reproduction of an original work published before 1923 that is in the public domain in the United States of America, and possibly other countries. You may freely copy and distribute this work as no entity (individual or corporate) has a copyright on the body of the work. This book may contain prior copyright references, and library stamps (as most of these works were scanned from library copies). These have been scanned and retained as part of the historical artifact.

This book may have occasional imperfections such as missing or blurred pages, poor pictures, errant marks, etc. that were either part of the original artifact, or were introduced by the scanning process. We believe this work is culturally important, and despite the imperfections, have elected to bring it back into print as part of our continuing commitment to the preservation of printed works worldwide. We appreciate your understanding of the imperfections in the preservation process, and hope you enjoy this valuable book.

# MANY MUMMIES DUG UP.

## A Great Discovery of Dried Corpses in Ancient Thebes.

At a time when so many reports are flying to and fro of the recent discovery of mummies at Thebes, a writer in the London *Times* says, it may be satisfactory to have some direct information from the highest authentic source. I am, therefore, glad to have it in my power to quote, in translation, the following extract from a private letter addressed by M. Grebaut, Director General of the Excavations, to his learned predecessor, Prof. G. Maspero, of Paris:

Here is some account of a fortunate discovery. Having found, in situ, at Deir-el-Bahari, a royal sarcophagus of a queen, and seeing that the surrounding ground had not been disturbed, I thought it worth while to make further excavations on the spot.

At a depth of fifteen meters we came upon the door of a rock-cut chamber, in which were piled, one above the other, 180 mummy cases of priests and priestesses of Amen, together with a large number of the usual funerary objects, including some fifty Osirian statuettes. Of these we at once opened ten, finding a papyrus in each.

There are a great many enormous wooden sarcophagi, containing mummies in triple mummy cases, all very richly decorated. Among these we have found a priest of Aah-hotep. These sarcophagi are of the time of the twenty-first dynasty. What we have found is, therefore, a "cache" of the same period as that of the royal mummies discovered in 1881, and made by the same priests of Amen.

Notwithstanding that the soil has remained untouched for 3000 years, some of these sarcophagi are broken, and many of the gilded faces of the superincumbent effigies are injured. The way in which they are piled up, their damaged condition and the general disorder, point to a hurried and wholesale removal, as in the case of the royal mummies. We find, for instance, a mummy-case inscribed with one name inclosed in a sarcophagus inscribed with another, while probably the inner cases may prove to belong to a mummy with a name different from both. May we here hope to find some royal mummies for which there was not space in the vault discovered ten years ago? I scarcely dare to hope it.

At the first glance it would seem as if the high priests had abstained from burying the mummies of their more humble predecessors with those of royalty. Everything must, however, be opened and studied.

About midway of the shaft now open may be seen the door of an upper vault, and, to judge by certain indications, there is also probably an intermediate vault. Had we, however, only the 180 sarcophagi contemporary with or anterior to the twenty-first dynasty, it would be a magnificent haul, the greater number of the sarcophagi being really splendid and in perfect preservation. There are, also, some charming things among minor objects.

The name has been purposely erased, or washed off, from several large sarcophagi, and the place left blank, as if the scribe had not had time to fill in that of the new occupant, but we may probably find the names of these later occupants on their inner mummy cases. One of the largest of these sarcophagi is surcharged with the name of the high priest of Amen, Pinotem.

As soon as we have cleared the lower vault I shall attack the upper chamber, or chambers.

A few words in explanation of some points in this extract may be useful. The high priests of Amen, at Thebes, were a line of powerful prelates, whose ascension must have dated back to the foundation of the great temple under the first kings of the twelfth dynasty. Thus supposed to be coeval with the visit of

twentieth dynasty (circa 1100 or 1000 B. C.) they had attained to such height of political supremacy that the first prophet of Amen not only unified in his single person the offices of Viceroy of Ethiopia and Commander-in-chief of the Egyptian army, but he actually took precedence of the reigning Pharaoh, assumed the titles and ovals of royalty, and founded the twenty-first, or Amenide dynasty of priest kings.

It was during the pontificate of the first of these royal priests, Her-Hor Se-Amen, that the mummies of a large number of kings and queens of the seventeenth, eighteenth and nineteenth dynasties were removed for greater safety from their sepulchres in the Valley of the Tombs of Kings to places where they could be more adequately protected from the depredations of the gangs of tomb-breakers which, at that time, infested the burial places of Thebes. These burial places were very numerous, comprising the two Valleys of the Tombs of Kings and the Valley of the Tombs of the Queens, the necropolis of the priestesses of Amen, and the great general necropolis, which also included the burial places of the kings of the eleventh dynasty. Now, although the necropolis of the priestesses of Amen was well-known, no necropolis of the priests had yet been found; and it, therefore, seemed reasonable to suppose that they were buried within the temple precincts.

Whether this was or was not the case, it would now appear that the high priests of the twenty-first dynasty became as much alarmed for the sanctity of their own sepulchres as for the safety of the royal mummies, and that they removed and concealed the mummies of these 180 priests of Amen as expeditiously and successfully as they concealed the remains of the heroic Pharoahs of the four preceding dynasties. There is, however, no ground for concluding that the evident haste with which the transfer was conducted points to a time of national peril. The period of the twenty-first dynasty was one of ignoble decadence and obscure peace, but the tomb-robbers were ever on the alert, and it is obvious that, unless a wholesale removal of this kind was accomplished under cover of night and with extreme rapidity, no precautions would avail. The well-founded hypothesis of Prof. Maspero, which attributed the concealment of the royal mummies to this standing danger of desecration, accounts, therefore, with equal probability, for the condition of the mummy cases just discovered.

As regards the Osirian statuettes mentioned by M. Grebaut, a large number of similar figurines carved in wood may be seen by the visitor to the Upper Egyptian rooms at the British Museum. These statuettes were made hollow in order to contain a roll of papyrus, but the documents thus preserved almost invariably consist of extracts from "The Book of the Dead," and, although in the present case we may expect to find such extracts varied with decrees of Amen and other religious formulæ peculiar to the members of the great Sacerdotal College of Thebes, it does not seem very likely that they will comprise documents calculated to throw much light upon the history of Egypt. Too much reliance must not, therefore, be placed on the prophetic utterances of those who anticipate large historic results from the bowels of this multitude of Osirian statuettes.

Speaking of the collection of Egyptian cloth and clothing in the possession of Herr Theodor Graf of Vienna, the correspondent of the London *Times* says:

That which ladies call the double chain stitch seams to have been as familiar to Egyptian seamstresses sewing with bone needles as it is to workers of the modern sewing-machine. The details of some of the garments seem, further, to prove, once again that there is very little new under the sun. There is a chemise of the sixth century which might be taken for a modern jersey of navy blue serge, and it is curious to find that the common blue check pattern of English household dusters and workhouse aprons was in general use among the Egyptians more than 3,000 years ago.

This is but one of almost innumerable evidences of the immense and practically incalculable antiquity of Egyptian civilization. Nor was that civilization, even in the earliest stages of which any relics have yet been discovered, either rude or only partially developed. It seems to have been complete and perfect of its kind. Those who visited the Paris exposition in 1867 will remember the little temple of Philæ, erected in the Champ de Mars for the Egyptian exhibit. It was a model of the exquisite original, located near the first cataract of the Nile; and the model contained a wonderful collection of ancient Egyptian curios of every description. There were seen coffins in the shape of mummies, entirely covered with elaborate figures in colors undimmed by the lapse of thousands of years. Beside them were two huge statues, one of diorite and the other of green basalt, which, as the inscriptions indicated, represented Chafra or Chephren, the fourth king of the fourth dynasty, and builder of the second of the great pyramids. Both of these statues were well preserved—so well that they looked as if "fresh from the hands of the able sculptor by whom they were carved more than 5,000 years ago." There was also a wooden statue, in equally good preservation, of a king named Ra-em-ke, which a competent critic declared not inferior, as a work of art, to the best productions of Greece. Of the jewels found at Thebes on the mummy of Queen Aah-ho-tep, mother of King Amosis—dating from the period when Joseph was the minister of the reigning Pharaoh—M. Lenormant says: "Neither Greece nor Etruria has produced any jewels which surpass them in grandeure of conception, in elegance and purity of form, or in beauty of workmanship." Among the smaller articles was a wooden spoon, representing a young and lovely Nubian girl swimming, and pushing before her on the waters of the Nile an oval basin of graceful design. This spoon belongs to the era of Moses, and may have lain upon the table of the royal lady who rescued and adopted him. A work-basket of parti-colored cane most skilfully woven might serve the same purpose to-day, though it is two centuries older than Abraham. In the museum at Berlin is the stone door of the pyramid of Sakkara, which is assigned to the first dynasty, and therefore nearly 6,800 years old. Bricks have been dug up in the delta of the Nile which, if the layers of mud deposited by the river were of the same annual thickness formerly as now, must have been manufactured 10,000 years ago. Everything pertaining to prehistoric Egypt yet found in that apparently exhaustless mine shows that in the remotest ages there was a highly organized society, with all the equipments of language, literature, science and art; an elaborate government, and still more elaborate religion. Of the splendor of the latter we may form some idea from the single temple of Karnac, four times as large as the church of Notre Dame at Paris, and reserved exclusively for the devotions of the king. We may remark in passing that, thus far, the investigations of Egyptian mythology have not revealed any allusions to a deluge, nor is there any visible connection with the Mosaic narrative in reference to the cosmogony and the early conditions of the human race.

In view of what has been brought to light in Egypt by modern research in various directions, it is impossible to doubt that man was there at a period far anterior to the date when it was once supposed he made his first appearance upon the planet; indeed, long before the date once assigned by the standard chronology for the creation of the world. If, as the highest authorities now admit, there was a thoroughly developed civilization in Egypt at least four or five thousand years ago, and probably much earlier, then when did that civilization dawn? When did Egypt emerge from a state of savagery and barbarism? When did the people who built these marvellous pyramids and temples, wrought these statues and jewels, wrote these manuscripts and inscriptions which the scholars of Europe devote their lives to deciphering—stand on the same social level with the cave-dwellers of Europe? Egyptian civilization certainly did not, like Jonah's gourd, spring up in a night. It was not a miraculous, but a natural growth, and we know how slow that growth always is, and necessarily must be. Centuries—how many none can guess—must have passed before it was possible for the prehistoric Egyptian to fashion the bricks lately resurrected from their deep grave in the Nile mud; and Abraham is a modern personage compared with the brickmakers. The imagination is staggered by the stubborn facts of Egyptian archæology, and that archæology is yet in its infancy. Sooner or later the whole of that vast volume, of which as yet we have only a few scattered leaves, will be opened and read, and when it is—if we may judge by the portion already in our possession—the earliest history of the world, and of man, will have to be rewritten. It is not impossible, hardly improbable, that an hundred years hence every school boy will know, with practically absolute certainty, that on the banks of the Nile were planted the first—the very first—seeds of science, art and religion; that there humanity first slowly and painfully struggled out of original brutishness into the dim and feeble beginnings of what it now is; that there began that upward fall of man, the achievements of which in the past are at once the inspiration of his present and the promise of his future. The pyramids have seen the rise of every society, every government, every religion now existing on the earth, and may see the end of them all.

# THEBES

LONDON
PRINTED BY SPOTTISWOODE AND CO.
NEW-STREET SQUARE

# THEBES

## ITS TOMBS AND THEIR TENANTS

ANCIENT AND PRESENT

INCLUDING

A RECORD OF EXCAVATIONS IN THE NECROPOLIS

BY

A. HENRY RHIND

F.S.A. &c.

LONDON
LONGMAN, GREEN, LONGMAN, AND ROBERTS
1862

DT73
T3R4

480819

STANFORD LIBRARY

# PREFACE.

WHILE describing the results of certain excavations which I made at Thebes, I have endeavoured in this volume to offer, at the same time, a general view of Egyptian sepulchral facts, as represented in the Necropolis of that city. Some of those disclosed under my own eye I have thought it right to set down minutely, and in doing so, to note others, even although, individually, they may be of no great importance. For, in any field, and especially where the fruits of few explorations have been circumstantially recorded, such personally observed details are useful, by helping to furnish practical conceptions as to the sources of evidence in the given branch of investigation. In particular, I have desired to offer a precise account of the large family-tomb of an official personage which a long search brought to light in undisturbed condition, not only because its contents are of interest, but because it is in certain respects the only known instance of such a discovery. With regard to the other products of my excavations, the more definite have been selected and grouped so as to illustrate the different kinds of tombs, and the state in which they are now usually found.

Indeed it has been part of the plan throughout, that the various details should exhibit some realisation at once of the conditions under which, and those by means of which, Egyptian relics have been procured. Thebes has therefore been treated of introductorily as the ancient Capital, but chiefly as the central source which has been archæologically so productive. The first six chapters and the ninth have directly this scope. The seventh (on the Theories explanatory of Egyptian Sepulture), is, as it were, complementary to the preceding five, by reviewing the psychological and religious questions connected with the origin of the customs of which these five chapters contain exemplifications. In dealing with this difficult subject I have had occasionally to dissent from the opinions of writers of distinguished merit in various walks; but I have done so always with a sense of the consideration due to deductions that may appear to be the product of thought or learning, and sometimes with diffidence as to the views which I may present. For, on such special points at least as relate to Egyptian metaphysical conceptions, I have a strong conviction that whatever can now be said is almost certain to be only provisional. And so far as I can judge (although I feel my imperfect warrant to do so), the materials as yet known are not likely to permit distinct definitions to be laid down with certainty, even when these materials have been rendered more fully available by inquirers who have made the ancient native literature a subject of technical study. But it is impossible to cease hoping that means may be found to obtain a clearer insight as to the exact nature of those religious and ontological speculations that, dimly descried through a haze of mystical allusion, still indicate the existence of ideas to which many of the sympathies of succeeding ages respond—ideas of whose history we should not willingly lose a trace.

The eighth chapter is devoted to one of those special ethnographical topics which vestiges from the tombs illustrate — the place occupied respectively by bronze and iron in the metallurgic economy of the ancient Egyptians. Certain remarkable relics discovered in the course of my excavations, required, and throw light on, the discussion of this subject, which has so many important points of contact with the early history of civilization.

I have not considered it out of place to exhibit in the two last chapters the more salient features in the life of the present native villagers — their social position, their habits, occupations, and relation to their rulers. As the reversionary tenants of the tombs which they have converted into dwellings, as active purveyors of antiquities, and as constituting in their capacity of workmen the machinery of excavation, they and their proceedings form a kind of province on the outskirts of Egyptian archæology. But whatever may be thought of this doubtful claim, it must be a very determined antiquarianism that, even on such a site as that of Thebes, can, under the circumstances, look so exclusively to the past as to close its eyes to the living interests of the present or the prospects of the future.

As the materials for that portion of the contents of this book derived from personal research among the tombs, were procured nearly five years ago, it may be necessary to explain why so long an interval has elapsed until the present publication. An early reason for postponement was that I contemplated being able to collect a farther series of sepulchral details in other parts of the country.* Subsequently, some retardation arose from its not having been desirable to remove the relics which I brought from Egypt, out of their packing-cases until the galleries for the Museum, in which they have now their place, were fitted up, and which were then about being prepared for the transference of that National Collection.† But the chief cause of the delay has been, that believing any work intended for publication to be entitled to at least such advantages as time and care may give, the demand for both in this case has been increased by the breaches in continuous progress involved in the circumstances of a lengthened annual absence abroad. Even now I have had to correct the proofs of two thirds of these sheets, about fifteen hundred miles from England.

In the following pages I have frequently had the pleasure, as occasion arose, to acknowledge obligations of various kinds interwoven with the preparation of this volume.

---

\* See p. 75.      † See foot-note, p. 90.

Although there has not been a similar opportunity to specify them, I am not the less mindful of, and would here convey cordial thanks for, other good offices, such as critical suggestions or additional information received from some friends, and assistance connected with certain of the illustrations obtained from others. The especial benefit which I have derived from Mr. Birch's philological aid various passages will show. But I must here again express my warm sense of having always personally experienced, what so many testimonies in works on Egyptian and other antiquities prove, that his learning is equalled by the liberality with which he diffuses its fruits.

# CONTENTS.

## CHAPTER I.

### THEBES.

|  | Page |
|---|---|
| Reasons for endeavouring to trace the condition of the City | 1 |
| Difficulty of following the links which connect the Present with the Past | 2 |
| The Characteristics of ancient Cities likely to be among the best aids | ib. |
| Their importance in historic Investigation generally | 3 |
| The details of few such Cities are known | 5 |
| Nature of the Data as to Thebes | 6 |
| Present Aspect of its Site | 7 |
| The Eastern Plain | 8 |
| Temples of Luxor and Karnak—prominent but solitary | ib. |
| This arising from the Disappearance of the more ordinary buildings | 9 |
| How to be accounted for | 10 |
| Temples on the Western Bank similarly isolated | 11 |
| The original growth of the City unrecorded | 13 |
| Its period of greatest prosperity | ib. |
| Its place in relation to ancient Records — Mesopotamian, Phœnician, Hebrew | 14 |
| Allusions to it in early Greek Literature | 16 |
| Herodotus silent on the subject | 17 |
| Later Writers could only describe the City in its Decline | 18 |

|   | Page |
|---|---|
| Early Greek Travellers did, however, see it ere its Fall | 20 |
| Their Works, especially those of Hecatæus of Miletus, may yet be recovered | 21 |
| Accounts of the City may also be discovered in Native Papyri | ib. |
| Instances which encourage this Hope | 22 |
| Enlightenment also to be expected from Babylonian Sources | 23 |
| Failing Narrative Description, the Nature of the Aid afforded by Egyptian Frescoes and Sculptures | 24 |
| Character of these | 25 |
| Deficient in scenic Effect | 27 |
| Pictures of Houses | 28 |
| But no Representation of the Arrangement of these into Streets, &c. | 29 |
| The Size of the City | 30 |
| How the Area was occupied | ib. |
| Probable Plan of the Streets | 31 |
| Many Phases of Theban Life in the Frescoes | 32 |
| Conceptions of it as a whole are, however, indistinct | 33 |
| This from the want of a Native Social Literature | 34 |

# CHAPTER II.

## THE NECROPOLIS.

|   | Page |
|---|---|
| Is one of the most Remarkable in the World | 36 |
| Its Extent, Nature, and Appearance | 37 |
| The Lake which Funeral Processions crossed | 39 |
| The Hills of the Desert in which the Tombs begin to appear | 40 |
| The Valley of Der-el-Medeeneh and the Tombs in it | 41 |
| The Hill of El Shekh Abd-el-Goorneh and the Tombs there | 42 |
| Tombs in the Valley of El Assasseef | 43 |
| Those around the Temple of Der-el-Bahrée | 44 |
| Those in and near the Hill of El Drah-aboo-Neggeh | 45 |
| The Tombs of the Kings | ib. |
| General Characteristics of the Necropolis | 48 |
| Periods to which the Tombs chiefly belong | 49 |
| Tombs of Various Descriptions intermingled | 51 |
| Including those of Animals | 52 |

# CONTENTS.

|  | Page |
|---|---|
| The present deathlike Aspect of the Necropolis | 53 |
| Its ancient Appearance | 54 |
| Shape of the Interior of the Tombs | 55 |
| The Scenes on the Walls | 57 |
| Tombs of Various Designs referred to | 58 |
| Nature of the Sepulchral Deposits | 59 |

## CHAPTER III.

### ON THE RESULTS OF FORMER SEPULCHRAL RESEARCHES.

|  |  |
|---|---|
| Want of precise Data as to the Details of Egyptian Sepulture | 62 |
| This chiefly owing to the Pillage of the Tombs from early Times | 63 |
| Instances of it under Native as well as Greek and Roman Rule | ib. |
| The earlier Attempts by the Arabs (*fellaheen*) | 65 |
| Explorations under European Auspices begin | 66 |
| Opportunities for accurate Observations neglected | ib. |
| The Excavations instituted by Salt and Drovetti | 67 |
| Those carried on by Dathanasi | 69 |
| His Procedure frustrated the recording of Sepulchral Details | 70 |
| Researches by Passalacqua | ib. |
| Excavations by Champollion, Rosellini, and Mariette | 71 |
| Various Points, Psychological and Ethnographical, which Sepulchral Details might illustrate | 72 |
| The Hope in which the Excavations, hereafter to be described, were undertaken | 75 |
| Preliminary Summary of their Nature | 76 |

## CHAPTER IV.

### THE UNRIFLED TOMB OF A THEBAN DIGNITARY AND ITS CONTENTS.

|  |  |
|---|---|
| Point at the Foot of El Shekh Abd-el-Goorneh selected for an Excavation | 77 |
| Arrangement of the Tombs in that Hill | 78 |
| Its present Aspect | 79 |

|                                                                                                              | Page |
|---|---|
| Such as to offer doubtful Prospects of Success                                                               | 80   |
| The Excavation commenced                                                                                     | 81   |
| The Native Method of Work                                                                                    | 82   |
| Discovery of a Doorway sealed with the Cartouch of Amunoph III.                                              | 83   |
| Description of the Tomb to which it led                                                                      | ib.  |
| Among its Contents, Tablets with Names of Princesses of the Family of Thothmes III.                          | 84   |
| Probable Explanation of their Presence                                                                       | 86   |
| The Excavation is continued along the same Scarp of Rock                                                     | 87   |
| Disclosure of another Doorway                                                                                | ib.  |
| The outer Chamber to which it gave Entrance, and the Objects in it                                           | 89   |
| Passages diverging from the Chamber                                                                          | 91   |
| Two of these found to be the Doorways of small Crypts — their Contents                                       | 92   |
| The third, closed by a Door, the Entrance of a Tunnel                                                        | 94   |
| Which terminated at the Edge of a Shaft                                                                      | 95   |
| Range of Vaults at the Bottom of the Shaft                                                                   | ib.  |
| Their Condition perfectly undisturbed                                                                        | 96   |
| Description of them and the various Mummies                                                                  | ib.  |
| Massive Granite Sarcophagus                                                                                  | 98   |
| Mummies of Animals beside it                                                                                 | 99   |
| Their Signification                                                                                          | 100  |
| Further Contents of the Vaults                                                                               | 101  |
| Opening of the Sarcophagus                                                                                   | 103  |
| Gilt Mask and Golden Chaplet on the Head of the Occupant                                                     | 104  |
| Use of Chaplets in Egyptian Burial                                                                           | 105  |
| Other Decorations of the same Mummy                                                                          | 108  |
| A Ritual Papyrus on the left Side                                                                            | 109  |
| The Accompaniments of the other Mummies                                                                      | 110  |
| Funeral Canopy from the upper Chamber                                                                        | 111  |
| Probable History of this Tomb                                                                                | 112  |
| Its earliest Occupants had been ejected                                                                      | 113  |
| Considerations as to Changes in religious Ideas which such Acts suggest                                      | 114  |
| The Sepulchral Customs themselves were, however, singularly permanent                                        | 116  |
| Comparison of some of these at different Periods                                                             | ib.  |
| Elements for such Comparisons offered by this Tomb                                                           | 118  |

| | Page |
|---|---|
| Its last Occupants—their Rank and Date determined by the Papyri | 118 |
| Details from the Papyrus of Sebau | 119 |
| Its philological Value as a bi-lingual Document | 120 |
| The Papyrus of Tabai, Wife of Sebau | ib. |
| The Connexion between all the Occupants of the Tomb not clear | 122 |
| The Vicissitudes in its Destiny | ib. |

# CHAPTER V.

## A BURIAL-PLACE OF THE POOR.

| | |
|---|---|
| Its Situation | 124 |
| Commencement of the Excavation | 125 |
| Disclosure of Groups of Mummies | ib. |
| Character and Description of the Coffins | 126 |
| The Objects which accompanied the Mummies | 128 |
| Frequent Presence of Shoes | 129 |
| Instances in which Scarabæi occurred | 130 |
| Presence of knotted Cords | 131 |
| Inequalities of Life stereotyped in Death by Egyptian Sepulture | ib. |
| The Occupants of the present Burial-Place evidently of the humbler Classes | 133 |
| Its Position in the Court of an older Tomb | ib. |
| Condition of that Tomb | 134 |
| Papyrus found near the Entrance | 135 |
| Frieze of Brick Cones above the Doorway | 136 |
| Probable History of the Interment | 138 |

# CHAPTER VI.

## EXCAVATIONS AMONG TOMBS OF VARIOUS GRADES.

| | |
|---|---|
| Tombs of the Kings | 140 |
| Ancient Statements as to their Number | 141 |
| Result of Trials at various Points in Bab-el-Molook | 143 |
| Disappointed of instituting Excavations in the Western Valley | 145 |
| Usual State of Painted-Chambered Tombs | ib. |

xvi   CONTENTS.

|  | Page |
|---|---|
| Opening of one with Frescoes of a House and Grounds | 146 |
| Another showing the Wall Subjects in Process of being drawn | 147 |
| Tombs consisting of horizontal Tunnels | 149 |
| Contents of one discovered near Der-el-Bahrée | 150 |
| Of another opened at the Foot of El Shekh Abd-el-Goorneh | ib. |
| Pit Tombs | 152 |
| Condition in which many of them were found | 153 |
| Relics from some behind the Memnonium | 154 |
| Miniature Coffin from one at the Foot of El Shekh Abd-el-Goorneh | 156 |
| Contents of another near El Assasseef | 158 |
| Painted Amphora | 160 |
| Tablets and wooden Dolls | 161 |
| Bows, Arrows, Clubs | 163 |
| Small Tombs in the Valley of Der-el-Medeeneh and their Contents | 165 |
| Account of a large Shaft Tomb opened at Geezeh | 167 |
| Excavations near the Sphinx | 169 |
| Description of two Tombs there met with | 170 |
| Their Contents unlike Egyptian Deposits | 172 |
| Skull recovered from one of them — its Fate | 174 |

## CHAPTER VII.

### ON THE THEORIES EXPLANATORY OF EGYPTIAN SEPULTURE.

| | |
|---|---|
| Egyptian Burial Customs psychologically a Subject of Interest | 175 |
| The possible Sources of Enlightenment as to their Development | ib. |
| How far we may be guided by Inductions from the Relics | 177 |
| Nature of the Connexion between Customs and Motives | 178 |
| Its Intricacy from the Relations of Man to the Physical World | 179 |
| General Bearings of the Question in Systems of Human Progression | 180 |
| Inquiry as to Laws applicable to Man's Procedure | 181 |
| Erroneous Results of Deductions merely from broad Propositions | 183 |
| Effects of Individuality and of Race must be also considered | 185 |
| This general Discussion illustrative of the special Subjects of this Chapter | 186 |
| Lepsius' Hypothesis with Regard to the Size of the Pyramids | 187 |
| Evidence of its Unsoundness | 188 |

CONTENTS. xvii

|  | Page |
|---|---|
| A Connexion between Egyptian Burial Rites and Religious Conceptions, certain | 189 |
| Its precise Nature as entertained by the Egyptians themselves, not handed down | ib. |
| Their Views as to the Relations of Body and Soul not clear | 191 |
| Difficulties in Hieroglyphic References to such a Subject | 192 |
| These specially applicable to the Ritual of the Dead,—its Nature | ib. |
| Diversity in its Allusions to the Results of Death | 194 |
| Doctrine of the Metempsychosis inharmonious with other Tenets | 195 |
| How such seeming Incongruities may be accounted for | 196 |
| Because the Religion of the Egyptians was developmental | 197 |
| Also because the existing Evidence as to their Ideas is heterogeneous | 198 |
| Their Conceptions as to Transmigration of the Soul | 199 |
| This stated to be connected with the Preservation of the Body | 201 |
| Arguments against certain Views as to the Nature of this Connexion | 202 |
| Objections to Modes of attributing Embalmment to a Belief in Resurrection | 205 |
| Egyptian Speculations too little known to warrant such specific Inferences | 207 |
| The local physical Conditions favourable to the Origin of Mummification | 208 |
| The Moral Causes which led to it gradual in Growth, and involved | 209 |
| Hasty Inductions on such Subjects to be guarded against | 211 |
| Causes of the Deposit of Objects in the Tombs also obscure | 212 |
| Various Motives might be alternatively assigned | 213 |
| Want of guidance from Facts duly classified as to Locality, Date, &c. | 214 |
| Chronological Adjustment, however, could only be relative | ib. |
| Provisional Character of Results in Egyptian Studies generally | 215 |

## CHAPTER VIII.

THE SEPULCHRAL EVIDENCE ON EARLY METALLURGIC PRACTICE.

| | |
|---|---|
| Absence of Iron objects among Egyptian Relics attributed to decomposition | 217 |
| Facts against this Explanation | ib. |

A 2

xviii                    CONTENTS.

|  | Page |
|---|---|
| The Question opened as to the Position of Iron-working in Ancient Egypt | 218 |
| Evidence from the Frescoes — significance of Colours | 219 |
| Representations of Armour | 221 |
| What the Paintings may be said to prove | 222 |
| Discussion of the Hieroglyphic interpreted to mean Iron | 223 |
| Statements in Texts where it occurs | 224 |
| Allusions to Iron in the Pentateuch | 225 |
| Mines of Iron Ore in Africa | ib. |
| The question, not Whether the Egyptians knew Iron, but How far they used it in more Ancient Times | 226 |
| Nature of the few Iron Relics hitherto found in Egypt | 227 |
| Uncertainty as to their Date | 229 |
| Evidence from the great Variety of the objects of Bronze found in the Tombs | 230 |
| Bronze, the Staple in early Egyptian Metallurgy | 232 |
| This fact of Importance in connexion with Ethnography generally | 233 |
| Inquiry as to When Iron assumed prominence in Egypt | 234 |
| Prevalent in the Time of Herodotus | 235 |
| Reasons for considering that it was Diffused by Phœnician Trade | 236 |
| Position of Iron and Bronze in the Ancient World | 238 |
| Their Relative Antiquity not to be determined | 339 |

## CHAPTER IX.

HOW THE DEMAND FOR EGYPTIAN RELICS HAS BEEN SUPPLIED, AND ITS INFLUENCE ON THE CONDITION OF THE MONUMENTS.

|  |  |
|---|---|
| The Earlier Draughts on Egyptian Relics by Rome, &c. | 242 |
| Labours of the First French Commission | 243 |
| Collections made by Salt and Drovetti | 244 |
| Also by Champollion, Rosellini, Mariette | 245 |
| Private Collections by Passalacqua, Cavigia, Cailliaud, Abbott, &c. | 246 |
| Native Traffic in Antiques | ib. |
| *Fellah* Dealers in Relics | 249 |
| Secrecy and cunning of the Finders | 250 |
| Concoction of Spurious Antiques | 251 |

|   |   |
|---|---|
| | Page |
| Forgery of Bronze Relics, and of Scarabæi at Thebes | 253 |
| Transference of Statues, Tablets, &c. to European Collections | 256 |
| Condition of the Temples | 257 |
| State of the Tombs | 258 |
| Destructive treatment of the Sculptures by Visitors | 259 |
| Mutilations by *Fellaheen* | 260 |
| Proceedings of the Prussian Commission | 261 |
| Bad Effects of authoritative Destruction of Monuments | 263 |
| Archæological Operations liable to Abuse | 265 |
| Recent Procedure at Carthage | 266 |
| Principles on which Excavations under Government auspices should be conducted | 267 |
| Mutilation of Edifices in general to be avoided | 269 |
| Grounds for Decision as to Removal of Relics | 271 |
| Egyptian Monuments have suffered much from Neglect | 272 |
| Supervision of them recently undertaken by the Native Government | 273 |

## CHAPTER X.

### THE PRESENT TENANTS OF THE TOMBS.

|   |   |
|---|---|
| Disposition and Capacity of the *Fellaheen* | 275 |
| Demoralizing Influences around those of Thebes | 277 |
| Deterioration of their Character | 278 |
| Their Inattention to Religious Formalities | 279 |
| A Muslim Festival—the *Moolid en Nebbée* | 280 |
| A Derwish *Zikr* | 281 |
| Ceremony of the *Doseh*, or Treading | 284 |
| The Coptic Christians at Goorneh | 286 |
| Degradation of the Copts, generally, and of their Clergy | 288 |
| Dwellings and Dress of the *Fellaheen* | 290 |
| Ornaments of the Women | 291 |
| Household Occupations and Dietary | 295 |
| Children and Family Relations | 296 |
| Social Severance between the Sexes | 297 |
| Evening Conclaves | 298 |
| The Nile an Engrossing Subject on those occasions | 299 |
| The River always Venerated by Egyptians | ib. |
| Legend as to its Source | 302 |

## CHAPTER XI.

### THE PRESENT TENANTS OF THE TOMBS AND THEIR RULERS.

|  | Page |
|---|---|
| Effect of lengthened Serfdom on the *Fellaheen* | 305 |
| Their Consciousness of their Wrongs | 305 |
| An Apologue on the subject current at Goorneh | 306 |
| Nature of Local Administration | 307 |
| Prevalence of corrupt Venality | 309 |
| Unsettled state of Upper Egypt fifty years ago | *ib.* |
| Outline of the ordinary tenor of life there now | 310 |
| The Conscription, a prominent episode | 311 |
| Condition of the Egyptian Soldier | 312 |
| Mode of Collecting the Recruits | 313 |
| Resistance to the Conscription at Goorneh | 315 |
| The Kasheff ensures Obedience | 317 |
| Result of the Turbulent Proceedings | 319 |
| Position of the Government with regard to the internal Polity of the Country | 320 |
| The Present degraded Condition of the *Fellaheen* | 321 |
| The Character of Turkish Rule | 322 |
| Its Prospects in Turkey — and in Egypt | 323 |
| Evils of "Enforced Labour" in connexion with the Suez Canal Scheme | 325 |
| What ought to be the first consideration of any Egyptian Government | 326 |
| The Future of Egypt | 328 |

# LIST OF ILLUSTRATIONS.

| | |
|---|---:|
| Funeral Canopy . . . . . . . . Frontispiece | |
| Map of Thebes . . . . . . *To face* page | 7 |
| View of El Shekh Abd-el-Goorneh . . . „ „ | 38 |
| Porch of a Tomb, from a Fresco . . . *In* page | 54 |
| Usual Plan of Chambered Tombs . . . „ „ | 56 |
| Section showing the Tomb of Sebau as discovered *To face* page | 89 |
| Statuette from the Upper Chamber . . „ „ | 90 |
| Plan of the Lower Vaults of the same Tomb . „ „ | 96 |
| Golden Chaplet . . . . . . . „ „ | 104 |
| Decorated Mummy . . . . . . „ „ | 110 |
| Shoe of Reed and Straw-plait . . . *In* page | 129 |
| Stamped Brick Cone . . . . . . „ „ | 137 |
| Miniature Coffin . . . . . . „ „ | 157 |
| Large painted Amphora . . . . . „ „ | 160 |
| Wooden Doll . . . . . . . „ „ | 162 |
| Section of Tombs opened at Geezeh . . „ „ | 172 |
| Modern Egyptian Silver Bracelet . . . „ „ | 293 |

# THEBES:

## ITS TOMBS AND THEIR TENANTS.

## CHAPTER I.

### THEBES.

As the tombs of the Thebans are chiefly the subject of the present volume, and as the various accompaniments with which that people surrounded themselves in death were interwoven so remarkably with the details of their life, it would seem a desirable preliminary to indicate what degree of knowledge we possess regarding their ancient city. The main outlines, therefore, I shall endeavour to trace, pointing out how far actual materials come before us for survey, where they at present fail, and whence it is possible they may yet be supplemented. In course of such a review, it will unfortunately appear that a great deal is wanting for clearness of result; and as very many features remain obscure, cause for regret will frequently arise. Nor will this be only from a feeling of disappointment, that a picture so interesting in itself must stand incomplete, but also on the higher grounds which in archæological inquiries, as constituting their real value, should be always more or less proximately kept in view, that the importance of the relics, and especially of such relics, of the Old World, is not in relation to the merely technical or isolated facts which they individually exhibit, but to the conditions of life and human development which they with others unfold.

The links which connect us with the past are as manifold as the springs of our inner life, and the external conditions which surround us. But by their continuity and fine gradation, they become attenuated so nearly to an impalpable essence, that a reconstruction, showing the chain in its completeness, while it might hardly be necessary to assure us of the reality of the intertwining strands, would, nevertheless, task or transcend the utmost powers of human perception to follow them. If one long gleam of light were to be thus thrown back athwart the ages, the most self-confident gazer would anxiously hope that it might hover luminously over the great cities, believing probably that from them he would derive the best aid to carry him on from point to point, by finding there contemporary characteristics as in a concentrated focus. For, although the seats in which men have gregariously assembled cannot in all respects, or at least in all cases, be regarded as a full embodiment of their condition, or a precise criterion of their peculiar civilization, they are, upon the whole, the most trustworthy and intelligible indices of both. Being, as it were, the adaptable matrix developed, often produced, by the requirements, tastes, habits of their occupants, or by the necessities and circumstances under which they lived, towns might naturally be supposed to bear the direct impress of co-existing public, private, and social life. Moreover, if they possessed a metropolitan character, they might also be expected to exhibit some evidence of the relative standard of skill and capacity, as well as of the general resources, of a country, no less than of the manner in which, as regards domestic affairs, these were directed either by the genius of the people, or by the exigencies of the rule under which they lived.

And since it is from facts like these that can best, or indeed, alone be traced the relationship of epoch to epoch, of country to country, of the present with all the past, they may justly be regarded as among the most valuable constituents for historic investigation. The area of History has been greatly widening since Thucydides, in his preface, proposed to himself to record past facts as a basis of rational provision in regard to the future. And if a corresponding ancient maxim is to retain any force, that the essential principle of the science is the practical benefit of "teaching by example," it can only be by an extended application. We may, indeed, vainly look for lessons deduced from consideration of political detail or individual career in the past, which would be directly applicable to the changed and changeful conditions that have succeeded. Any such hope should recall all that is included in the truth thus condensed by De Tocqueville:—"Il faut une science politique nouvelle à un monde tout nouveau." But as even in this view we cannot afford to lose the advantage of gaining some experience of what has been the sequence of events, and to abide in the inexperienced boyhood, which the ancient orator not inaptly attributed to those who were ignorant of precedent occurrences, it must be recognised that any really practical teaching can only proceed from the very same comprehensive plan of treatment as systematic ethnography also requires. There is but one pathway to substantial results, and that lies through not solely or chiefly the annals of government, but through the analytical process which would exhibit the various developments of nations and races, the circumstances of their growth, their efforts in the scheme of human action and progress, as shown by the actual products, material and moral, of their existence. And what should be sought as the true studies for such pictures are photographs, so to say, of public and social life,—not compositions sketched according to assumed laws of reaction and causation, filled in with realities, it may be, but so grouped and interpreted as merely to reflect the mind of the artist instead of the spirit of the past.* The value of broad

---

\* " Was ihr den Geist der Zeiten heisst,
  Das ist im Grund der Herren eigner Geist,
  In dem die Zeiten sich bespiegeln."—Göthe, *Faust*.

Or, as Sir Thomas Browne expresses it: "And truly since I have understood the occurrences of the world, and know in what counterfeiting

conceptions, if well balanced, is at once to be admitted; but all the more requisite is the corrective and vitalising influence of such series of facts, as might help to show the life of a people or period, not merely from one or two external points of view, but in its actuality and, as nearly as possible, in its aggregate.

From the degree, therefore, in which cities receive the stamp of contemporary thought, manners, and general development, they ought to be, in connection with relative chronological aid, one of the sources richest in illustration : and the ruins of those which have sunk are the depositories of more than curious architectural fragments. But, unfortunately, although very naturally, when their period of active existence lies far back into the past, the great majority have left in written records as little memory of the life once enclosed within their walls as the changeful course of events and the laws of resolution into crude matter have spared of their actual vestiges. Yet such recorded pictures, and such tangible remains, are each the necessary complement of the other. For, as we have not succeeded to the inheritance of the eastern prince, no wizard has for us combined both by freezing up actual examples of town life into petrifactive unity, if Vesuvius has partially embalmed for us two inferior specimens. Indeed, of many even of the great cities whose names are synonymous with central points in

shapes and deceitful vizards times present represent on the stage things past, I do believe them little more than things to come." —*Religio Medici*, xxix.

the history of the world, we have so few authentic details, or so few remaining relics, that it is impossible clearly to reduce, into definite shapes, the mere hazy phantoms of their ancient renown hovering over more or less doubtful sites. Of not more than one or two, namely Athens and Rome, whose prosperity lies beyond a period so comparatively near to us as the Revival of learning, is it practicable, from a sufficient body of evidence, to form a reasonably full conception as to their structure, civic arrangements, and daily routine; and it is remarkable how very few are so happily circumstanced from the kindly dealing of time with their own vestiges or with coetaneous documents which more or less directly portray their characteristics, that they are capable of yielding even such modified result as the partial gratification of that instinctive desire which seeks to recall in something like their reality, the dwellings, haunts, and surroundings of the men of the past, and so to impart to history that body and consistency which scenery gives to the drama.

In the case of one of the most celebrated of all the cities of antiquity, Egyptian Thebes, the data bearing upon what its condition had been, are in certain respects unusually expressive, and in others anomalously silent. The site is certain. The remarkable preservation of individual ruins of singular extent and magnificence, show the peculiar development of native art as conjoined with architectural design, the direction of its bent, and a capacity for vast under-

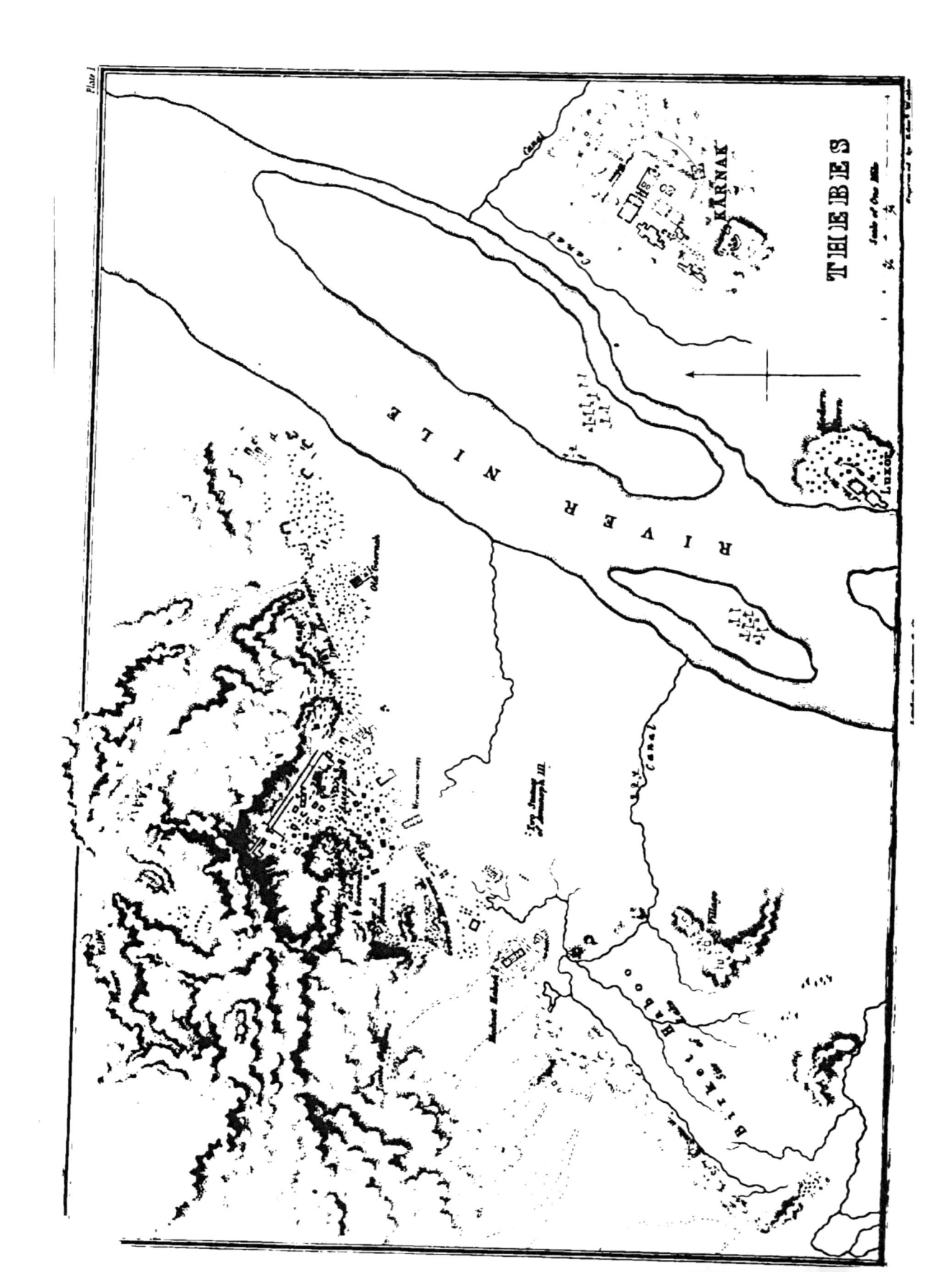

# THEBES

takings. Recovered relics and pictorial details from various sepulchral sources offer a key to a large number of the incidents of life which had concurrently performed their part. But of the actual structure of the city, of its general outline, much more of internal details, it is possible, from the very limited amount of attainable guidance, to speak only inferentially and in the highest degree vaguely. In the first place, the present aspect of the plain on which it stood is such as to offer almost no assistance on the subject. Not merely does it fail to present a sufficient body of vestiges for a reconstruction satisfactory to technical rules, but in itself it might equally defy the efforts of any beholder scanning the scene untrammelled by rigid procedure, and striving only to shadow forth to his own mind something like a resuscitation to satisfy the natural impulse which endeavours to conjure up dead cities when gazing on their graves.

Whence this arises will be more readily understood if, aided here by the map*, Plate I., we glance for a moment at the principal features of the wide prospect across and along the valley of the Thebäis, commanded from a lofty peak of the mountain range of the Western Desert, immediately overhanging the Necropolis. A rich plain of intensest green lies stretched out with unnatural minuteness under that cloudless sky. It is

* In this map prominence is given to the chief points, and the obscurity of overcrowding is as far as possible avoided. In the relation of the outlines I have with his friendly approval always had reference to Sir G. Wilkinson's excellent large Survey published in 1830.

cut into two very unequal divisions by the sweeping curves of the broad and gently flowing stream of the Nile, which glides in where a bend in the hilly outline of the desert bounds the horizon to the south, and similarly is lost towards the north. First, as being immediately in front, although three miles distant on the eastern bank of the river, and almost casting its shadow upon the water, the eye rests on the great Temple of Luxor, with its obelisk, its low heavy towers, and its sturdy columns struggling in noble contrast with the mud or crude brick hovels of the modern village, which crowd around and even on them. A mile farther and to the north, the massive portal towers of Karnak overtop a grove of palms which partially hide the forest of clustering pillars, the avenues of sphinxes and bulls, the obelisks, the statues, the endless sculptured halls, and cells, and colonnades, covering an area full half a mile in diameter, amid acres of mounds which bury other buildings within the precincts of this sacred range, where age after age had lavished its efforts of religious zeal, grafting temple upon temple.* Between these two grand groups of

---

* It is scarcely necessary to say that it is no part of my plan to enter into minute descriptions of the various Theban temples, repeating details already elaborately set forth in the well-known repositories of Egyptian research, and which those who prize them in their completeness will prefer to seek there, — *e.g.* in Wilkinson's earlier work, *Thebes and View of Egypt*, or in its subsequent editions under different titles, the last being the *Handbook*, 1858; in his *Architecture of Ancient Egypt;* in Champollion's *Lettres écrites d'Égypte et de Nubie*, and his *Monuments de l'Égypte;* Rosellini's *Monumenti dell' Egitto;* Lepsius'

Luxor and Karnak, on either side of them, and beyond to a distance of perhaps twelve miles, where the hills of the Eastern Desert spring up in waving lines, the dead level of the green and fertile tract is unbroken, save by an occasional tiny village, clumps of palm trees, the rough embankment of a modern road raised above the reach of the annual inundation, vestiges of two small Ptolemaic temples in the far distance, and here and there white low-domed tombs of Muslim saints. Yet there stood the principal portion of ancient Thebes: and although the ruins of the two masses of

> "High built temples fit to be the homes
> Of mighty gods,"

are noble relics of its greatness, the want of other traces, gives them only the significance of mere individual structures. Nor is it to be wondered at if even a bold imagination should there at least refuse the attempt to re-embody the vanished city; for the eye roves hopelessly over the plain seeking in vain for any adequate groundwork for the reasonable exercise of constructive ingenuity.

This thorough disappearance of the more ordinary portions of the old metropolis, is partly accounted for by the probable fact, that the material most commonly

---

*Letters*, and the plans and sections in his magnificent *Denkmäler*, in which, at length, after fifteen years of labour, he has the satisfaction, denied under similar circumstances to Champollion and Rosellini, to see completed, at least pictorially, the results of the three years' sojourn in Egypt of the Prussian Commission, of which he was the head.

used for dwelling-houses was sun-dried brick, which under circumstances of decay would readily become disintegrated. But considering the prevalence of luxurious taste, opulence, and structural ability, it is not to be doubted that other buildings besides the temples, whose vestiges have come down to us, were of hewn stone. Still, whatever might have been the proportions in which the work of the mason and the bricklayer had been employed, it is not difficult to see why the labours of both, except in the case of the most massive edifices, should, as they are now, be equally destroyed. In England even we have a humble parallel in Roman towns and villas which have become as though they never were, the disclosure of their substructures alone evincing their former existence.* And Thebes had even less chance of exemption from the common fate. Not merely the subject of ordinary decadence, when it ceased to be the seat of a native government, but also a victim to the fierce violence of eastern war, its powers of resistance against the local obliterating influences which are peculiarly active, have been crushed out for some two thousand years. The sedimentary alluvium constantly brought down by the Nile has continued its unresisted deposition, until at length the soil has accumulated in this part of

* The tendency of the soil to accumulate into so thick and impenetrable a shroud is remarkably manifested in the case of what was Roman London, whose vestiges are found about fifteen feet beneath the level of the present streets.—Roach Smith's *Illustrations of Roman London*, p. 18.

the valley, to a height of seven or eight feet above the level which the basements of certain monuments show to have prevailed when the great city was in full prosperity; and rich harvests now wave over its buried wreck.

Nor is the portion which covered the western bank more prominently marked. Surveying its site from the same elevated position in the mountain, there is nothing but one or two villages, sheltered by solitary palms, to break the green plain stretching towards the spectator from the margin of the river. Where it is bounded by the edge of the desert, almost at his feet, there are indeed splendid vestiges of this, which, in Ptolemaic times, was called the Libyan suburb, studded at irregular intervals along the sweeping curve of more than three miles in length, hemmed in by the circling hills. But here again their isolation tends only to individualise them, and we more readily associate them with the Necropolis which in palpable impressiveness lies immediately behind, rather than with the idea of a reconstructed city rising up in front.

Of these surviving fabrics, all of which are religious in character, the farthest to the north, as may be seen by a glance at the map, is a small and not very ornamental temple and palace, encroached upon by ruins of ancient brick-houses, at Old Goorneh, nearly opposite the gateways of Karnak, which spring up a mile beyond the bank of the main channel, on the other side of the river. Next, at the distance of nearly two miles along the curve of the cultivated land, comes the Memnonium or Rameseseum, as from the actual name of its builder it is more properly called, reduced now, as seen from a distance, to its crumbling towers and a graceful cluster of columns. Another segment of half a mile is marked by the protruding basement of the temple whose dromos or avenue was guarded by the two colossal statues of its founder Amunoph III., one of which was the celebrated vocal Memnon of antiquity, for whose low tones, as they greeted, or were called forth by, the rising sun, early Greek and Roman travellers declare themselves anxiously to have listened.* With the soil of the valley stretching flat and unbroken around them, and the harvest ripening at their feet, they now sit solitary sentinels surviving their ancient trust. The large, well preserved and richly sculptured temple and temple-palace of Medinet Haboo, embedded in the brick ruins of an early Christian town, are, with the interval of nearly another half mile, next in order towards the south; and the view in this direction is closed by high mounds to which we shall revert when describing the Necropolis, as they define a wide rectangular area, reasonably surmised to have been an artificial lake whose banks and surface were traversed by processions preliminary to entombment of the dead.

But besides there being thus no actual skeleton, so

* "Claudius Emilius has heard Memnon," is a short record inscribed on the statue itself by a Roman governor of the Thebaïs. — Letronne, *Recherches pour servir à l'Hist. de l'Égypte*, p. 274.

to say, of ancient Thebes, which might be dealt with by inductive treatment, there is a hardly less complete want as yet of the other supplemental sort of evidence, which descriptive allusions in contemporary narrative could supply. The position which the city occupied in the past, when compared with what we are in the habit of terming ancient literature, will show how little of this kind of aid might be expected from external sources; and the internal have hitherto failed to make good the deficiency. Not only does this refer to the early and literally unknown growth of what was to be the future capital, when the already mature Egyptian civilization had its principal seat lower down the Nile, at Memphis, but the same remark equally applies to the time when Thebes had become the heart of the country, and was the representative, as vouched for by monumental remains, of all that was most developed in native art and power. This period of greatest glory may be said to have been spread between 1500 years and 1100 years before the Christian era. There are, indeed, imbedded in the mass of temples at Karnak, a few pillars of the time of Osirtasen I. whose date goes back to 2000 years B.C.; and half-buried fragments have been observed by Sir G. Wilkinson at El Assasseef, near the Memnonium, with the name of a preceding king, giving tangible evidence of full vitality, under the earlier of the Theban dynasties, whose memory the historic lists and genealogies have preserved. But it was during the reigns of the Eighteenth, Nineteenth, and Twentieth of those Dynasties, that the city, and indeed Egypt, attained their zenith. Then it was that all those temples were reared, whose existence the foregoing hasty glance at their sites will recall, and although they were in some cases the subject of repairs and additions in subsequent years, their early splendour was barely maintained, rather than surpassed. It was then also that Egyptian influence was more dominant than ever before or afterwards, within the range of our knowledge, and really filled a cycle in the history of those eastern regions. Conquests to the north and south, distant expeditions by land, and even partially by sea\*, tribute or plunder of all that was richest and best on every side, great internal prosperity, if great luxury be evidence — these were the characteristics that marked this epoch.

And of all this energy Thebes was the centre, and must have been the reflex. But where shall we look for descriptions of its then condition? The thirty years' study of Egyptian writings which has followed the discovery of the key to them, has yielded almost no results in this direction, chiefly from the merely technical religious character of the great proportion of the documents hitherto brought to light. The Mesopotamian nations were in full activity, were in more or less constant communication with the Nile

---

\* See on this more peculiar and disputed point, curious evidence in Birch's *Mémoire sur une Patère Égyptienne*, pp. 31, *seq.*; ext. vol. xxiv. Mém. de la Soc. des Antiquaires de France.

valley, and were leaving records which marvellous ingenuity has only just begun to decipher. But although facts illustrative of the history of Egypt are being recovered from them, it was hardly likely, although it is not impossible, that many details bearing upon the capital of that country should be found in muniments of the public character, which distinguishes the cuneiform imprintings on cylinders or incisings on slabs. Phœnicia, again, was in active intercourse with her neighbours in those distant ages, and also possessed the perpetuating power of the pen; but a few lithic inscriptions of slight importance, and fragments of a mystical theogony at second hand, are nearly all the remnants of her literature which have weathered oblivion. If we turn to the Hebrew Biblical writings, which have preserved for us the earliest continuous narratives of ancient events, we find them so exclusively occupied with the national life and action of their race, that contemporary accessories meet with no more than rare incidental allusion. It is only in the later books, the Prophecies, that we hear of Thebes in the vaguest terms, and then of its passing glory, as the populous or prosperous "No Amon that was situate among the rivers"—"Egypt and Ethiopia were her strength, and *it was* infinite." * From Greece, too, comes only a similarly inarticulate echo of the

---

\* Nahum, iii. 8, 9. The last clause is rendered by Baron Bunsen: " Ethiopia was her strength, and Egypt without end."—*Egypt's Place*, vol. iv. p. 610.

traditional fame of the city. Indeed, during the period of Thebes' greatest vigour, the home of the Hellenic people, if not itself absolutely unlettered, left no heritage of writing. And when somewhat later the poems of Homer appear, as the first instalment of Greek literature, we have, indeed, presented to us a dim vision of the power and splendour of Thebes, by a twice-repeated * reference to its wealth. But there is only one actually pictorial allusion, the use of the well-known distinction "hundred-gated;" and *that*, as suggesting the idea of a fortified wall, of which, at all events on a great scale, there was probably none, is so far inaccurate or misleading, that a subsequent writer, Diodorus†, offers as a commentary, whether the word may not be a mere general reference to the stately porticoes of the numerous temples.

As the Greek States and their literary development advanced, some of their inquiring travellers are known, from the remarks of later authors, to have been attracted to Egypt even at a very early stage of their national progress. But to what extent, if any, they preserved records of their personal topographical investigations can only be surmised, as their works, in which such passages might have been sought, live in many cases not even by name. One, although not one of the earliest of their number, however, Herodotus, whose literary labours have enjoyed a

---

\* Iliad, ix. 381, and Od. iv. 126. † Lib. i. c. 4.

happier fate, strangely omitted to embellish his pages with some definite narration of the glories of Thebes. It is true that even he, far back into the past (460 B.C.) as his narrative would bring us, could only have depicted a languishing magnificence, for that city had ceased to be the royal residence and the centre of government more than 500 years before his day. Internal dynastic changes, and new channels of commercial activity, had turned the main but diminishing stream of national vigour, back towards its old course in Lower Egypt. Moreover, the decrepitude which must thus have been gradually overtaking Thebes was not likely to be retarded by the Persian subjugation of the country under Cambyses, when an unbelieving conqueror thought it no sacrilege to despoil the temples of the ancient capital. And this had occurred about sixty years before the visit of Herodotus. Whilst any description which he could have given, must, therefore, if accurate, have contained as an element the evidences of decline, it might yet have been sufficient to explain details of plan, structure, aspect, and civic arrangement. He has, however, handed down nothing of the kind, and, in consequence, has been rather daringly accused * by some of never having journeyed so high up the Nile, not-

* The risks of this rough and ready style of criticism are well marked off in a sentence of Niebuhr's, which insists on the fallacy of the inference, in discussing ancient literature, " that a man is ignorant of a thing because he does not mention it."—*Lectures on Ethnography*, vol. i. p. 14.

withstanding his express statement to the contrary, reiterated in at least two, and I think in three, different passages of his work. But whatever may have been the cause of this omission on the part of him who, to us, in this matter, stands, for the present at any rate, practically as well as titularly, the Father of History, his silence might be said to frustrate the best, if not the last, hope of a foreign contemporary account of Thebes in anything like the reality of its early condition. For, gradually advancing ruin had all but overwhelmed it, before the main body of what, looking to Classical sources, we are accustomed to term ancient literature, had fairly begun to flourish.

Other Greek chroniclers did indeed continue to pass over the scene, and particularly after Egypt was more fully opened up to intercourse with their countrymen by the Macedonian conquest in 323 B.C., and by the subsequent government under the Ptolemies. That some such visitors wrote accounts of what they saw, while this great dynastic change was yet recent, we know by a general reference to their statements made two hundred and fifty years thereafter by a later traveller, Diodorus Siculus, in confirmation of his own. But except the citations thus embalmed, they too have written in vain for late posterity; and the first descriptive notices of Thebes which we possess are those, sufficiently meagre, drawn up from various sources by Diodorus himself, who speaks in a manner not easily distinguishable of what the Egyptian priests declared *to have existed*, quite as much as of what his countrymen had stated themselves actually to have seen. He himself had been in the country, although not, it would appear, in the Thebäis, about eighty years before the Christian era. But nearly the last episode in the downfall of the old metropolis had just been accomplished. Dynastic intrigues and intestine struggles in the reigning family of the Greek Ptolemies, accompanied by civil commotions, led to a rebellion on the part of the Thebans, with freedom from foreign rule most probably as its aim. For three years they were able to defy the armies of Ptolemy Lathyrus; and the stubbornness of their resistance exasperated their conqueror to a sterner revenge when his triumph came. Such fines were levied upon them, says Pausanias [*], that no vestige of their former prosperity was left; and after this infliction, added to massacre, sack, and pillage, the city rapidly hastened to decay. A century later it is mentioned by Tacitus [†] only as magnificent in its ruins. And visitors of that period, such as Strabo and Juvenal, while recording like the former the wide expanse covered by vestiges [‡], or appealing like the latter to the wail of the colossal Memnon [§], could but speak of a majesty entirely of the past, and furnish another evidence for the philosopher, another simile for the poet, of the transitory character of worldly glory.

Thus it is that we do not now possess one single

---

[*] Lib. i. c. 9.      [†] *Annal.* ii. 60.
[‡] Lib. xxii. p. 561, ed. Casaubon, 1587.
[§] "Magicæ resonant ubi Memnone chordæ."—Juvenal, xv. 5.

available contemporary description portraying, we need not say details, but even a general outline of the internal structural arrangement of Thebes. Diodorus, indeed, while handing down the repute which in former ages it had held as the stateliest city of the earth [*], adorned, as he adds, with great edifices and magnificent temples, and enriched with vast revenues, concludes by stating that the founder had built the houses of private persons, some of four and some of five storeys in height. Even this glimpse, however, comes to us at second hand, is offered by the writer only on the vague authority "they (namely, his predecessors) say;" and in assigning such dimensions to all private residences, the account probably, as we shall subsequently see, embodies an exaggeration.

But it is not altogether forbidden to hope that something distinct and definite may yet be known of ancient Thebes, as it was seen by the eyes of dwellers in its streets, and it may be, described by their hands. Time entombs the past in oblivion and marches on; but he does not always so thoroughly efface his footsteps that fortune, or the energy of advancing intellectual ingenuity, may not, after the lapse of ages, find the clue to retrace them, and re-embody the spirit of the buried ages. The works of some of the earlier Greek travellers may yet be discovered mouldering in a forgotten crypt, or covered by later writing in some unsuspected palimpsest. The narrative of Hecatæus

[*] Lib. i. c. 4.

of Miletus, a guest of the Theban priests\*, about the time of the Persian conquest †, may one day be restored to the world; for, as late as the fifth century of our era, it was probably in existence, having then been largely quoted by Stephen of Byzantium; and there is every reason to believe that it contained much curious and graphic information. The notes of another Hecatæus, distinguished by the name of his birthplace, Abdera, may also come to light, as Diodorus Siculus‡ refers to them familiarly for particulars respecting Thebes, which had been visited by this Hecatæus some two hundred years after his namesake, but still an equally long period before the retribution of Lathyrus had dealt the last great destructive blow.

Nor need we, moreover, entirely despair of some happy circumstance bringing to light a still more precise account of many characteristics of Thebes, the legacy of some native scribe committed to writing when the Greeks were illiterate freebooters, and the capital of Upper Egypt in the full blaze of its prosperity. Mr. Harris of Alexandria is the fortunate

---

\* Herod. lib. ii. c. 143.

† Mr. Sharpe (*History of Egypt*, vol. i. p. 110, *pass.*) places the visit of Hecatæus some years before that event, in which case he would have seen the city as it stood, unscathed by its first foreign conquerors. But a consideration of the facts in the life of this traveller would seem to show that he had not been in Egypt until ten or twelve years after Cambyses subdued that country. Vide *Hecatæi Milesii Fragmenta*, ed. Klausen, p. 9. Mr. Birch dates this visit in 521 B.C., or not more than about two years after the Persian conquest. *Egyptian Hieroglyphs*, p. 180.         ‡ Lib. i. c. 4.

possessor of a splendid roll of Papyrus, procured, I believe, at Thebes, and dated in the reign of Rameses III., about 1200 years B.C., which, so far as it has been unwound, as yet but a little way, describes with a minuteness hardly less elaborate than the terms of an architect's specification, an extensive building, which the owner of the manuscript, after laborious comparison, was inclined to regard as one of the temple-palaces of Medinet Haboo.[*] That other scrolls of more special interest than those which accompanied the dead as ritualistic formulæ, may yet give similar evidence respecting other more secular structures or portions of Thebes, and generally of its urban characteristics, is not beyond the range of hope. But besides the possibility of such descriptions coming to us in a manner so precise and formal[†], they may be found imbedded incidentally in some such carefully-drawn deeds and conveyances of property as are known to have been used, from specimens, almost barren, however, in this respect, collected by Dr. Young[‡]; or they might be allusively interwoven in fictitious narratives[§], whose creation might

---

[*] I have since heard that this extraordinary papyrus has just been entirely unrolled, measures 150 feet in length, and is supposed to contain a kind of rent-roll of Rameses III.

[†] Clement of Alexandria, in the second century A.D., mentions the existence of a work, among many others in the native language, on the Chorography of Egypt, &c. *Stromat.* vi. 4, p. 633, ap. Birch, *Hieroglyphs*, p. 185.

[‡] *Discoveries in Hierog. Literature.*

[§] *Revue Archæol.* vol. ix. p. 385.

be predicated, and of whose composition there is also proof, in the romance translated by De Rougé, and entitled "The Two Brothers," dating from the thirteenth century before the Christian era. Based upon an incident very much like that in the early life of Joseph in Potiphar's house, this story, in accordance with the ordinary idea of narrative common in the ancient world, has little or no regard to scene or outward circumstances beyond mere locality, and introduces only the actors, their deeds, and their relation to supernatural agencies. Still its mere existence, and that of the other species of documents adverted to, is some sort of augury that the city and inner life of the ancient Thebans may be destined to be yet disclosed with fuller illustration than hitherto, from sources like these.

We are reminded too of the hoards of primeval knowledge stored up for future ages in the vast mounds of Babylonia; and even on Egyptian subjects there might be looked for from them an unanticipated wealth of enlightenment, especially if further research should confirm the authenticity of certain remarkable documents which a distinguished orientalist has just reintroduced to prominent notice.[*] These are Arabic manuscripts of the tenth century, purporting to be translations of Babylonian books, written about thirteen hundred years before the Christian era. They are of

---

[*] *Ueber die Ueberreste der Altbabylonischen Literatur in Arabischen Uebersetzungen*, von D. Chwolson. St. Petersburg, 1859.

marked importance in themselves, but their striking, and, indeed, startling interest, consists in pointing to what might be really called a literary activity, not only in operation then in Babylon, but also very much earlier, and having reference to a great variety of topics at home and abroad.

But while contemplating with more or less reliance the prospect of a further harvest of old world literature, it might be thought that in the actual absence of descriptive narrative bearing upon the flourishing condition of Thebes, the deficiency ought to be largely supplied by the products of that genius for pictorial decoration which distinguished the ancient Egyptians, "catching the manners living as they rose," and transferring them to the walls of tombs and temples. On one important branch of the subject, the manners of the people and the general nature of their civilization, they present an unexampled body of evidence: as to the appearance, structure, and special characteristics of the city, they offer almost or absolutely none. In these remarkable delineations nearly every episode in social and public life, where individual and even collective operation is implied, is depicted with dramatic precision. But the spirit of the style is only restrictedly scenic, being content for the most part if, by a bare representation of the *action*, the subject intended to be portrayed is, as it were, emblematised, there being generally no effort to exhibit the external accessories. Thus all the labours of tilling and reaping are often depicted with an accuracy so scrupulously minute as regards the actors, that touches are introduced into the picture almost superfluous, save in the eyes of a very honest copyist, or of a more ingenious draughtsman artistically exercising his power of composition to impart reality by throwing in characteristic details. At one corner of such a field-view may perhaps be seen a thirsty gleaner on his knees drinking from a water-skin, suspended in the lower branches of a tree; at another point a colley, or cur, stands with airy impudence at the heel of his master the overseer, who leans upon his staff. But with all this fidelity of design there may not be the slightest hint as to the nature of the country in which the operations are going on, and the information deducible will generally be restricted to the various phases of action in the piece. Again, a yoke of oxen with curving neck and steady step bend willingly to the plough, but there is not a trace even of the furrows which they are making. Hounds and huntsmen with the lasso and the bow pursue the flying and wounded deer, whose drooping head and faltering step are sometimes rendered with pathetic simplicity; but the waving line over which they career is all that represents what probably was the rough undulating desert where the chase takes place. A king on his throne receives the homage of his subjects, and the spoils of his enemies, but the palace, the temple, the hall, or the court where the ceremony is held is not attempted, or only, as in a few cases, by the confused insertion of a stray pillar. A festive party enjoy the luxuries of a hospitable feast listening at the same time to bands of music; but the chamber in which the banquet is spread is left to the imagination.* Craftsmen of every kind diligently ply their trades; the materials they employ, the tools they use, even the manufactures they produce are minutely set forth; but the workshops in which the various processes were performed have no place. In short, the actors and what objects may be necessary to identify them with their pursuits, are alone depicted — a species of *tableaux vivants* without the scenery.

It cannot be said that this peculiarity or imperfection of style was inevitable from the medium through which the representation was to be expressed. No doubt it to a great extent was so, when an incised surface was made to bear the subject in bas relief or intaglio, for then the piece being sculptural, its components, almost of necessity, were limited to the frigidly statuesque, from which they could only have been relieved, and that but partially, by a highly artificial elaboration. But the artists of ancient Egypt did not confine themselves to this mode of perpetuating their works. For although on the temples in nearly all important cases, and in very many of the sepulchres, it is found to prevail, there is still a large number of other tombs on whose smoothly-plastered walls *fresco*-painting (if the term may be used with-

---

* In these allusions I am referring to the actual scenes in the tombs as I have noted them. Copies of specimens of most or all may be found in the illustrated works on Egyptian Antiquities, mentioned in a previous note (p. 8), and in many others.

out confusion), was the method of decoration. There the colourists might have been as pictorial as the extent of their skill admitted, or the canons of taste to which they adhered, allowed. But they followed with the brush the same rules which guided the chisel, the same conventional perspective, the same characterisation of action and individual objects to the neglect of efficient scenic composition, which distinguish the sculptured bas-reliefs. In short, this was the peculiar or limited development of Egyptian art,—and not of Egyptian art alone; but it is remarkable that, although in a few instances there are traces of something better, beyond this rudimentary stage, which was very early attained, it never progressed. So it first dawns upon us in the most ancient tombs around the pyramids of Geezeh; so it remained practically unchanged until its final extinction, having descended unaltered through ages of flourishing national existence, of foreign aggression, and repeated conquests. With reference to this permanence of style, Plato, alluding to the subject in another aspect, expresses, save as to lengthened duration, only what the monuments plainly testify, when he says,—that statues and pictures produced by the Egyptians ten thousand years before, were in no respect better or worse than those executed in his own time.

And even when the artists, as in several still-existing examples, touched subjects in which life or action was in the nature of the case subordinate, and general outline everything, their conventionalism of perspective, or rather their ignorance of it, was fatal to their success. Their deficient apprehension, too, of the pictorial idea, or their inability executively to realise it, narrowed down their efforts in this direction to the mere presentation of individual forms or objects. Thus, in a few, I would add too few, of the wall paintings, we have crude representations of houses[*] of two or three different descriptions, but they are never grouped,—never so set forth as even to produce an approach to the most limited panoramic effect. They are, in fact, mere emblems or hieroglyphics on a large scale, with less actual suggestive scope than analogous embodiments in the most angular specimens of mediæval needlework. They are, however, sufficient, and no more, to give some sort of idea of the appearance, and partially of the structure, of certain Egyptian houses individually, as inhabited three thousand years ago. It may thus be gathered that the general plan seems to have been that still so common in the domestic architecture of countries to the South and East, in which the chambers enter from an open central court, subdivided if large, and planted with single branching trees according to its dimensions. The external or street-elevation depended of course upon the importance of the house. The paintings show some to be mere

---

[*] Copies of some of these, and an elaborate elucidation of them, will be found in Wilkinson's *Ancient Egyptians* (vol. ii. pp. 93, *et seq.*), where so many details of Egyptian archæology are so carefully stored. For plates of houses see also Rosellini, *Mon. Civ.* t. lxxxviii. *et seq.*

quadrangular cubes pierced by a doorway with fillet and bead mouldings, and by one or two corresponding windows, answering to a height of two storeys. The loftiest of which any example is given, cannot be set down at more than three storeys; and its exterior is much more ornate. In this case, spaces not occupied by windows, are panelled; and slender columns rise from the ground to the flat corniced roof, which rests upon short pillars springing from the walls, thus forming on the top a sort of verandah sheltered from the sun, and open to the cooling breeze. Other houses, surrounded by gardens and pleasure grounds laid out with ponds and trees, had massive gateways or pillared porticoes; and, confined apparently in great part to the height of one storey and a basement, they were spread over a more considerable space.

But how any or all of those dwellings were collocated together—in streets, or squares, or quarters, or suburbs, or what was the general aspect of the city or of any portion of it, cannot be gleaned from the fresco subjects. Its great extent in mere area the position of the present traces and ruins may so far testify; and Diodorus, quoting predecessors, gives its *circuit* at one hundred and forty stadia, or sixteen English miles; while Strabo mentions that the vestiges in his day covered a *length* of eighty stadia or nine English miles and nearly a quarter.\* It has been pointed out that

---

\* The enormous areas stated to have been occupied by a few of the ancient cities may be noted by way of comparison:—Babylon about 14 miles square (Herod. lib. i. c. 178); Syracuse 22 miles in circuit (Grote's *Greece*, vol. iii. p. 481); Carthago 23 miles in circuit (Liv.

in actual numerical strictness there is a very great discrepancy between those two statements *; but both were most likely mere approximate estimates, and Strabo when writing of length may by no means have had in view a medium, or even a direct diameter. Moreover, the stadium having been fundamentally an indicator of distance with reference to time of transit †, like the German *stunde*, need not always in general description be considered a precise definition. In any case there is every reason to believe from the existing state of matters, that an average segment of the ground on which Thebes stood would measure from four to five miles. But in what way this space was occupied or apportioned we can only conjecture. If we suppose it filled up and peopled in accordance with modern European conceptions, the result would be vast even in this which has been called "the age of great cities," ‡ the dimensions above indicated being very little less than those of the present site of London.§ But looking to a characteristic feature of

---

*Hist.* ii.); and an Arabic traveller of the end of the twelfth century, Abd-Allatif (*Relation de l'Egypte*, trad. par De Saucy) avers that the ruins of Memphis in Lower Egypt covered, in his time, a space half a day's journey across in each direction.

\* Wilkinson, *Thebes and View of Egypt*, p. 42.

† See summary of Ukert's discussion,—Smith's *Dict. of Ant.*, sub *Mensura*.

‡ This title as supposed not unreasonably to be characteristic, has been selected for a work on social polity, of some ingenuity,—Vaughan's *Age of Great Cities*, 1843.

§ Although the greatest length of street in London is about 14 miles from east to west, the estimated admeasurement of the occupied area as computed in a solid mass, is about 7 miles by 4.

large eastern towns, — to the pleasure grounds, even the fields and orchards included within the limits of ancient Babylon[*] — to the numerous gardens which diversify modern Damascus, and comparing the Egyptian plans of villas surrounded each by what our older writers would term a spacious pleasaunce, it seems most probable that a certain proportion of the expanse of Thebes was taken up by luxurious dwellings like these.

As to the roadways, if we also seek an analogy in long prevalent oriental custom, we must imagine them to have been in large proportion as narrow, gloomy, and cavernous, as the powerful rays of a southern sun are supposed to demand.[†] It is true that we might expect wide thoroughfares [‡] to the splendid temples

---

[*] Rawlinson's *Herodotus*, vol. ii. p. 570. See corroborative notes; and also the remarks by Layard on ancient Nineveh. *Nineveh and its Remains*, vol. ii. p. 243.

[†] On the other hand, we may bear in mind that Herodotus in describing ancient Babylon, dwells upon the straight streets by which it was all transversely intersected (Herod. lib. i. c. 180). Mr. Grote (*Hist. of Greece*, vol. iii. p. 394) in commenting upon this passage remarks, that the traveller could not fail to "have his astonishment heightened by remarking the *broad* and straight streets, unknown in a Greek town until the distribution of the Piræus by Hippodamus, near the time of the Peloponnesian War." I do not find, however, that Herodotus, in stating the streets to be straight, makes any observation as to their having been broad (τὰς ὁδοὺς ἰθείας, lib. i. c. 180, as above), and his mention of there having been small gates at the end of certain of them would rather point the other way.

[‡] Amunoph III., who added at least two great temples to the city, is stated in Papyri to have made the "Royal Street" at Thebes; but of what nature the avenue so distinguished was, it is impossible to say.

with some corresponding architectural pretensions; although we may at the same time remember the fact of mediæval cathedrals rising up amid compact masses of contemporary hovels. Upon the whole, looking to the style of Egyptian architecture and to the paintings, the probability is against lines of handsome façades to any considerable extent; and in the portions of the city more particularly devoted to residence, the streets were most likely flanked by elevations either blank or rarely pierced, or by high dead walls which, in the case of some of the more important dwellings, enclosed them and their appendages. An allusion by Homer [*] goes to show that a Greek house of that early period was surrounded in this manner; and among other similar examples in Egyptian paintings, I uncovered one on the wall of a tomb, afterwards to be described, in which this arrangement was very plainly to be seen.

But even if we may thus endeavour, vaguely and indefinitely it is true, to conceive something of the shell, we would naturally, as of still more importance, desire some knowledge of the life which circulated within it. The paintings have indeed preserved the reflex of a number of phases such as Thebes might have presented. There are tradesmen of various kinds, as they might have worked in their shops; guests at table, as they may anciently have feasted; conquered tributaries bearing the spoils of their countries, as they

---

[*] Odyss. i. 441.

may actually have borne them to the foot of the Diospolitan throne in a military triumph; funeral and other religious processions, as they may have wound their way to the Necropolis, or marched through the avenues of the stately temples. A recent writer * has strung together these various episodes as rendered in the mural decorations, with the view of constructing a Theban scene of the time of the great Eighteenth Dynasty. But although he has used his materials with considerable boldness, and strained some of them, as was almost inevitable, into rather dubious points of contact, the result wants the cohesion of natural connexion, and the individual subjects, being such as I have just mentioned, merely stand as a few of the active incidents of Egyptian civilization.

The integral character of life in the great city, fails to come before us from these and the other sources as yet at command. The specialties of trade, the powers of production, the fountains of supply, the relation of classes, the ordinary occupations of those not engaged in handicraft, the channels of mental culture, the administration of law, the relation which religion in its ceremonial and directer influences bore to daily cares and duties, the springs of common inte-

---

* Feydeau, in his *Histoire des Usages Funèbres*, pp. 136, *seq.* the finish of whose plates is remarkable even in these days of skilful illustration. His attempt referred to above has been popularised or paraphrased — and, as regards accuracy, not, it may be supposed, improved — in a fantastic novelette entitled *Roman de la Momie*, by Th. Gautier.

rest or sectional action — these, the true peculiarities of status, can be but imperfectly traced in their elements. It is true that by proceeding deductively the rough outlines might to some extent be predicated, and by reasoning on theoretical principles it might be assumed that a given series of conditions would prevail in a society living under the general circumstances which records and vestiges reveal. But such inferential portraiture would, for purposes of inquiry, amount to little, as it would want that realism which could alone assure us that we had caught the features of a special or national development. And while this essential quality is too deficient for the actual depicting of city life in ancient Egypt, it is curious to remark how a very few touches might have supplied it to a degree almost unequalled. For, most significant indications do abound, in the painted representations of so many facts in pursuits and in manners; and it is easy to perceive to what extent these would have acquired unity and vitality, if supplemented only by a little more of the scenic effect of art, or by a little of the informing spirit exhaled from the pages of writers unconsciously embodying the circumstances which surrounded them. They are in truth, as the dry bones in the prophet's vision, fit to be thus clothed upon and animated—ready for the invocation, "Come from the four winds, oh breath, and breathe upon them that they may live." But the breath we seek, is a breath bearing the echoes of a contemporary social literature. And we have no orations of an Egyptian Demosthenes or Æschines instinct with allusions to the condition of the people to whom they were addressed, or dealing specially with discussions of public and even personal career. We have no odes of a Theban Horace lightly reflecting the city life, whose incidents were mainly their theme; no Juvenal broadly depicting the follies and vices, but concomitantly, with some exaggeration, the habits and manners of his time; no letters of a Cicero or Pliny, not only preserving the motives and lines of thought which actuated statesmen and other members of the then great intellectual world, but also detailing the routine of their relaxations and their cares. And so, while the old Egyptian metropolis breaks the indistinct horizon of the past with impressive vastness, the cloud which overhangs it lifts only here and there, disclosing specific points with anomalous minuteness, and shrouds its general features as well as the full current of existence which gave them form, with a thick gloom, now nearly impenetrable, but not perhaps destined never to be rolled away.

## CHAP. II.

### THE NECROPOLIS.

But if the memories of Theban life have been, in so great a measure, swept away with the dwellings in which it had developed itself, the realities and accessories of death have been largely handed down in, and along with, what the ancient people themselves termed their "eternal homes." The beliefs and practices connected with the close of the earthly career, and the disposal of the deserted wreck of mortal humanity, have been prominent influences in the character of all races, but they were very specially so with the Egyptians. And the Necropolis of Thebes will share with that of Memphis the distinction of being the most remarkable exemplar in the world of that peculiarly human phase of action which, whether guided always by dim forecastings of futurity or not, deals with sepulchral usages. Its great extent, and the elaborate nature of many of the tombs, would also, if the temples had been levelled and history silent, be very certain evidence of the size, magnificence, and resources of a city whose people, being dead, yet speak thus far through the medium of their vast abode.

The now cultivated land on which the western or Libyan district of the town stood, bounds with the rocky desert for almost three miles and a half; and back from this line along nearly its entire and somewhat circuitous length, the pits and doorways of the sepulchres are closely crowded together. They commence immediately behind the range of temples, mentioned in the previous chapter as planted at intervals along the curving boundary which, with more than figurative propriety, linked, as it were by religious ties, the activities of life in front with the solemnities beyond. And stretching over every available spot, the flats being occupied with shafts perpendicularly cut down into the rock, the low hills and crags being pierced with horizontal chambers similarly tunnelled, the tombs (those of the kings not here being referred to) cover a space varying from a few hundred yards to nearly a mile in breadth, ceasing only when the mountains of the Libyan Desert present too impracticable a face. The shifting sands, drifted like snow-wreaths over slope and hollow, partially hide the surface of the rock beneath, but neither so completely nor extensively as to conceal how closely it is perforated throughout nearly all the tortuous windings given to this tract by the configuration of the desert range. The mountains, unsubdued by any softening influence of vegetation, here bound the Nile valley with something of the rugged character of a bold coast line. A projecting spur called El Drah-aboo-Neggeh abuts like a headland near the northern extremity of the Necropolis: the southern may be said to be marked by a similar but insulated hill called El Goornet Murrawée. Between those the main chain recedes westwards with a circular sweep; but a third hill, El Shekh Abd-el-Goorneh, rises up in the bay thus formed which, with irregular undulations of rock and sand, stretches to the foot of the precipitous cliffs, here constituting the first deep stratum of the base from which the mountains in the background spring into pyramidal peaks.

The three spurs just named, and particularly the last from its central position, and the numerous doorways of tombs which pierce its sides at every point with nearly the frequency but less than the regularity of windows in some gigantic ruin, give its chief character to any comprehensive view of the Necropolis as seen in approaching it from the river. Something of this general effect can be gathered from Plate II. the details of which a subsequent chapter will more fully explain. But the map (Plate I. p. 7) is necessary to show the actual topography; and by referring to it, a few pages, indicating the main points as they occur in proceeding from one end to the other, may give a fair approximate conception of the Necropolis as a whole.

Starting at the southern extremity we find, first, a large flat oblong space referred to in the former chapter, and measuring about a mile and a half in length and more than half a mile in breadth.

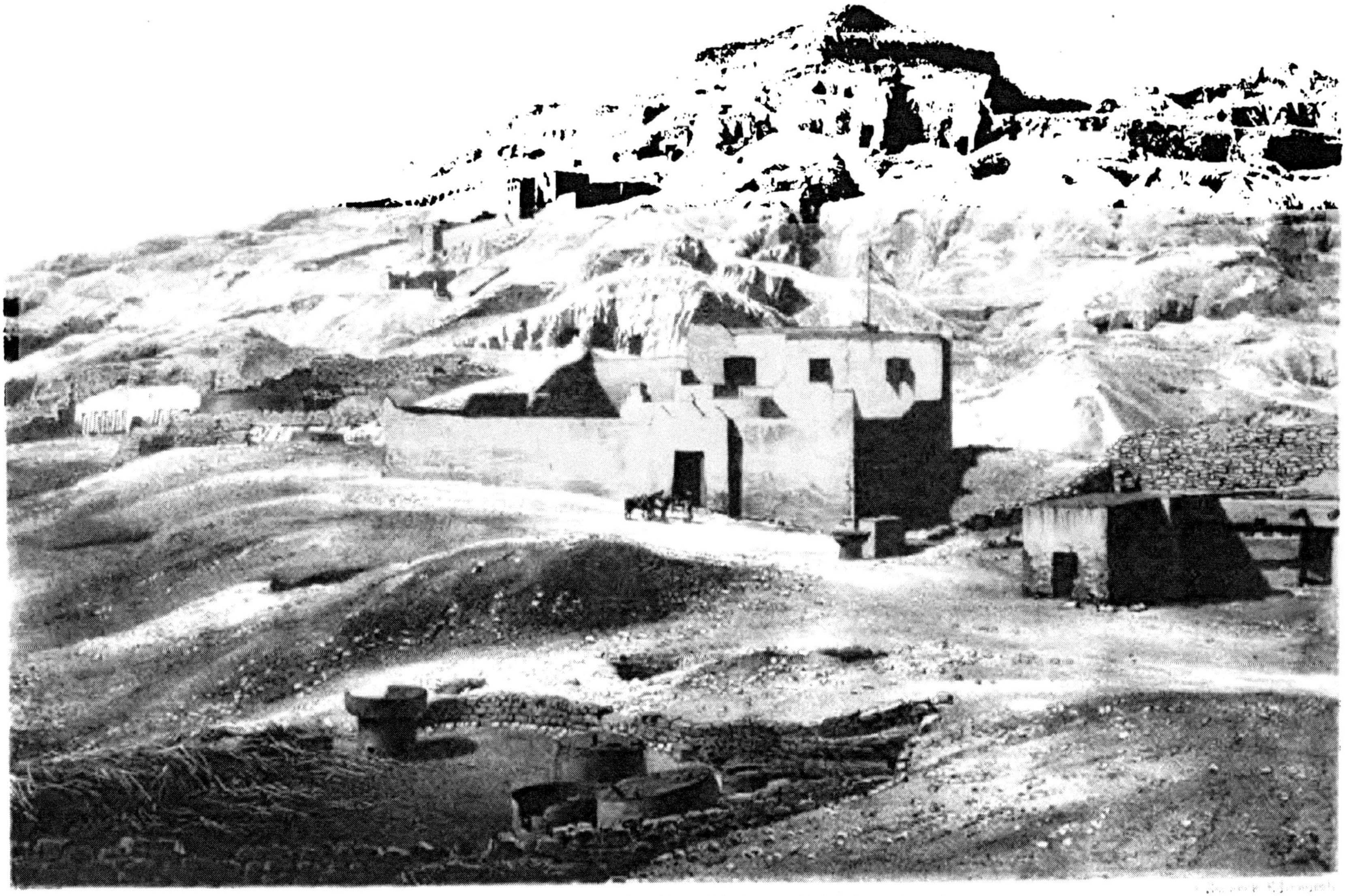

It lies just at the edge of the desert, is somewhat depressed with reference to the surrounding level, and is defined along the greater part of its outline by high mounds* of sand on the one side and of the soil of the valley, on which it trenches, on the other. Besides coming naturally first in order by position, it might also not inappropriately be the commencement of a survey of the Necropolis, having been, as it were, the threshold over which the old denizens of the tombs themselves passed on to their sepulchral city. The fresco and relievo mural pictures of funeral subjects frequently represent ceremonial processions of boats or barges. Diodorus Siculus, copying, perhaps, as was his wont, from more ancient observers than himself, describes a lake as playing an important part in the rites of Egyptian sepulture, and tells of forty judges holding solemn court upon its margin to decide whether any accusation raised against the moral life of the deceased person brought so far on the way to burial, was such as to prevent his being ferried over, the symbol of his having earned an honourable rest.† It is not improbable that, as regards the details of this remarkable judicial procedure, Diodorus, or his authority, may have trans-

---

\* Cutting a section through one of those mounds was one of my unexecuted designs.

† Diod. Sic. lib. i. c. 7. He is here describing Egyptian burial without direct reference to locality, but it may be said that the lake he had particularly in view was at Memphis, as he names it a few pages further on in the same chapter.

muted or, by error, transferred to an earthly ceremonial, the mystical teaching of the ancient Egyptian ritual, wherein such an ordeal is set forth as awaiting the disembodied spirit. But, considering the specific mention of a lake, considering the processions in the fresco scenes, and the appearance and situation of the large basin-like enclosure above referred to, it would seem to be the excess of pyrrhonism and the adoption of a mere conjecture in opposition to the force of what evidence exists, to agree with a recent French writer in supposing that the statement of Diodorus is throughout, including the alleged existence of the lake, a confused adaptation to real circumstances of the native doctrine as to the soul's futurity,—that the barges in the mural subjects have only reference to the funeral cortege on its passage on the Nile,—and that the area in question, instead of a sheet of water, had been a sort of Champs de Mars for military spectacles or reviews.

A flat tract of desert about a mile in width lies between this enclosure and the Libyan hills to the north-west, in whose skirts the tombs begin to appear. Those scattered at intervals in the lower slopes, and none are here to be seen high up, are little more than cell-like apertures, neither numerous nor of very definite character. In one, however, of the short ravines, which, like a deep cleft runs into the mountains, an important range of sepulchres have their place. They are tombs of a few of the queens and princesses of the Eighteenth and Nineteenth

Dynasties as identified by the inscriptions. They are of no very considerable dimensions, consisting each of a small cutting about nine feet high by five or six broad terminating in a corresponding chamber—all hewn into the hill-side. The sculptures or paintings with which their walls were covered have suffered so greatly, that in none are they in good condition, while in some they are almost entirely obliterated.

In all this back district of the southern end of the Necropolis, sepulchral cells and tablets cut in the rock, occur here and there in the ravines formed by the lower clustering hills, but the first continuous grouping of the tombs is met with in the gorge which insulates El Goornet Murrawée, and which is named after a small Ptolemaic temple, Der el-Medeeneh, standing at its innermost angle. From side to side and down towards the mounds of Medinet Haboo, the whole valley is filled with pits half hidden by the crumbling brick mould of the superstructures which had covered them. Many of those very probably belonged to the comparatively late time, between one and two centuries before Christ, when the neighbouring temple of Der el-Medeeneh was built and kept in repair, the sculptures on whose walls are prominently sepulchral; but amid the general ruin and overthrow of the brick erections, some with interior paintings on a coating of clay or stucco, have been recognised and described by Sir G. Wilkinson as dating from a period as early as the Eighteenth Dynasty. In the rocky sides of the valley the usual excavated chambers are studded, and these extend at intervals around the southern end and along the front of El Goornet Murrawée, where they first form part of the general expanse of the Necropolis facing the river. Here, however, they soon cease for a space as the hill sinks into the level tract which divides it from El Shekh Abd-el-Goorneh, and which is partly occupied by the pits or perpendicularly excavated tombs adapted for the flat surface. But whenever El Shekh Abd-el-Goorneh springs up, and the strata again offer available angles for horizontal cutting, the chambers reappear, and the whole of that hill, on every side and at every elevation, is completely perforated, as a subsequent page will more fully point out. The sepulchres there belong chiefly to high officials of priestly, military, or bureaucratic rank under the Eighteenth, Nineteenth, and Twentieth Dynasties (1500 to 1100 B.C.), and they are of the highest interest from the great variety of the subjects illustrative of life and manners preserved in the paintings and sculptures on their walls.

These house-like tombs again give place to others of more decidedly subterranean character, when El Shekh Abd-el-Goorneh slopes in turn to the northward, into the valley of El Assasseef; but many of those with which the greater part of this comparatively level valley is occupied, are of different design and frequently of vastly greater dimensions than the perpendicular shafts with terminal crypts, to which the flat districts of the Necropolis were mainly devoted. A rectangular cutting, as large in area as a considerable house (say 80 or

100 feet on one side by 40 or 70 on the other), sunk into the rock to a depth of 10 or 12 feet, and bounded along the surface edge by the crumbling vestiges of a brick wall, once, no doubt, ornamented—might be said to describe the visible externals of one of these tombs. In one of the sides of this sunk court, chiselled it may be into architectural outlines, appears a doorway leading to the penetralia, which are more or less elaborately worked out of the rock, according to the extent of the design. In some a passage of moderate length leads to a single chamber. In others there are several sculptured chambers connected by a tunnel, which afterwards, leaving these in the rear, pushes onwards and downwards for such extraordinary distances to the ultimate repository for the mummies, that in one, after penetrating two or three hundred feet, I have been obliged to return without reaching the end, warned back by the choking sensations, and the flickering of the candle, indicative of the mephitic character of the air. Another executed for a High Priest, Petamunap, is celebrated as perhaps the most remarkable subterranean work in Egypt, from its enormous extent and the involutions of its design. Long painted corridors measuring together more than 800 feet, passing through various halls and chambers, and doubling upon each other rectangularly, offer very nearly such a plan as if the longitudinal galleries of the Museo Chiaramonti in the Vatican, with two or three of their transverse junctions, were embedded in the rock; and two yawning pits in the floor

of certain of the interior chambers, communicate besides, with minor excavations beneath, where the dead had most probably lain.

With such, but, of course in most cases, much smaller tombs than those, the greater part of the valley of El Assasseef is filled, until the hills are approached. At its innermost extremity, where these take the form of abrupt perpendicular walls of cliff, a temple joins its solid outline to theirs claiming to itself such sublimity as the natural accessories of the spot might give. Known as Der el-Bahrée from having been for a time, after its original uses were past, the abode of an early Christian community (Der signifying convent), it owes to that occupancy some of its preservation, and, no doubt, some of its dilapidation.* Its size is not very considerable, and its general structure is that of the similar edifices on the plain, including an avenue still clearly defined, although the rows of sphinxes are gone, which, lining it on either side, led through the tombs towards the river for the third part of a mile in length. The temple itself is also in the closest proximity to tombs, which, indeed, almost undermine it. The doorways of horizontal chambers pierce the crags at available points around it, and the dark shadows of similar openings speckle all the lower slopes of the range which sweeps round El Assasseef on its north-western border, terminating in the protruding buttress of El Drah-aboo-

---

* The early Christians mutilated the walls of many of the temples and tombs to deface the graven images.

Neggeh. In this hill the tombs are, in some places, clustered almost as closely as in El Shekh Abd-el-Goorneh; and here as there, many of them, from their convenient shape, are now the homes of living occupants.) On certain of its ledges of moderate height, but mostly above the elevation devoted to the excavations, some small brick pyramids (a feature peculiar to this spot), hand down a link from their ancient gigantic prototypes in Lower Egypt. And in the desert flat beneath to its junction with the fertile· alluvial soil, groups of sunk doorways, and yawning shafts, and the heaps of drift sand drawn from them and covering others, show how fully the ground was appropriated, giving it over a wide tract a curiously dappled, uneven, surface which might suit Dante's description of the plain of Arles, —

"Fanno i sepolcri tutto il loco varo."*

¹ Here, in respect of its circling along the site of the city, and as the grand general receptacle for so many classes of the dead, the Necropolis ends. But deep in the mountains behind, the kings of the great Theban Dynasties had their tombs, in some cases so vast and splendid, that their royal owners, in going to their last rest, could by no means be said to lay down their state with their lives.† In the rear of that field of pits, which has last been mentioned,

* *Inferno*, ix. 115.

† "Et rien enfin ne manque dans tous ces honneurs, que celui à qui on les rend."—Bossuet, *Oraison Funèbre de Louis de Bourbon*.

and almost in a line from the temple of Karnak, on the opposite side of the Nile, a break in the desert range opens up a narrow defile which, with many windings, leads to a desolate glen closed in by the arid hills. The Valley of the Shadow of Death could offer no picture more sternly emblematic. No flower or shrub, intruding its message of vitality, fringes one single spot in the whole parched outline. Stray footprints in the sand of hyenas and jackals, although dim evidences of life, speak rather of the haunts of death. The cavernous entrances to the tombs, marked by deep dark shadows where they pierce the crags, look more than figuratively the gloomy portals of the grave. But if selecting, for example, the most important of these, that known by the name of Belzoni, whose energy its discovery rewarded, you enter, conceiving that, as a natural sequence to the external accessories, the next step might even be into the actual presence of mortality, the surprise would hardly be less than a sudden plunge into Aladdin's cave. The glimmering lights are not, it is true, reflected back by the sparkle of his jewelled trees, but they flare upon a whole legion of quaint and monstrous celestials, busy in the exercise of the functions which fell to them respectively to perform, when a disembodied human soul entered their shadowy land. In bright colours, more stable than the deities whose effigies they tint, and hardly tarnished by the lapse of three thousand years, the walls and roofs of long corridors and pillared halls are covered with subjects ideally representative of the spirit's progress in the unseen world. The portraiture of certain of the gods determining their personality — the known attributes with which these were accredited — the aid, often unfortunately slight and uncertain, of accompanying inscriptions — and the general scope of Egyptian theology, as partially unfolded in the available sources, give intelligibility to many of those scenes. But some are so entirely mystical, that any pretence to exhibit the exact measure of their expressiveness may be ranked as little more than conjecture, until some contemporary commentary on the ultimate religious mysteries and their symbolism, shall haply be discovered, much more direct and articulate than the now known ritualistic books.

Twenty-one tombs, generically the same but in no case so splendid as this of King Sethi I. of the Nineteenth Dynasty, are now open in this desolate ravine, which possesses the modern Arabic name of Bab el-Molook. And four more similar royal sepulchres have their place in what is conventionally called the Western Valley, a branch of the same defile, lying still deeper in the heart of the mountains of the desert. In a future page, while describing excavations among those truly regal tombs, I shall have to refer more precisely to circumstances connected with their number and their occupants. But neither there nor here do I propose to myself to enter into any account of the respective specialities of their dimensions and the subjects on their walls.* That is to say, with regard to them, as with regard to the other localities of the great burial-place of Thebes, I only contemplate offering here such a chart as will identify their characteristics, and afford a preliminary view of the Necropolis as a whole.

In endeavouring, however, to do so, it will be desirable to indicate, cursorily, a few prominent points in the general conditions affecting this vast sepulchral field. And, first, as to its age, or rather the dates represented within its limits. We have already seen that, of the earlier vestiges of the city, only the merest traces have come down among the existing ruins, and that in the temples we have, almost exclusively, relics of the great period of Theban power, from 1500 to 1100 years B.C. (under the Eighteenth, Nineteenth, and Twentieth Dynasties). What further can be gathered from them in this respect is evidence of later repairs at some points while general ruin was advancing elsewhere, and proof of additions, and some minor works attributable to the succeeding times, even as late as the period of Roman rule. And so is it in like manner with the tombs. Any clearly referrible to the more

---

* For lengthened details on these points, which, if they cannot be said to be exhausted, have at all events been treated with very full illustration, those seeking them would rather refer to the works I have already indicated in a note to the foregoing chapter (p. 8), and to several others which are sufficiently well known. Excellent copies of some of the walls of the royal tombs, recently published after drawings by M. Prisse, may be specified. They are included in Feydeau, *Usages Funèbres*.

ancient days of the growing city are not to be recognised. They may have been comparatively few in number or, in certain cases, so little elaborate that, from the absence of decoration, no mark remains to distinguish them; or some may have been reduced to the same indefinite condition by the more lengthened action of time on their painted walls. But without any of these suppositions, the circumstance is not difficult to account for if we remember that under the nurture of the three Dynasties named, the changes and the prosperity were so great, as the monuments show, that the stamp of that period was essentially impressed upon the city. In the Necropolis, with an increasing demand for space, it was not likely that the older tombs would be preserved untouched in perpetuity, and that they should escape the vicissitudes of reappropriation which circumstances invited and practice sanctioned. It is sepulchres dating under those three of the Diospolitan Dynasties, which now present themselves so frequently at nearly every point, that they almost give the whole assemblage a representative character as regards that flourishing period. From the Valley of the Tombs of the Queens to El Drah-aboo-Neggeh they are to be found — not in any topographical sequence according to relative age,— and they, although not they exclusively or without intermixture, occur at nearly every part of the range, wherever paintings or sculptures on the interior walls enable dates to be determined. A prominent exception, is, indeed, to be made in favour of the valley of El Assasseef, where the large subterraneans mentioned previously in this chapter, belong almost, if not quite all to the days of the Twenty-sixth Dynasty, in the sixth and seventh centuries B.C. It is also to be borne in mind that only a certain proportion of the tombs have mural decorations, and that a vast number are without any such index to their history. Only those which take the shape of distinctly formed rock chambers are so distinguished, and not even all which are so planned, while the simple horizontal tunnels, and the very numerous perpendicular shafts show no more chiselling than was necessary to cut them out. To these and other such unchronicling receptacles of the dead of many descending generations, there is therefore no guide for chronological definition; but among them there are, no doubt, representatives of every age in the long centuries of Theban life, until its extinction. Occasional discoveries of relics, as we shall presently see, have brought to light sepulchral deposits in them, not merely of various earlier epochs, but of the periods of Greek and Roman supremacy. And, as the last stage of all, I have known among the sand-heaps and surface-*débris*, imperfectly preserved mummies to be met with, bearing on their breasts, entwined with necklaces of beads, the Christian cross.*

As the tombs are ranged in no progressive order

---

* Some of the early Christian Fathers denounced embalmment as a pagan practice, showing that it was then in use among adherents of the Egyptian Church; and St. Anthony, in the fourth century, was not, perhaps, the last of the preachers against it.

according to their age, so neither do they fall into strict groups with reference to their importance as indicated by the elaboration of their finish or the rank of their owners. In El Drah-aboo-Neggeh, El Shekh Abd-el-Goorneh, and indeed at most points where the rising crags admitted of excavations taking the form of horizontal chambers, the painted or sculptured tombs occur; and these, in nearly all ascertainable instances, belonged to dignitaries of the priesthood, the government, or the army under the three so often mentioned dynasties. But amongst them are many of obviously inferior class, although of indeterminable ascription from their plain unornamented walls; and in even not less close juxtaposition are some of the large catacombs in which the bodies of workmen and others of humble degree, as inferred from accompanying tools, were interred in great masses together. The imposing subterraneans dating under the Twenty-sixth Dynasty, and already mentioned as the distinctive feature in the Valley of El Assasseef, do indeed engross to themselves the greater part of its central space; but the humbler pit tombs swarm up, so to say, among them, as in fact they do everywhere throughout the whole of the sacred tract. Nor for other than human occupants of the Necropolis was there a defined locality, although it does not appear how far the few known tombs here, in which certain animals were buried, were quite indiscriminately embedded among those of men. But in perfectly close proximity to the latter, if not actually always surrounded by them, the former have been observed in several of the districts. In a ravine near the Valley of the Tombs of the Queens, mummied apes used to be discovered. At points in El Assasseef and El Drah-aboo-Neggeh, mummied fish, cats, snakes, and cows have been found.\* And from a sunk tomb on the southern outskirts of the sandy flat, at the foot of El Drah-aboo-Neggeh, I have known many hundred mummies of hawks and ibises, carefully rolled in ornamental bandages, to be procured along with jars of white eggs, probably of the ibis, and sundry small boxes each containing a mummied mouse †, whose effigy, cut in wood and in some examples gilt, was stuck on the lid.

Of one and all of those tombs, or rather of the external appearance of them all taken together, it may be said that their aspect is more truly deathlike now than when they were actually dedicated. The care once withdrawn which in the days of their sacredness kept them exteriorly in harmony with the native

---

\* The localities of these are indicated in Wilkinson's large Survey of Thebes. In his list of mummied animals (*Anct. Egyptians*, vol. v. pp. 116—126), he mentions several others as having been found at Thebes, as rats, sheep, geese, crocodiles, &c.

† It was as the respective emblems of the gods Horus and Thoth that the hawk and the ibis were objects of care; and the shrew mouse owed its sacredness, if we are content to follow such later theosophic explanations as Plutarch has preserved, to the circumstance, that it was considered as blind, and that the Egyptians believed darkness to be a more ancient condition of being than light. (Plutarch, *Symposiaca*, iv., *Problema*, v. 2; cf. Wilkinson's *Man. and Cust.* 2nd series, vol. ii. ch. xiv. pp. 133—136) ap. Greswell's *Origines Kalendariæ*, vol. i. p. 152.

standard of taste and feeling,— this care once withdrawn, the order which had prevailed became the prey of time and circumstance. And nature had not here the germs of another form of life, forced into abeyance only by the active presence of man, but ever ready to spring up and enwrap the traces of decay; for the necessary condition of a site beyond the fructifying influence of the waters of the overflowing river, is parched, unbroken sterility. Another obliterating agent she did have, the wayward drift of the desert, but this having done its work of submergence with fitful irregularity has only given intenser expression to the characteristic desolation, without reducing all things to the still equality of primitive repose. Pits in constantly recurring succession gape through the shifting sand. Doorways cast across it the deep shadows of the cells or tunnels into which they lead. The ruins of brick outworks and superstructures struggle with it. Torn cerements, fragments of rifled mummies, or dismembered bones, dragged forth by more than one generation of careless searchers, protrude through it here and there, or lie blanching but not decaying on its rainless surface. And more palpably than when the ancient dead were laid to their rest, more literally than in Wordsworth's mountain churchyard, the whole expanse is now in appearance, if not also in reality,

"ground
Fraught with the relics of mortality."

What the general aspect had been during the period

of Theban prosperity, may with some precision be gathered, from certain of the existing vestiges, when compared with the few pictures, among the very numerous mural subjects, in which funeral processions are represented approaching the end of their march. It would thus appear that the exterior portal of the tomb was commonly a quadrangular, corniced, and

PORCH OF TOMB FROM A FRESCO AT THEBES.

pyramidally roofed erection, which fragments of actual ruins prove to have been built of sun-dried bricks, that had no doubt been plastered and probably painted in bright colours. An outline of one from a fresco at Thebes is here given, which shows its form, and what represents the slope of the mountain of the Desert, upon or against which it stood.* It quite corresponds with the few other wall paintings referred to, and with the more frequent vignettes on papyri depicting similar buildings fronting, as in this case, the march of a funeral procession.

The undecorated doorways were flanked by porches such as this; the shafts were covered by mausolea of the same or a similar type; the large sunk tombs were surrounded by ornamental walls. The two latter occupied the flats; and how the porches would cluster on the hill-sides, may in some degree, and allowing for the absence of colour and the diversity of architectural outlines, be realised in a portion of the Campo Santo of Naples, where tiers of small projecting sepulchral façades cling, as it were, to the face of a steeply sloping eminence.

Of the ancient condition of the inner penetralia of the tombs we can also know much, although not, unfortunately in all respects, with precision. Their shape of course remains the same, and, from the conservative character of the climate, the paintings and bas-reliefs on the walls of a large proportion of those which were so adorned stand more or less clearly to the present hour, with marvellously little alteration. The general character of the interiors, as illustrated in the great sepulchres, has already been touched upon by a cursory reference to

* The whole subject, printed chiefly in colours, is copied in Rosellini, *Mon. Civ.* tav. cxxix.

the extent of their galleries and halls and the subjects (in them chiefly religious) with which these are covered.

The smaller decorated examples, if less magnificent, are not of inferior interest. They are those which have been mentioned as mostly belonging to official personages. What may be called their elementary

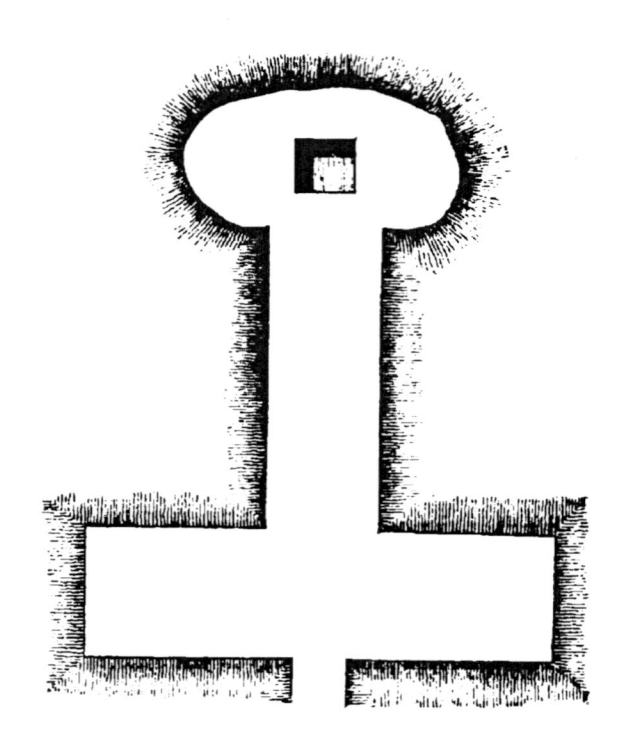

USUAL PLAN OF CHAMBERED TOMBS.

typical plan is shown in the accompanying outline, but the variations are frequent in the relative proportions, and not less so in the design. Commonly, however, they consist of a rock-cut chamber some eight feet high and eight or ten feet broad, extending laterally from twelve to twenty feet on either side of the entrance doorway, opposite which a passage of very much the same height and breadth as the chamber runs from the back wall for about twenty or forty feet into the rock, terminating either in a widening crypt, or in a sunk shaft, or both, wherein the mummies had been deposited. The whole available wall space, both of the outer chamber and the passage, is fully occupied by representations either in colours laid on the stuccoed surface, or sculptured in very low relief (often also with the addition of colour), in the smoothed limestone itself. At a prominent point in each will be seen the figure of the owner seated not unfrequently with his wife, or standing, or in the act of being presented before the judge of the dead, the great god Osiris; and immediately around him will often be found other religious episodes. But it is the peculiarity of those tombs that the scenes they offer are mainly secular, being such as have handed down those vivid expositions of the ancient manners and civilization which modern research has rendered so familiar. Sometimes in groups of which the figures are given in more than half life-size, but more usually in longitudinal zones, each about eighteen inches high, continued in rows round the walls, these phases of life in the old world are embodied, accompanied often by a few descriptive hieroglyphics, and broken by longer ritualistic inscriptions. The various operations of agriculture and wine production are among the most common subjects, as well as banquets, processions of conquered races bearing tribute* like prisoners in a Roman triumph, craftsmen of many kinds at work at their trades, fishing and fowling scenes, funeral processions; and, in short, a large proportion of the ordinary occupations of contemporary life are depicted in one or other of these enduring chronicles. Certain additional particulars as to this class of sepulchral chambers will be found in future sections descriptive of explorations; and as there likewise will naturally occur details showing the structure of the other tombs of different designs, it will not be desirable here to specify the varieties in their form.

To those pages also I would rather refer for facts bearing on the remaining ingredient necessary for a fair conception of the ancient condition of the Necropolis, namely, the nature of the contents of the tombs and their arrangement. But it will be well in general terms, not perhaps, as will subsequently be seen, admitting of literal application—it will be well to glance at a few of the broader outlines by way of completing the introductory scheme of this chapter.

In some of the great sepulchres, the bodies embalmed with the utmost care, swathed in very numerous folds

---

* Of those very valuable ethnographic delineations, the tribute-bearing processions, it may be noted, that one of the most important is vividly copied at length, and coloured after the original, in Hoskins' *Travels in Ethiopia*. Special references to plates of specimens of certain of the other scenes here indicated will hardly be necessary.

of the finest linen, bearing ornaments of gold or precious stones, chiefly in the form of religious symbols, and accompanied by rolls of papyrus inscribed with ritualistic guidance for the soul's career, were deposited in admirably chiselled sarcophagi of alabaster or granite, covered with incised religious effigies and inscriptions. In minor tombs the occupants had been similarly treated, but more or less according to a correspondingly descending or varying scale. The preservative processes, of which there were several, might be less delicate; the bandages coarser; the ornaments, of pebble or pottery; the papyrus, diminished in size or altogether wanting; the coffins, of wood shaped usually in close resemblance to the contour of the swathed mummy within, and brightly painted both inside and outside with sacred figures and columns of hieroglyphic texts. In these are entered the name and position of the deceased with various prayers, of which this to Osiris is one of the most important, "That he may be allowed to enter into the union, whereby he may see as the devout souls see, hear as they hear, sit as they sit." *

But besides the dead thus carefully disposed of and accompanied, as they frequently were, by four vases containing the principal viscera, closed by covers representing the heads of the four minor deities or

* Lepsius, *Todtenbuch*, S. 13; cf. Duncker, *Geschichte des Alterthums*, vol. i. p. 75.

genii of the Amenti (Hades), who had each tutelar functions in regard to these respective portions of the bodily frame, and their influences upon it — besides the dead

"Packed to humanity's significance,"

the tombs were the depositories of other and very remarkable contents. Tablets inscribed with prayers or invocations, numerous small symbolical effigies of the deceased, and statuettes of certain of the deities, were the chief accompaniments of a specifically religious character. And just as the wall paintings have preserved such numerous phases of life and manners, so the tombs of one kind or other have yielded corresponding tangible relics in nearly as great variety. Vases of all kinds, baskets, stools, chairs, a chariot, a boat, musical instruments, bows and arrows, ink-horns, workmen's tools, personal ornaments, children's toys, fish-hooks, fruit, corn, bread, even a roasted duck, and the many other articles in our museums, have come from those rich treasuries. Unfortunately, as we shall have again to remark, adequate data are wanting for the accurate or even approximate apportionment of those and other such objects according to their original collocation in the tombs. And so, thus much of the internal arrangements of these, either in their individual character, or in their classification with reference as well to their plan as to their relative dates and locality, can be but partially and indistinctly made out. Nor is it only as a breach in mere barren antiquarian completeness that this is to be regretted, if it be remembered that through the sepulchres and vestiges of Egypt, the path lies to so large a proportion of the few now available sources of knowledge of the ancient world.

## CHAP. III.

ON THE RESULTS OF FORMER SEPULCHRAL RESEARCHES.

With Egyptian museums of extraordinary variety and extent formed under national auspices in at least eight capital cities, not to speak of many minor gatherings in other towns and in private hands—with all those masses of relics, procured in the great majority of instances from tombs, it might seem paradoxical that the details of Egyptian sepulture should be known only from exceedingly slight and often indefinite data. Amid this vast profusion, except one group in the royal collection at Berlin, and two at Florence, to which I shall presently refer, I am not aware that there can be found the contents of a single sepulchre duly authenticated with satisfactory precision as to what objects were present, and as to the relative positions all these occupied when deposited by contemporary hands. Indeed, for many of the Egyptian sepulchral antiquities scattered over Europe, there exists no record to determine even the part of the country where they were exhumed. Of many more it is known only from what necropolis they were obtained. And of a very few can it be stated from what tomb, and under what circumstances they were discovered; while as to these it has almost invariably happened that they were but the leavings of former spoilers, and could bear only a very imperfect relation to the original character of the respective deposits.

To a great extent this result has inevitably arisen from the constant pillage from very early times, and from ordinary motives of cupidity, to which Egyptian burial-places have been subjected in course of the vicissitudes through which the country has passed. But unfortunately, also, there is much room for regret, that even after Egyptian antiquities began to be comprehensively studied and sought after by systematic research, attention was almost exclusively directed to obtaining possession of the relics, without sufficiently careful reference to the circumstances under which they were discovered. It is true that those excavators who then came upon the field might not have had many opportunities of observing the funeral arrangements of the ancient race as preserved in intact tombs; for, as I have already said, their predecessors, during many centuries, were numerous and active. Already in the flourishing days of the native monarchies, robbery of the dead appears to have been known as a form of sacrilege; and a contemporary papyrus recently acquired by the British Museum, is found by Mr. Birch to contain a species of report by a commission appointed to investigate the condition of some sepulchres which had been violated. When foreign and conquering nations succeeded to the dominion of the country, the sanctity of the old tombs was not likely to be more inviolate, and the description of one, which is presently to follow, will show one form of the treatment to which they appear to have been liable, for example, in Ptolemaic and Roman times. But besides such authoritative and open appropriation, robbery not only of ancient but of contemporary sepulchral deposits was probably as common as the temptations they might offer would suggest.* Letronne has translated a papyrus in the Louvre, dated under Philometer and Euergetes II. (180 to 116 years B.C.) in which an official owner of tombs, called there a Colchytus, complains to a Theban magistrate that one which was his property had been broken open and rifled.† Lastly, as we approach nearer our own day, a stronger impulse was given in the same direction, for, at a very early period of modern European intercourse with the East,

---

\* This seems universally, in early days, to have been a subject of dread. See among many well-known instances the curious one in the Phœnician inscription on the sarcophagus of Esmunazar, found at Sidon. *Mémoire sur le Sarcophage d'Esmunazar par le Duc de Luynes:* Paris, 1856.

† Note to Didot's *Aristophanes* ap. Feydeau, *Hist. des Usages Funèbres*, p. 167. It is needless to refer to the narrative of Strabo as to the tombs open and penetrable in his day, or to point to the scribbles by Greek visitors on their walls, showing that then, as now, they had ceased to be sacred, and were liable to the same inexcusable defacement from which they still suffer.

Egyptian relics, whether of material intrinsically valuable or not, began to possess (as indeed it is probable they had to some extent in Roman times) a certain pecuniary worth. As long ago as the middle of the seventeenth century, a traveller complains that he could not induce the Arabs of Sakkara to aid in finding for him there an unopened tomb, as it was their habit to make their own explorations in secret, with the view of securing any relics they might discover, to sell to the Franks in the neighbouring city of Cairo.* This traffic must have easily spread up the river; and when, with reference to its contents, the Necropolis of Thebes first comes prominently before us in the elaborate volumes of the first French Commission†, and in the narratives of Belzoni and Dathanasi descriptive of the ordinary details of collecting antiquities, as well as in the more general allusions of passing travellers, we find the native villagers experienced and expert investigators, digging on their own account with secret assiduity, and perfectly practised in dealing in the products of their work.

It therefore may readily be supposed that when, within, as we may say, the present generation, Egyptian research began to be the object of sustained effort,

* Pour les venir vendre à la ville aux Francs. — Thevenot, *Voyage au Levant*, p. 431, 12mo edition, Paris, 1689. The journey was accomplished in 1655—1659.

† Jomard describes the Arabs or rather *fellaheen* as diligently transporting antiquities to Cairo to sell to Europeans. "Ils sont donc continuellement occupés à fouiller les catacombes avec une patience infinie."—*L'Egypte*, folio ed. *Ant. Des.* t. i. p. 36.

the chances were not likely to be numerous, especially in the more celebrated burial-places, of tombs having escaped in their original integrity, for inquirers who had come so late in the day. Some, however, doubtless, did remain in this condition, as subsequent results have shown; and it is with regard to such of those instances, where the opportunity to note their details was neglected, that a feeling of disappointment cannot but arise. For there have thus been swept unrecorded into the past illustrative facts of very great interest, which cannot now, according to any reasonable probability, be replaced, at all events in the degree which there are grounds to believe was then possible. However true it may be in all which relates to the increase of Egyptological knowledge, that "in this land of wonders mystery hath yet unfolded but half her treasures,"[*] unfortunately we cannot expect in a literal sense that any such balance of actual vestiges remains to be disclosed. I do not doubt, and, indeed, besides mere conjecture, there is warrant to hope, that from the drifting sands may still be unshrouded fresh proofs of the profuse monumental genius which distinguished the past of the Nile valley. But looking, in conjunction with the known spoliation they have experienced, to the present appearance of the great burial-places, burrowed, so to say, from end to end, the prospect is not very hopeful that future discoveries will include

---

[*] Moore's *Epicurean*.

many tombs with their old occupants undisturbed as venerating hands had placed them.

It is difficult to determine in what proportion sepulchres in this rare condition occurred in the progress of those excavations, the first undertaken on a systematic scale, to which I am now particularly alluding.* Of nearly all of those researches there remain only the most imperfect records: of the great majority there are absolutely none. Prosecuted with ardour more than forty years ago, the mode of procedure adopted was by no means of a satisfactory nature. Mr. Salt and Signor Drovetti entered at the same time actively on the pursuit, and their official influence, as Consuls-General for England and France, obtained for them the necessary permission and facilities from the native government. Various of the ancient sites were fixed upon, and in particular the Necropolis of Thebes was, so to say, mapped out between the working parties employed by these two gentlemen. But nearly all their explorations were conducted under the supervision of agents whose instructions, while it is only just to believe that they had in some respects broad scientific ends in view, would seem, by some oversight, to have been to attend

* As to an earlier period, if we accept the encyclopædic research of the French Commission as an adequate summary of then existing experience, we find the avowal that there was no sufficient light as to the arrangement of objects in the tombs: — "Il en serait autrement si l'on pouvoit pénétrer dans *un seul* hypogée que n'auraient pas encore violé les Arabes." — *L'Egypte, Ant. Descrip.* t. i. p. 354.

to the accumulation of relics, rather than to the circumstances under which these were found. At least we look in vain for sufficient accounts of the latter. As regards Drovetti's collection, now at Turin, there are, I believe, no means of ascertaining the individual history of its constituents; or rather, there are no particulars preserved as to the previously undisturbed tombs, if any, which fell to the lot of those who formed it. In the case of Salt's collections, one in the Louvre, the other partly in the British Museum and partly dispersed, there is a similar want: for it cannot be said that this is in any proper sense supplied by the narratives of those who acted for him, Belzoni and Dathanasi. In both there are interesting generalities on the subject of sepulchral deposits, but hardly any details, and none of the nature of regular specifications of the contents of given tombs. It would seem, however, beyond doubt, that some of these in their original integrity came under their observation. In Belzoni's volume, containing the history of his celebrated discovery in the Bab el-Molook, and generally of his proceedings, first on Salt's account and then on his own, there are several allusions which would indicate that the good fortune was not unknown to him of meeting with intact deposits.* Dathanasi again unmistakeably refers to

---

\* See, for example, *Narrative of Operations, &c.*, p. 167; and p. 158 where he remarks that "ordinary travellers being shown only grottoes already plundered, can form but a poor idea of the real tombs where the remains were originally placed."

such, as having been frequently under his eye.* But it is more than doubtful if ever he preserved or had in view any description of these; as the notes subsequently drawn up by or for him, as the prefix to the sale catalogue of Salt's second collection were prepared, apparently, from memory, and embody, with occasional illustrative reference to individual objects, only outlines of generic sepulchral arrangements. His long residence at Thebes must in practical exploring have given him unusual opportunity and experience; but it is curious to know that, on the spot, he was as reticent and secret in his proceedings as the Arabs themselves. I have been told by two distinguished travellers of those days, whose names are well known in connection with Egyptian research, that it happened to them respectively to try to induce him to allow their examination of any tomb in its untouched condition, which he might so discover. The one, after repeated disappointments, offered him a considerable sum as a reward contingent on compliance, but quite unavailingly. And the other was not more successful, for although he was long established at Thebes prosecuting those studies, which have since been so fruitful, and although promises were not withheld, Dathanasi constantly succeeded in frus-

* *Brief Account of Researches, &c.*, p. 117, in which he states, in a general way, the ordinary appearance of tombs when first discovered with unbroken entrances; and p. 70 where he implies having been familiar with such at Thebes, in contradistinction to his inability to find any at Abydus.

trating the accomplishment of his wish, by invariably arranging to remove the relics so as to prevent their being seen *in situ* (or probably in some cases at all), afterwards alleging some frivolous excuse. It is not worth while inquiring, as the conclusion might hardly be satisfactory, what was the probable motive for this secrecy; but thus it has been, that in all the excavations carried on under Dathanasi during a long course of years, whatever opportunities may have presented themselves for recording observations of the nature of those whose absence we have been regretting, were so to say blotted out.

About the same time the Necropolis of Thebes was further laid under contribution, somewhat extensively, for the collection brought together by Passalacqua, subsequently purchased for the Museum at Berlin. Of these relics the sufficiently well known "Catalogue Raisonné" was published with many illustrative notes by the finder, containing the fullest sepulchral details we possess, as well as the most accurate, if their precision be not always reliable; and to him also are we first indebted for a distinct description of a tomb with its contents as disclosed in undisturbed condition. But it is worthy of notice, as evincing the rarity of such good fortune even then, that the solitary instance which occurred to him among excavations prosecuted during several years, was this small but interesting sepulchre discovered in 1823.[*]

[*] *Catalogue des Antiquités découvertes par* Passalacqua, pp. 117, *et seq.* and p. 144.

Not long thereafter, the French and Tuscan Commission, headed by Champollion and Rosellini, appeared upon the same scene. Among the fruits of the explorations instituted by them, were not more than two previously unrifled tombs, both of very moderate dimensions and simple character, whose arrangement and contents are carefully described by Rosellini.* It is unnecessary here to refer to other excavations, more or less considerable, which have been prosecuted both before or since, some of which have resulted, if not in disclosures of the peculiar character in question, in other discoveries of the highest interest and value. Among the most recent and most important are those, so generally known, of M. Mariette, embracing the Serapeum, tombs of the older Dynasties in its neighbourhood, and, according to recent reports of the Paris press, the mummy of a Princess at Thebes, found, I am informed, among some *débris*, as if ejected from a sepulchre, but accompanied by jewels of a beauty and finish which illustrate in a wonderful degree the resources of ancient art manufacture. The fruits of these highly successful discoveries are as yet but partially published, but it does not appear that among their important products they included any intact tombs. Nor, so far as I know, are there in the literature of Egyptian research, accessible accounts of any further examples except the three which have just been mentioned; and no others would seem to

* *Monumenti dell' Egitto — Mon. Civ.* t. i. pp. 99, *et seq.*

have been met with in the course of such excavations as have been observantly conducted.

If, however, instead of such slight and imperfect glimpses of the mortuary practices in their completeness, a concurrence of fortunate circumstances had added a lengthened and precise series of such facts to the material of Egyptian archæology, it is not difficult to conceive how greatly they would have aided in the elucidation of obscure points which, in some respects, must lie at the root of a just conception of the genius of the ancient people. There would then have been a body of evidence, capable of being interrogated for clearer and more sequential traces of the nature of some of those religious changes and developments, of which there is evidence, notwithstanding the remarkable permanence in the main elements of worship, and which, vital as they may have been in the character of the nation, remain so indefinitely obscure. There would then too have been satisfactory means of discriminating with some precision, how far certain sepulchral practices were merely local, how far they were thus local as matters of diversity in social custom or as connected with divergences in belief and worship; and within what limits such differences of whichever description ranged. And the questions arising from indications of such discrepancies might have been more directly approached than hitherto; for, although recognized, they have upon the whole, chiefly we may believe in consequence of the absence of minuter data, been usually swamped by what I venture to think will ultimately be found a too generic treatment on the tacit assumption of homogeneity. Again, a similar class of facts, intimately intertwined with the religious idea, might also ere now have yielded more definite illustration of it. It would have been something had a sufficiently long record of observations existed, to form a basis for adequate inductions with reference to the accompaniments of the dead, in some of their more important relations. For example, as to whether any marked distinction might be drawn between those of a sacred character, as the effigies and emblems of deities, and those of a secular nature, as the implements and instruments of actual life? Whether at any period or different periods the presence of either class or both seemed to have been essential religiously, or ceremonially optional? Whether the latter class were found in such circumstances as might offer a practical commentary on certain passages of the Ritual, by showing that they had reference directly or symbolically to the perpetuation of mere earthly life beyond the tomb; or whether they testified memorially to the past and not to the future of the deceased; or whether, indeed, in every case they had individual significance at all? Nor are there wanting various topics connected with the progress and practice of the arts of life and the collateral subjects of external influence and commerce, as illustrated by the introduction of some, or disuse of other foreign materials,— there are various topics of this nature which might have been capable of similar elucidation, had the means existed for a more rigid classification of that knowledge of the manufactures of the ancient Egyptians, which the contents of their tombs might have afforded. In short, it is no mere acquaintance with, in themselves, insignificant minutiæ which might alone have been increased — no mere accumulation of barren trivialities, if, indeed, any elements of a civilization, at once our oldest discoverable type and a highly diffusive source, can be so regarded. On the contrary (and independently of strictly archæological considerations), from the place among the institutions of this remarkable people, which sepulchral customs occupied, from the pre-eminent manner in which the tenets of their belief twined round the sepulchre, not merely in abstractions as to the soul's futurity, but in an elaborate ceremonial attendant upon every stage of sepulture, the more we could learn of their burial customs, the more should we be likely to know of the springs of their inner life and their psychical condition in one of its most important developments — the more, in short, should we be likely to know of that which it now mainly concerns us to comprehend in the case of this dead nation. For its earlier history, at least, seen imperfectly through the vista of so vast an antiquity, possesses now, in any general view of the world's career, the concrete form of an ethnographic problem, rather than the pictorial vitality of a stirring series of eventful efforts.

To have expected, at any period, say within the last two thousand years, the recovery of a complete

## OBJECT OF UNDERTAKING EXCAVATIONS. 75

body of such evidence, would have been as chimerical as to look for a visible reconstruction of the past, or to count that after a lengthened unresisting submission to the progress of oblivion, all that Time had won might be reconquered. But although success approaching to this would ever have been impossible, we cannot but be conscious that in the field we have in view, much has been lost that might have been gained, and that, to supply the void, there is only too strong a necessity to have recourse to conjecture and inference to piece out what fragments there are. In the hope, by no means sanguine from the considerations already stated, that even by an individual attempt, details of the nature that seemed so highly desirable might still be somewhat supplemented, I undertook some excavations during the spring of 1856 at Geezeh, in the neighbourhood of the Pyramids, and during the winter and spring of 1856—57, on a much larger scale, in the Necropolis of Thebes. I had the intention, at first unavoidably frustrated and now unnecessary even if practicable[*], of pursuing them there and elsewhere in subsequent years.

It is needless to say that the disappointments, if not always vexatious because anticipated, were frequent and numerous. Sometimes whole days or even weeks of labour directed to one spot failed to discover the en-

---

[*] Not long ago the Egyptian Government having, as was proper, undertaken the supervision of the monuments, placed them under the charge of an efficient curator, M. Mariette, I believe, and means were provided, at least for the present, for carrying on systematic researches.

trance to any tomb, and the shafts had to be abandoned. Sometimes entrances were disclosed leading only to interiors which had long before been more or less completely rifled. Sometimes, in the lower ground, the sepulchral chambers were gained only to exhibit the remnants of their contents sodden and decayed by the moisture of the constantly encroaching inundation. There were, however, occasional comparative successes, where facts of interest presented themselves, the principal of which shall be elsewhere set down. But in only one instance did it happen to me to discover a sepulchre of importance in point of magnitude and accompaniments, in which the repose of the last occupants had remained entirely unbroken until then. Its first tenants, whose surroundings would have been of more interest still, had been dispossessed. But the very manner in which this had been accomplished, the perfect integrity in which the arrangements of their successors were found, the nature of these, and the remarkable realization of funeral customs existing at Thebes about five hundred years after the fall of the last native Egyptian dynasties, will render it desirable that a minute description should be offered, the more especially as no record, so far as I know, has hitherto been published of any tomb belonging to this period discovered intact.

## CHAP. IV.

### THE UNRIFLED TOMB OF A THEBAN DIGNITARY, AND ITS CONTENTS.

DIVIDED into several working parties, I employed my men simultaneously in the various districts of the Necropolis — one body in the Valley of the Tombs of the Kings; another at El Drah-aboo-Neggeh, the western extremity of the vast cemetery of the city; another in the direction of Goornet Murrawée, the eastern extremity; another in El Assasseef; and for another, after various imperfect results in the same neighbourhood, I had selected what appeared a promising point nearly at the foot of El Shekh Abd-el-Goorneh. This well known hill, projecting and isolated by deep ravines from the mountain range of the Desert, rising steeply and almost pyramidally, as is indeed the typical geologic outline in that region, and standing centrally in advance, breaking the sweep of the valley, forms the most prominent feature in the Necropolis of Thebes. Its rocky face, from base to summit, is pierced with the doorways of tombs, many of which are those whose painted walls have become classic as among the most important illustrations of the best period of ancient Egyptian civilization. The tombs, while occupying every available point, are not generally ranged in regular lines or shelving rows: but although there are instances of such symmetrical distribution, and although in the original adjustment some regard to method must have been pursued with a view to general facilities of access, the main guiding plan which appears to have been followed, was simply that indicated by the structure of the crag. Wherever the facets of the rock afforded an opportunity for scarping them down into perpendicular walls of ten or twelve feet in height, there, without reference to uniformity of position, a rectangular area was formed, open generally in front, bounded by two walls of rock, and having the door of one or more tombs cut in its inner face, that is, the side of the hill. Sometimes this inner face is chiselled into panels, or other similar devices, and ornamented with a few sculptured hieroglyphic subjects; but as a rule the rock is only rough hewn, presenting a bald unfinished look which, doubtless, in the old days did not exist. For, in the rare instances where the later scenes of funeral ceremonies are depicted in the frescoes, the procession approaches a square porch, of which an example is shown above in page 54.

An idea of the original arrangement and present aspect of El Shekh Abd-el-Goorneh may be readily gained from the view\* in Plate II. Taken from a point some distance up the slope, and at an angle aslant the hill, the bold isolated contour is modified; and the doorways of many tombs, concealed by intervening projections of the crag or heaps of drift sand, appear less numerous than they strike the eye, when the whole rocky mass, seen in full front from a greater distance, discloses at once its outline and all the perforated crannies in its rugged face. But in this view may be well observed the general plan of the entrances, the forms of protruding ledges, and the glacier-like deposits of sand intermixed with fragments of stone, being the subsidence from the disintegrating rock, often, in the course of years, shifted and helped to its ultimate descent by recurring attempts to uncover the tombs which it engulfs. The turreted erection of sun-dried bricks standing at a considerable elevation to the left, flanks a now deserted abode, occupied in former years by Sir Gardner Wilkinson, by Mr. Hay, and still later by the Prussian Commission under Dr. Lepsius. The similar building in a central position lower down was raised as the head-quarters of Mr. Salt's excavating operations, and in it two friends and myself found an excellent shelter for several months.† The stone wall and clay fabrics to the

---

\* For this view (see p. 38) I am indebted to a photograph taken when the excavations were in progress, by a friend, Mr. J. Nicholson.

† The occupation of this house, as well as the *firmán* from the Egyptian Government, which empowered me to excavate, and other facilities, I owed to the kind intervention of Mr. Bruce, her Majesty's

right are outworks of the tomb-dwelling of the Shekh of the troglodyte villagers scattered in this immediate neighbourhood; and the cylindrical objects in the foreground are keeping places formed of a crust of baked mud, as the manner of the country is, raised in front of another *fellah's* subterranean habitation.

Burrowed so completely as it is, this hill could not fail to excite hopes in all past times, when any motive for examination existed, of whatever nature it might be; and, accordingly, the cell-like entrances are disclosed in such numbers or, where more or less hidden, are replaced by such perpetually recurring marks of disturbance, that it was difficult to find a spot which did not offer all the evidences of having been thoroughly explored. At various points, comparatively easy to test, and which seemed to hold out certain vague chances of success, I had already been repulsed by discovering that I had only followed in the wake of previous searchers, and succeeded merely to what they had despised. It has happened, both in the experience of European and Arab explorers, that accident has led them to intact tombs, so easy of access, that it was almost miraculous how they had escaped so long. But as none of those pieces of good fortune fell to me, I was forced to recognize the only reasonably probable prospect as likely to result from a search where

ambassador to China, then consul-general in Egypt, in considerate furtherance of an introduction with which I was obligingly furnished from the Foreign Office through a friendly application.

the difficulty of the undertaking might have deterred, at all events, native precursors.

A survey of the ground appeared to show that this condition, at least, would be fulfilled in a sort of bay or circular depression between two projections of the crag, almost at the foot of the hill, and about forty yards to the west of, and on a lower level than, the tomb with chiselled front, at the extreme left of Plate II., which, having been photographed before this particular excavation was commenced, just stops short of including the site in question. It was plain that the amount of labour necessary here would be very considerable, from the extent of the deposit which had settled down by natural subsidence aided by frequent former operations at higher elevations; and from the indefinite manner in which the tombs were placed, as I have already pointed out, there was no approach to certainty that any might be concealed at this spot. But there always remained the hope that, were one found, its position and the consequent difficulty of reaching it, would have saved it from molestation in modern times. Accordingly, as in this part of the Necropolis especially, there are none but remote and doubtful chances to select from, this had in any case something to recommend it, and a party of forty strong were set to work.

After the excavation had been carried on for several days, a ledge of rock was reached running inwards; and although this could not absolutely be pronounced to bear marks of artificial cutting, it was an excellent guide to follow. The process, however, was exceedingly slow, in consequence of the mass of accumulated drift which the nature of the place required to be removed. Nor is the native method of work expeditious. The *fellaheen* (the native peasants), stripped to the skin except their waist-cloths, certainly make a considerable show of activity, at least when well overlooked; and there is often no want of effort, and even constancy, in their labour. But the result is, after all, unsatisfactory, from the inefficient appliances which they employ, notwithstanding that they use them with great aptitude. Their implement is the *fass*, a short-handled hoe. With it, one set of men, grubbing and scraping, fill little round baskets, which others lift, placing them on the heads of boys and girls and the weaker men, waiting thus to carry the rubbish from the trench, in revolving files, singing together as they march off with their loads.

By a system such as this, the waste of power is so great as to require an inordinate number of hands for a cutting of any size. But besides the delay incident to the style of labour, a most vexatious source of retarding progress, at the point to which I now refer, arose from the peculiar nature of the ground. The excavation being at the foot of a steeply-angled slope of loose detritus, gave occasion to frequent landslips; and a breeze of wind, a dog or goat passing above, the flutter of a little bird's wing setting a few pebbles in motion, or any other trifling cause, would sometimes give the work the character of digging in the face of a constant avalanche. The people occasionally got disheartened, and the overseers would at such times urge that the attempt should be given up, expressing their own characteristic feelings, that it was a pity to undertake the expenditure of so much labour, not only with no prospect of a speedy termination, but with no certainty of success in the end. As, however, the ledge which I have mentioned gave stronger indications of having been hewn the more it was exposed, the course was manifestly to persevere, especially as, in due time, it was proved to be the boundary of an area of the usual kind already described, its junction with a scarp of rock at right angles to itself being reached.

The mode of operation which the disclosure of this new line pointed out was more hopefully entered upon; and at the end of seven weeks a doorway was uncovered in the face of this rock. When originally secured it had been carefully built up and the outside plastered with clay impressed in regular rows with a large seal, bearing an *oval*, somewhat indistinct, yet preserving the name of King Amunoph III.; but an aperture was found in this building boding ill for the state of the interior, which it had been intended to protect. And every fear was realised. The tomb was a large, undecorated, rectangular chamber, measuring from forty to fifty feet in each direction, with six square rock-pillars supporting the roof. At one of the inner corners a sunk passage led to another vault on a somewhat lower level, the entrance to which, also once closed and sealed, but with another cartouch\*, had likewise been broken through, and with what object was sufficiently manifest. The floors were strewn with bones, torn bandages, fragments — but these not numerous — of mummy-boxes, and (in the lower chamber) with mummies themselves, their wrappings ripped up along the throat and breast. A careful search, which I caused to be made among the *débris*, only produced fourteen small inscribed tablets of thin wood, about two inches and a half long by two broad, and rounded at the top, each pierced with a hole for the purpose of attaching it to a body. Similar slabs of a larger size, but with Greek inscriptions, are not unfamiliar Egyptian relics; and during the previous summer a considerable number of this kind, several of which I procured, were found at Goorneh, although in what precise locality I could not correctly ascertain. The legends on those Greek examples for the most part contained the name of the deceased and the age at which he died.

The hieratic inscriptions on the fourteen tablets in question likewise present names, and names of a very unexpected kind, being those of princesses of the family of Thothmes III. The inscriptions will be published along with facsimiles of the papyri which

---

\* This seal, which bears a jackal and three rows each of three kneeling men with their hands tied behind them, Mr. Birch remarks to be the same as the stamp used hieroglyphically by the sealer for stamping cattle pronounced to be clean, and refers for a similar representation to *Horapollo*, ed. Leemans, Pl. III. fig. 47 a. He adds, that in inscriptions he has found the tomb often called *khatem*, the sealed place.

TABLETS WITH NAMES OF PRINCESSES.

are presently to be mentioned, and will then receive full philological elucidation from Mr. Birch, who, considerately, as always, has communicated to me what he finds them to be. Distinguishing them by numbers, they are as follows:— No. 1. The Princess Nefru amen. No. 2. The Princess Han en annu. No. 3. The Princess Ptah meri, or Meri en ptah. No. 4. The Princess Uai. No. 5. The Princess Sat [en] Hara. No. 6. The Princess Pet pui. No. 7. The Princess Pet pui surnamed Ta . . . en aui. No. 8. The Princess Pet aha of the sun, placer of the world [Thothmes III.]. No. 9. In the year 27 the 11th day of the month Pharmuthi, the Princess Neb tu aa, daughter of the Princess Sat [en] atum. No. 10. The Princess Ta enti of the sun, the placer of creation, of the house of the royal family who are after her (or behind her) —

    The Mason Tukai.
    The Guardian Tsa.
    The Guardian Nef ru er ha t f.
    The Embalmer Nefer renpau.

"Of No. 11 the lines proceed thus:—

    The Princess Nini . . . . .
    House of the royal children . . . .
    The Mason Moa . . . . .
    The Guardian . . . . .
    The Guardian Nefer . . . .
    The Embalmer . . . . . . .

"The other three are duplicates of Nos. 2, 7, and 8;

and all are more than usually interesting as being the first reference yet found to the family of Thothmes III."

How those tablets came to be in this tomb, or rather what their presence there may be held to imply, I have great difficulty in conjecturing. Such distinguishing slips, known as tesseræ[*], were attached to bodies, and this was obviously their destination here, some even retaining pieces of the cord which had passed through them. But it is inconceivable that the rifled mummies among which they were found should have been the daughters of a king, whose power and architectural works were so considerable as those of Thothmes III. The tomb itself, although undecorated, might, possibly, be considered, from its reasonably large size, to be sufficiently fitted for such occupants; but the sepulchral accompaniments, as shown by the fragments of common coffins, and somewhat coarse linen swathings, not abundant in quantity, are not to be easily reconciled with the idea that the bodies were actually those of princesses of the royal blood. The wooden tablets, themselves, would also perhaps have been inappropriately rude media to have borne their epitaphs. If, therefore, the inscriptions upon them are to be held to have had a personal relation, I should be inclined to surmise that it must be by sup-

---

[*] Mr. Birch, in alluding to tesseræ as having been fastened to bodies when transported from place to place, points out to me that such are mentioned in a papyrus in the British Museum. Peyron, B., *Pap. Grec.* p. 40.

posing that some of the mummies in this tomb had been slaves or attendants of the palace, and that the names with which they were ticketed were those of personages whose special guardianship they thus, as it were, assumed, or to whose suites they had been attached. The cartouch of Amunoph III., with which the door was sealed, although also countenancing the supposition, does not necessarily indicate that the tomb had any connexion even of this sort with royalty, as the monarch's name was so generally used in various ways; but at any rate it proves that the last burial had taken place in his reign, which began (*circa* 1400 B.C.), about ten years after the death of Thothmes III. At what time the sepulchre had been broken into there was nothing to show, or by whom the ransacking had been accomplished.

A result like that which it exhibited when I gained an entrance, if not altogether unexpected, could not be otherwise than vexatious. But the work here was not yet concluded, and there was still a chance of a more successful issue, or rather, as I then feared, of another disappointment. While the entrance to the tomb which proved such a comparative failure was being reached, I had another party of workmen engaged clearing farther along the same face of rock in which it was cut. At a distance of twenty feet, a brick wall* built up to the rock was a favourable sign, and fifteen

---

* This wall had no doubt been part of a porch such as is described in p. 54.

feet beyond there was certain promise of another door. This point was attained almost simultaneously with the fruitless opening of the other; and, with so little encouragement to persevere, it was a spiritless task to attempt, what would still be a laborious affair—gaining an entry into a sepulchre which, it could hardly be doubted, was of the same uninteresting class, and had shared also the same fate as that in such close proximity. The discovery of two coarse jars and a small plain mummy-box within the brick wall and near the rock, was also a bad omen; for it had already several times occurred to me to meet with such evidences of meagre burials, in the rubbish at the entrance of previously-rifled tombs.

Although the doorway, as I have said, could almost be detected, the sloping mass of superincumbent stones and sand was for many days an effectual barrier, constantly pouring down like a torrent until a gradient of a sufficient angle was formed. A fortnight more was, therefore, consumed before all doubts were to be resolved; and then appeared another unfavourable symptom, that although the entrance was built up, the rock above had either been broken through, or had fallen in from natural decay. At length a passage to the inside was cleared, and the time had come to ascertain the result, expected with some anxiety but with hardly any hope. The sun was setting ere ingress was obtained, and shedding its last rays on the eager faces of the workmen, who crowded round at a prescribed distance from the entrance, anxiously on the alert for some report

PLATE II

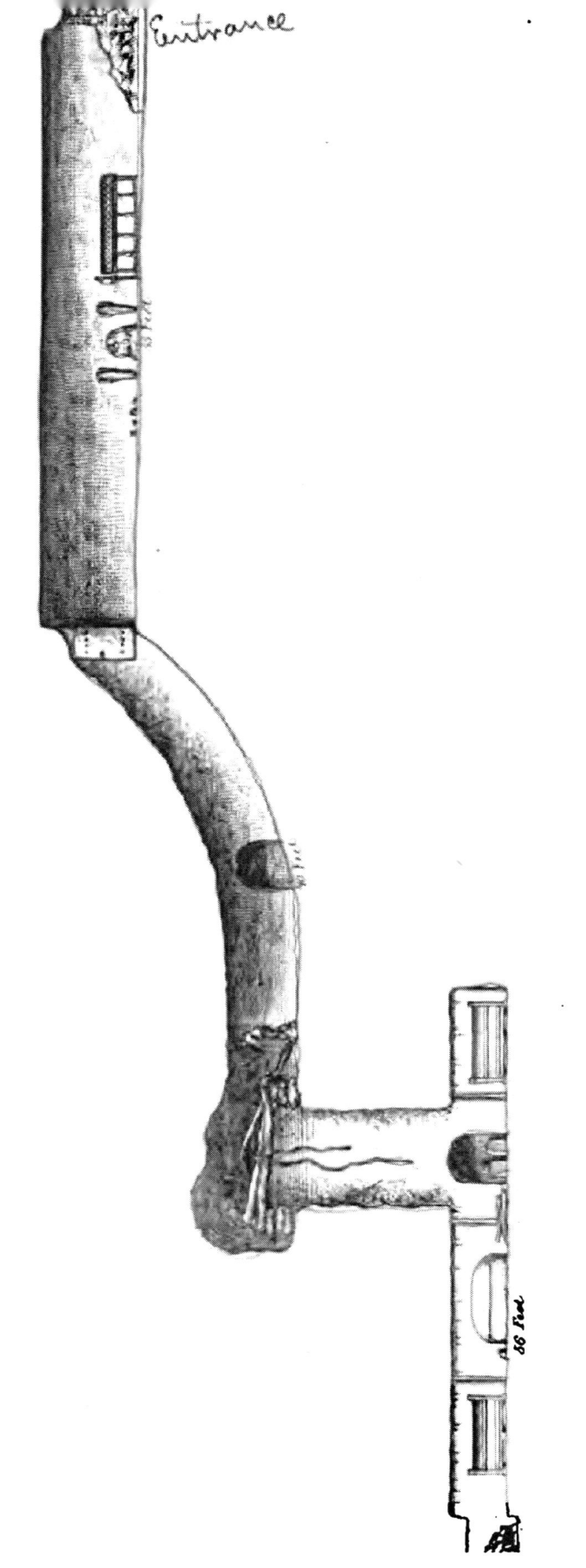

Entrance

86 Feet.

SECTION SHOWING THE TOMB AND ITS CONTENTS AS DISCOVERED.

from the interior. Many, being old hands at this sort of business, felt all the interest of a rude professional keenness; but it was natural that the whole of them should manifest some excitement at the moment which was to determine the fruit of a labour on which they had been for more than two months engaged, while it also perhaps acted as a stimulant that a contingent *backsheesh* depended on the event. The word was speedily passed out descriptive of the state of matters within, and was received by a shout from the expectant band, some of them, naked as they were, dancing about in their peculiar way, in slow circular hops, with their hands raised in the air. It was the evidence, however, of what might be anticipated, rather than the actual disclosure presented at the moment, which warranted this demonstration.

The chamber into which entrance had been thus effected was eight feet and a half broad, about eight feet high, and penetrated the hill to the length of fifty-five feet, as shown in the section Plate III. It was found to be quite clear of rubbish, except about the doorway, where the rock above (as I before mentioned) had been broken or had fallen; and the walls, unfortunately undecorated, were smoothly plastered with clay. About half-way along, a curious object stood upon the floor, the more remarkable and striking because to me it was altogether unexampled; and indeed it is, so far as I know, of its kind unique. This was a funeral canopy of wood, brightly painted, and in perfect preservation, as represented in the plate forming the frontispiece to this volume, to which I shall presently revert.*

Near it lay, tossed together, chipped, and fractured, four stones, not hollowed, but cut each in one piece, as is sometimes the case, in imitation of the common viscera vases, with the heads of the genii of the Amenti; and farther inwards, close to the wall, was a statue in limestone, two feet high, of a pair of figures seated lovingly together, as was the Egyptian fashion of conjugal portraiture, although here, in point of fact, the relationship was fraternal.† This group (Plate IV.) represents a person named *Ur en ma* [tai] a chief of mercenaries, a military officer attached to the police of the temple of Amun Ra at Thebes, along with his sister‡;

---

* It may be well to state, for the information of any who might wish to know where this and the other relics of mine mentioned in this volume are to be seen, that they and all such antiquities as I have had opportunities to collect are now in the Royal Museum at Edinburgh, to which I have had satisfaction in presenting them, in the belief that objects of this kind are best deposited in a public collection the property of the Government, where their presence is more likely to be useful, and security against loss or dispersion is ensured.

† This circumstance in some sense reminds us of the fact, that intermarriages, even between brother and sister, took place in Egypt, at all events in the later royal line.

‡ In addition to this, Mr. Birch gives the following note as to the inscriptions:—On the dress of the figures is the beginning of the formula: "All food off the tables of Amen Ra and Mut are given to the deceased." The six lines on the back are the dedications; and the reading commences from the right:—

1. His sister beloved from the depth of his heart . . . .

2. Consecrated to Amen Ra, lord of the Horizon, who let the Osiris *Ur en ma tai* [chief of mercenaries], see the sun at its rising.

PLATE IV

SARCOPHAGUS WITH FIGURES FROM THE ROCK CHAMBER

and while it may be regarded as a direct memorial of the first or an early owner of the sepulchre, it likewise, from being mutilated, was another evidence of the changes which had taken place — evidence which subsequently became more clear when further research demonstrated that there had been a double appropriation of the tomb. There were also, one on either side of the statue, two tall cylindrical jars (amphoræ) with conical pointed bottoms, and handles attached where the contraction for the lip rises from the narrowing bulge. Finally, the innermost corner to the right was occupied by a large coarse clay platter, half filled with dry mortar, the rest of which had probably been used to complete those arrangements, whose appearance gave rise to such sanguine expectations.

The assuring features were the entrances, carefully built up and intact, of two passages diverging from the chamber, one at the inner end, the other about midway along the left-hand side. Nor were these the only or

---

3. Consecrated to Mut, the great mother, mistress of Askeru, who gave food to the Osiris *Ur en ma tai* [chief of mercenaries].

4. Consecrated to Khunsu in Gami, Neferhetp, who gave water and incense to the Osiris *Ur en ma tai* [chief of mercenaries].

5. Consecrated to Osiris Un nefer, who gave food and air to the Osiris *Ur en m. . . .* [chief of mercenaries].

6. Consecrated to Isis, the mother goddess, who gave incense and libations daily to the Osiris *Ur en m. . . .* [chief of mercenaries].

The mutilation of the lower part of the statue leaves some doubt as to the fact of the name or title being expressed by *Ur en m. . . .* The group is perhaps as old as the Eighteenth Dynasty, but the style of hair rather resembles that of the Nineteenth. It was dedicated to the Theban and Abydene Triads.

the most encouraging signs, for at the farthest corner of the same side was the opening of another cutting in the rock, secured by a massive wooden door, barred, locked, and protected by a barricade of large stones built in front of it to half its height.

Those details ascertained, there was still to be a probation of suspense before the barriers could be removed that guarded the penetralia; for the night was falling, and besides, it was necessary to have the outer entrance more thoroughly cleared to facilitate operations inside. I had, therefore, reluctantly to postpone the examination, leaving the place in charge of a guard chiefly composed of Nubian sailors from our boat, which lay idly in the river. They were posted outside the tomb, and relieved and visited from time to time during the night; for the *fellaheen* of Goorneh are little to be trusted in anything, and least of all where antiquities are concerned, to the traffic in which so much of their demoralization is owing.

Early next day the preliminaries were completed, and the men selected to break through the built-up doorways were soon set to work. A few minutes sufficed to remove the obstructions, and, with them, almost every foundation of hope. The side entrance led to a small cell about eight feet by six, and that at the end, to another rather more than twice that size. Instead of an untouched deposit in each, both were in confusion. The mummy-cases had been broken open, and the bodies, denuded of many of their wrappings, were, for the most part, lying beside them, not having even been replaced except in one or two instances. Their date was to some extent defined by the style of mummification, the arms being crossed over the breast, and the conserving substance being a dark pitchy bitumen; but the double wooden shells in which they had been placed being quite unlettered, and externally plain black, indicated nothing. Nor was anything discovered by a careful examination of the rifled bodies. Among the *débris*, however, were several painted funeral tablets of wood of the usual character, boxes that had contained sepulchral clay images, wooden jackals, hawks, the common upright swathed figures on pedestals, and a torn scrap of a hieroglyphic papyrus. In the innermost cell one of the very lamps whose light had aided this destruction, or the consequences of it, stood in a corner. Of the plainest circular form, conventionally termed Roman, moulded of coarse terra cotta, and bearing the evidence of use on its blackened nozzle and half-exhausted wick, it had not been removed when, nearly two thousand years before, the contents of the rifled crypt had been huddled in, and the doorway built up as if to show that, while the intruders thought it no sacrilege to despoil, the common tribute paid to the mortal vestiges of man as such, constrained them not to deprive these utterly of shelter.

Kept for the last, there still remained the most important-looking passage — that closed by the massive door; and now beginning to suspect what might have been the sort of treatment experienced by the tomb, I still trusted that this might lead to something of interest, notwithstanding the disheartening condition of the two chambers, which were quite as effectually, if not so elaborately, secured. The door itself was a remarkable object, from its strength and the perfect freshness of all its parts, including two wooden pin-locks of the kind now used in Egypt, the iron nails with large heads with which it was fastened together, and staples of the same metal, in which a bar slipped to and fro. Indeed, so sound and substantial was its whole fabric, after having done duty in this grim abode for at least twenty centuries, that in a region where timber is scarce, it was regarded by wise householders who subsequently saw it, as a most desirable piece of property. And my native servant, a Copt who, about that time I ascertained, was curiously enough in deacon's orders, seeing I did not propose to carry it away, begged that from among the numerous aspirants to the gift, including a bishop, a consular agent, and two shekhs, he might be selected. If he kept his word, which I am obliged to confess is somewhat doubtful, it now hangs in the portals of a church or convent in Cairo.

On it all interest was now concentrated, and it speedily swung round, disclosing a tunnel nearly six feet high. Winding slightly and sloping downwards, this cavernous passage led on through the rock for about seventy feet, terminating at the edge of a shaft ten feet by six. But considerably before the tunnel reached that point two cuttings diverged, one on either side, with their entrances firmly built up. For a few minutes attention was diverted to them, that each recess as it occurred might be examined in turn; and again the result was miserably unsatisfactory. These openings were the doors of cells, which were similar in size, and had been treated in a precisely similar manner to those connected with the outer chamber; and from among the shattered vestiges, which partly filled them, only a few such objects were recovered as I have described those last to have contained. There was now no further reason for delaying the examination of the well-like pit, the final, and not for that reason only the most exciting repository. Reared above it, an erection supporting strong beams, over which the very rope of twisted palm fibres still hung, that had lowered to their resting-place the tenants of the sepulchre beneath, appealed with striking force to the imagination, and presented one of those telling pictures which, from the very simplicity of their details, are often the most suggestive exponents of the acts in which they have borne a part. In due time a pioneer was let down to the bottom of the shaft, a depth of nearly twenty feet; and he reported the existence of chambers penetrating from each of the four sides — one being closed by a strong wooden door. To ascertain this was the extent of his commission, but soon a careful examination followed, and showed the chambers to contain the last funeral deposit they had received, in undisturbed security.

Thus far a reference to the general section of the tomb, Plate III., will aid the description; but with regard to the account which must now follow of the lower chambers, the plan \* of their arrangement in Plate V. should be kept in view. In it they are distinguished by numbers, which may be conveniently used as a means of designation.

No. 1, being not quite ten feet long and five feet six in breadth, was little more than large enough to accommodate its contents. Side by side on the floor, and almost in contact, there were a heavy, rather ill-finished mummy-case, shaped in the usual form of the swathed body, with bands of blue hieroglyphics on a white ground — and a plain unsmoothed deal shell or box dove-tailed at the corners. On the breast of the former a wreath of leaves was twined, and above the knees there rested the tiny bodies of two very young children, covered only by a few folds of simple bandages, the outer rolls of which encircled them together. The latter also bore a similar but a heavier burden — the mummy of a full-grown man carefully swathed, the exterior cloth being painted to represent the lineaments of the face, the hands, and the feet, with

---

\* For laying down the measured draught of this plan I was indebted to the readily volunteered assistance of Mr. Wenham and of Mr. Frith, who was then in the neighbourhood filling up the series of his admirably successful photographic views of Egypt and Syria.

PLATE V

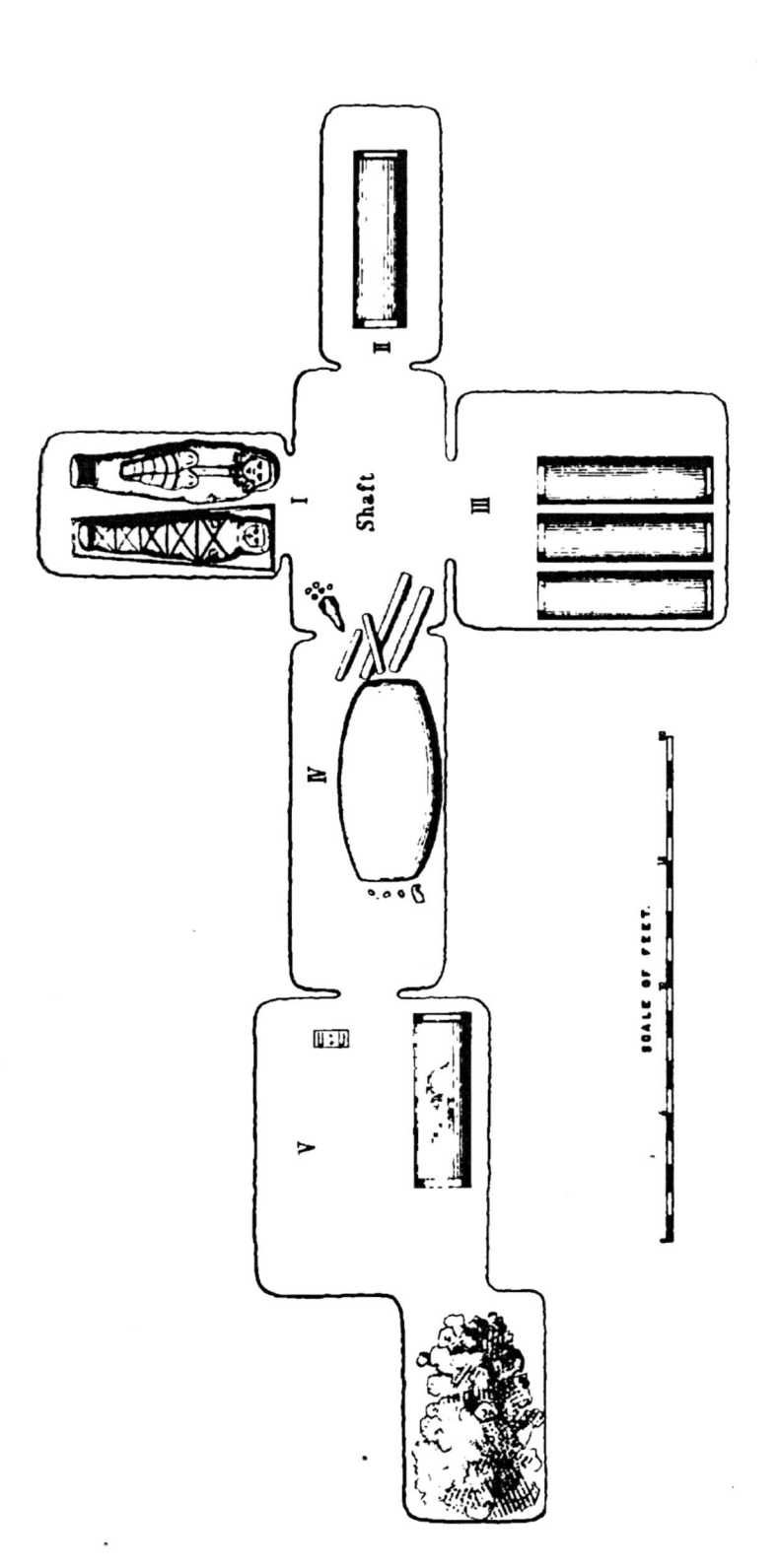

PLAN OF THE LOWER MUMMY VAULTS.

SCALE OF FEET.

a line of hieroglyphics from the neck down the front to the extremities. And this was the common method of decorating the corpse during the Roman dominion in Egypt.

The box, which was merely the simplest form of a deal coffin, contained an undecorated mummy. The large case, its neighbour, enclosed two, one the body of a man, the other that of a young girl, bearing two bracelets of bronze or copper, two coarse anklets of iron, and an ear-ring of the same metal, whited in a peculiar manner, as if with silver or tin. The prominent circumstance connected with these two bodies was the slight degree of trouble that had been expended to prepare the mummy-case for them. It had undoubtedly been constructed for a very different tenant — for a tenant of a much earlier time, and probably had held the remains of one of the first owners of this tomb; but whether it had been thus procured on the spot where it was again employed, or not, the method of appropriation had been very summary. For the lid, which showed marks of having once been violently wrenched off, was only laid loosely on, the fractured slips or tongues of wood, which had originally secured it, not having been restored to efficiency, while they were in some cases completely broken away. Nor could this be explained by assuming, with reference to the presence of two bodies, that the coffin had first been deposited with one, and subsequently, as a continuation even in death of earthly affection, opened to receive the other, that of the young girl, which was uppermost; for, besides the evidence of rough usage, it was plain that the case was made having regard to a mummy of different dimensions from either of those within it, and intended to be differently disposed. The corroborative analogy of other facts observed in the tomb likewise went to prove, that here was one of the instances of appropriation of a quite improvised and certainly undisguised character.

Chamber No. 2 was closed by a wooden door, and contained one large coffin, of the plain uninteresting type, constructed with square pillars at the corners, one long panel in either side, and a semicircular top. In this instance a demotic inscription on the end of the case, which will be considered along with the papyri, was a distinguishing peculiarity.

Chamber No. 3, being ten feet four by nine feet seven, afforded ample space for the three similar mummy-cases, which were stored in it.

In chamber No. 4 stood a massive sarcophagus, of the dark granite of Assouan, quite unpolished, and chiselled no more than was necessary to bring it into shape. Immediately in front of it, and protruding into the shaft, lay some of the appliances which had doubtless been used to move the cumbrous mass,— and the presence of the old workers was singularly recalled, even here in the depths of the grave, by rollers and planks which they had left on the spot, where, as mechanical aids, they had employed them. The planks, too, were another proof of the disregard with

## GRANITE SARCOPHAGUS AND ITS ACCOMPANIMENTS. 99

which the older occupants of the tomb had been treated, for they were the sides of broken mummy-cases, covered with hieroglyphic groups, in the style which is usually met with on coffins of the period of the Eighteenth and Nineteenth Dynasties.

Likewise at the doorway of this vault lay a tall, cylindrical jar, precisely like the two formerly described as discovered in the upper chamber of the tomb. It is inscribed near the neck with what appears to be a short line in demotic, almost entirely defaced; and it was nearly filled with the fruit of the Dom palm. Several more nuts of this tree were also strewed about: and they were very frequently accompaniments of the Egyptian dead. I have several times found them in tombs, sometimes along with the common date, sycamore fig, and other fruits.

At the head of the sarcophagus four curious objects were placed upon the floor. First came a figure about eighteen inches long, being the body of a dog very nearly of the shape and size of a small Italian greyhound [*], imperfectly preserved with natron, and swathed in osiers. Then followed a mummied ibis; a copy of a small hawk perched on a pedestal, considerably decayed, but apparently constructed of folds of linen cloth gummed together; and an oblate ball of bitumen from three to four inches in diameter. There

---

[*] The wall paintings preserve, among the numerous representations of dogs, figures of one breed "with a pointed nose and prick ears," to which the above most probably belonged. An example may be seen in Wilkinson's *Egyptians in the Time of the Pharaohs*, p. 83.

can be little doubt that we are to regard these accompaniments of the departed as significant, in a religious point of view, with reference to the ritualistic teaching on the subject of death and its sequel. Not that in the canine mummy we may perceive an illustration of a simple creed, like that of some untutored nomad,

> "Who thinks, admitted to that equal sky,
> His faithful dog will bear him company."

We shall have to look farther for the explanation, and find it in the never-ending symbolism of Egyptian worship, when it will probably stand thus. The dog[*] was one of the emblems of Anubis, who ranked as the genius of tombs, and who, as in the gold ornament on the breast of the mummy in Plate VII., is constantly represented as bending over the dead body. His special duty was to guide the newly disembodied soul as it passed from the present life to the future, and to aid at the final judgment in weighing the actions which constituted its earthly career. In the ibis, again, we have the emblem of the recording angel, if from this one of his attributes we may so name Thoth, who wrote down and recounted to Osiris the deeds of the deceased. And the hawk was the symbolic bird of that other important functionary of Amenti, Horus, who, after having first taken part along with Anubis,

[*] Herodotus affirms that when a dog died a natural death in a private house all the inmates shaved not only the head but the whole person.—*Lib.* ii. c. 66. It was death to kill a dog according to Cicero.—*Nat. Deor.* i. 29; *Tuscul. Qu.* v. 27.

in weighing the good and bad actions of the trembling souls, ushered those whose welcome was secured into the presence of Osiris. In the ball of bitumen was imbedded a coiled snake, of what species the thoroughly amalgamated character of the mass renders it difficult or impossible to determine. But most probably the mummy is that of a horned snake. This variety being sacred to Amun, it was a custom, Herodotus states, to bury it in his temple at Thebes, of which city we know he was pre-eminently the god, his title on the monuments there being generally " King of the Gods:" and Sir G. Wilkinson intimates that it was "not unusual to find these snakes embalmed in the tombs of Goorneh."*

The inner end of chamber No. 4 communicated with another, No. 5, which contained one more pillared mummy-case, with a festoon of crumbling evergreens resting upon it. And lying, as it were carelessly, on the floor, was a block of stone bearing on one side a portion of a decorative subject, showing that it must have been carried from the ruins of some building, probably the Ramseseum, already dilapidated, which stands at no great distance, and with the materials of which, as indeed with those of any temple, it perfectly accords. The presence of this stone is perhaps to be accounted for on the supposition that it had been used like the rollers and planks to move the granite sarcophagus, as a fulcrum or otherwise.

At the farthest corner of this vault was the en-

---

* *Ancient Egyptians*, 2nd series, vol. i. p. 248.

trance to yet another, on a slightly lower level, and nearly filled with stone chips and rubbish, among which were no traces of sepulchral remains. This was the limit of the subterranean gallery, whose extreme length from the end of this chamber through Nos. 5 and 4, across the shaft and on to the end of No. 2, was fifty-six feet. The height of the vaults was within two or three inches of five feet; and their roofs were encrusted with dependent crystals proceeding from the nitrous and calcareous constituents of the rock.

Such were the deep recesses of the tomb, such the method in which the dead had been left to their rest, as every object evidently remained in precisely the position it had occupied when the funeral rites were performed over the last who had "*gone down into this pit.*" For had its gloomy silence been ever broken by explorers during any of the subsequent centuries, through whose long course treasure-seeking has more or less vigorously flourished, it would not be conceivable that the mummy-cases should stand intact, and particularly that an imposing receptacle like the sarcophagus, so well calculated to excite the hopes of searchers, should be permitted to retain, unattempted, the mystery of its interior. But the time had come when those who had reposed so long were to be disturbed in turn, although there were no successors to be established as they had been in the place of which some of them were to be dispossessed. The tunnel above and the vaults beneath were fully lighted up, the grim corridors resounded with the song of a band of excited *fellaheen*, as they pulled at the hoisting ropes, and the old beams, erected over the shaft, once more bore the unanticipated weight of the coffins, which they had helped to lower to a home that might almost have been deemed as permanent as the duration of time itself.

The size and weight of the granite sarcophagus would have rendered it extremely difficult of removal from its site had that been desirable or necessary, but every purpose was answered by subjecting it to examination where it stood. The solid cover, freed from the cement with which the joint was seamed, was easily raised from the bed on which it simply rested without any of the contrivances for fastening it down that sometimes are seen to have formed part of similar relics. And then the subject of all this care was disclosed, surrounded by yet another precaution for its security. Under, above, and around the mummy, the whole sarcophagus was filled with bitumen which had been poured in hot, forming a compact mass adhering at all points with such tenacity as to require the most patient labour for its liberation. During the greater portion of this long and tedious work, Mr. Wenham, whose help I have already referred to, very kindly undertook to remain for me on the spot to watch and direct the progress of the operation. At length the object was safely attained, and subsequently, in the upper air, the crude encrustation of bitumen peeled readily away from the outer wrappings of the mummy.

At a very early stage of the process, the bright glitter of the leaf of a golden chaplet aroused to the wildest pitch the extravagant speculations which the *fellaheen* always entertain with regard to the probable contents of tombs of considerable extent. The presence of treasure was whispered about; and as many of the people in the neighbouring villages had been looking forward with great interest and absurd anticipations for the final result of this particular excavation, a marvellous report, magnifying as it spread, found willing ears, and, in an incredibly short time, pervaded the whole district for miles on either side. The story is now probably a fixed tradition, and it might be attempted in vain to shake the established belief that I procured a profuse amount of gold and jewels of dazzling value.*

And this was what gave origin and colour to the fable: the head of the mummy was cased by a gilt mask, outside of which, around the temples, a circlet reposed (Plate VI.). It consists of a ring of copper, whose metal, about half an inch in diameter, is thickly gilt; and eleven bay leaves of thin gold are attached to it by pliant stalks. Chaplets, if not of this precise arrangement, at least of golden leaves, were frequent accompaniments of burial in the ancient classical lands

---

* This notion of the rich harvest to be gleaned from old world vestiges, founded in some degree on fact, is by no means confined to the imaginative Easterns. I have found myself locally accredited with the same kind of good fortune while excavating among humble primeval remains in a remote part of Britain.

GOLDEN DIADEM FROM THE HEAD OF THE MUMMY IN THE GIANT'S "APPLE TART".

of Europe, and various collections, such, for instance, as that of the University of Palermo, and the Museo Gregoriano at Rome, contain examples, the one from Greek the other from Etruscan tombs. I cannot remember whether any evidence has been met with to show if the Egyptians in earlier times, under their native Pharaohs, decked, in any case, the brows of the dead with similar natural emblems. But of circlets of another kind, a notable specimen is preserved among the chief treasures of the museum at Leyden, which, instead of leaves, bears on its circumference the symbolically royal asp.\* It rested on the head of a mummy found, it is said, in El Drah-aboo-Neggeh, the western hill of the Theban Necropolis, under circumstances not certainly determinable, so far as I could learn, by inquiry on the spot. The mummy is stated to have been enclosed in a coffin bearing the name of one of the family of the Nentefs, whose chronological place is as remote as the Eleventh Dynasty†, or approximately from 2000 to 2500

---

\* Leeman's *Lettre à Salvolini.* Compare the asp-formed crowns mentioned on the Rosetta stone.

† In the adjustment of the Dynasties, as given by Mr. Poole (*Horæ Egyptiacæ*, p. 136, *et seq.*, and later, in the article *Egypt*, in the *Encyclopædia Britannica*) the Nentefs are placed in the Ninth, a Heracleapolite Dynasty; and they are similarly allocated by Sir Gardner Wilkinson (Rawlinson's *Herodotus*, vol. ii. p. 99, note 8), who has elsewhere shown reason for regarding them as Heracleapolites from the constituent letters of their name. This does not affect, according to the same view, the question of date, as by this arrangement the Ninth and Eleventh Dynasties are regarded as contemporaneous. But the fact of the coffin of the Nentef referred to having been found at

years before the Christian era. But as a jasper scarabæus, asserted to have been found upon the mummy, bears the name of *Sebek-em-saf*, of the Twenty-fifth Dynasty, some seventeen hundred years later, there would seem to be room to believe that the coffin of Nentef had undergone various vicissitudes, and that its last occupant, and therefore the crown, are not the representatives of an antiquity at all corresponding with that of their covering.

Another remarkable diadem from the head of a mummy, is a hoop of gold nearly an inch wide, graven and studded with scarabæi, now in the Mayer Collection at Liverpool*; but the character of zodiacal figures, which appear upon its inner surface, leads to the inference that it is to be attributed to a comparatively late time. One more exhausts the list of those which, within my knowledge, have been preserved. It is, save as to the leaf, nearly identical with that in Plate VI., and is described by Cailliaud†, who engraves it, as a chaplet of olive in copper gilt. The mummy whose head it decorated was one of several found in a tomb at Thebes, where the family to which they belonged held a high official position, one

---

Thebes, if we may infer that his tomb was there also, is certainly so far confirmatory of the family having been of the Eleventh, a Theban Dynasty, for this would accord with the analogy of all the royal sepulchres known in that necropolis being of kings of other Diospolitan Dynasties. Other more precise considerations of a chronological nature appear also to fix the Nentefs as the Eleventh Dynasty.

* See *Catalogue* of that collection, 1852.
† *Voyage à Meroë*, vol. iv. pp. 1, *seq.*

having been Archon of Thebes about the close of the first century A.D. This sepulchre appears to have fallen a prize to the *fellaheen* of Goorneh, for there is no minute account of it, and portions of its contents have found their way into several different hands. In many respects it presents a close analogy to the tomb I am in these pages describing. The occupants of the latter, or at least its principal tenant in the granite sarcophagus, as his papyrus shows, lived about a hundred and twenty years earlier than the personage whose mummy is depicted by M. Cailliaud, and who died in the nineteenth year of the reign of Trajan. But in a general way the dead in both tombs may be said to have belonged to the same period. The shape of their wooden coffins was the same, only, in the one case, these were plain, in the other covered with figures and hieroglyphics. The outer covering of the mummy copied in Cailliaud's plate is decorated with the identical pattern which I shall presently have to describe. The chaplets were almost correspondingly alike; and with one of the Archon's family was found a papyrus, deciphered by Champollion, in which his name, at least, (Cornelius), occurs not only in Greek but bilingually in Egyptian — in demotic and hieratic, — just as in the papyri about to come before us are longer passages in similar duplicate, and otherwise blending these two forms of writing. As to the golden ornament which has introduced this comparison, upon the whole it seems probable that the use of the sepulchral chaplet in Egypt was a direct graft of a Greek practice.* And we are reminded of the touching incident in the life of Pericles, when he, who had shown the Athenians how to meet evil fortune manfully, as the plague struck down one by one his family and friends, burst into an irresistible torrent of grief at the funeral of his last and favourite son, Paralus, when the time came for him to lay a garland on the body.†

✗ While the head of the mummy in question was decorated with this ornament set on a gilt casing, the outer cloth covering of the rest of the body was painted in colours designed in a diagonal pattern known in earlier Egyptian decorative work‡, but which seems to have been very popular in the Greek and succeeding period. The exteriors of two other mummies from this tomb were similarly painted. The same design is found on that copied by Cailliaud, as already alluded to, and, not to specify other examples, it appears again on a curious double mummy-case which I procured at

---

* It should, however, be observed, that although details are wanting to show whether in actual practice the use of such chaplets was an ancient native custom, there are two chapters, the nineteenth and twentieth, of the *Ritual of the Dead*, relating to what is called the "Crown of Justification." Whether this was intended to be something entirely symbolical it is difficult to know; but the illustrative vignettes of these chapters in the papyri represent just such chaplets resting upon a small altar, on one side of which stands the god *Atmou*, and on the other the deceased in an attitude of adoration. See copies in De Rougé, *Études sur le Rituel, Rev. Arch.* Fév. 1860.

† Plutarch, *Pericles*, c. 36.

‡ See a specimen on a boat, primarily, though not precisely the same, in a funeral procession. Rosellini, *Mon. del Cult.* tav. cxxx.; and if I remember aright the same or a nearly similar design may be seen on the roof of one of the very ancient grottoes at Silsili.

Thebes, and which, as a singular and rare relic, I may mention, contained two infants, side by side, with necklaces, small papyri over their left arms, and figures of Pthah on their breasts — all fastened to the folds of the outer bandages. But the diagonal pattern on the mummies also challenged remark, as additionally connecting them with the wooden canopy in the upper chamber, on the top of which the same ornamentation occurs.

Beneath this painted shroud of the occupant of the sarcophagus were numerous plain folds which, after a certain depth, were so saturated with fine bitumen and pungent gums, as to form one concrete mass with the body which they encased. Imbedded among them it was difficult to detect various small thin plates of gold (some being in the shape of winged scarabæi), and several pieces of vitreous composition — portions of emblems which had been studded in the bitumen after the fashion, better illustrated in the case of another mummy which I shall subsequently describe. From the usual position on the left side a large Ritual papyrus was recovered in excellent condition, and besides proving to be highly instructive philologically, it throws light as we shall presently see on the less important subject of the status and family relations of its bearer. Physically, he appeared to have been, as in reality he was, a man of mature years, with features strongly marked, but of their special characteristics it would be impossible to speak definitely, on account of the adhesive nature of the cerements. The skin of the upper part of the body had been gilt with thick gold leaf; and the arms, first bound round by a single bandage, were brought down by the sides, with the hands resting under the thighs, and then embedded in the general swathing. That is to say they were not rolled up apart according to the practice commonly attributed to Greek times, by which also each finger was often separately bandaged.

All the mummies in the pillared cases, being five, and, indeed, all the others in the tomb, were laid in the same attitude, and the upper portions of several of the former were likewise gilt. Of these, one of a lady from chamber No 3, the wife of the occupant of the granite sarcophagus, bore also on the left side a papyrus, to which we shall hereafter return. Another was decorated with a gilt mask. And another, being a handsome specimen of the style of ornamenting externally, by means of inlaid or impressed emblems of gold and coloured vitreous composition, in the manner which, to a greater or less extent, prevailed on all, I removed and have retained in the condition in which the Plate (VII.) represents it. In this instance the compact bitumenised cloths began to occur beneath not more than two outer layers of the ordinary linen, and here, in the black glutinous substance, are embedded the figures. The genii of the Amenti are on the left side, over the spot probably of the ventral incision; Pthah above the knees; Anubis with the corpse, on the breast; the hawks of Horus on the shoulders; the pillar of stability on the forehead;

PLATE VII

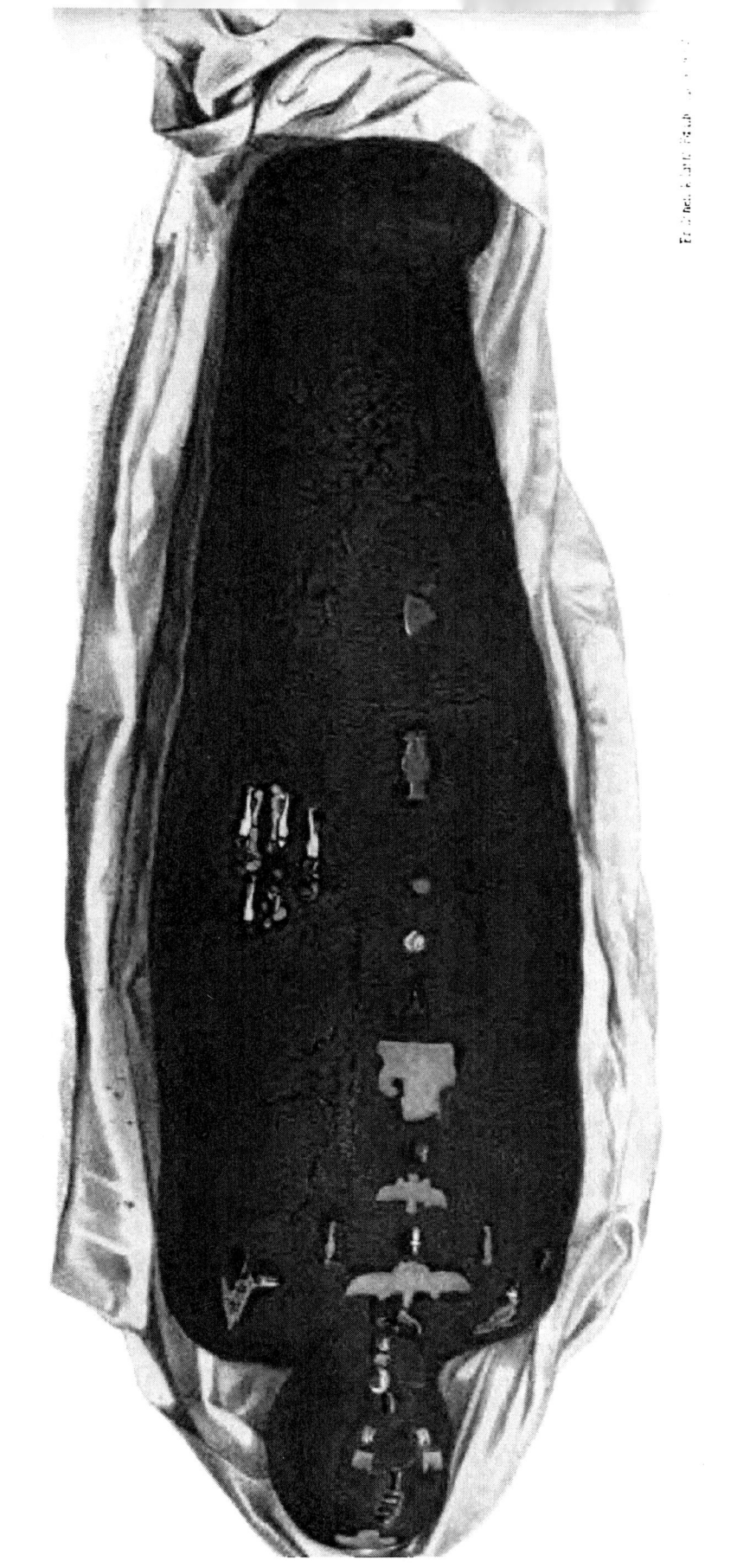

eyes of Horus over the eyes; vultures and scarabæi with outstretched wings; and other emblems of the same nature.

Reverting now for a moment to the funeral canopy, there can be little doubt that this designation correctly describes the service in which it had been employed. The sculptures and wall paintings constantly exhibit, in mortuary processions, the mummy resting in a boat, sledge, or car, as the case may be, covered with a species of shrine. Those shrines usually appear to have been large and cumbrous, presenting to the eye almost the architectural solidity of dwarfed temples; but I remember at least two or three instances in which they are represented with something like the lighter proportions of that in the frontispiece. One occurred upon the bandages of a mummy[*]; another is part of the model of a boat found by Passalacqua[†] in an undisturbed tomb at Thebes, already mentioned. Although the nature of objects of this kind has therefore been sufficiently familiar, there is, I believe, no evidence of any actual example having before been met with. The inscription[‡] which it bears along the

[*] The group has been frequently engraved. See Wilkinson's *Ancient Egyptians*, or his Notes to Rawlinson's *Herodotus*, vol. ii. p. 108.

[†] The plate in his *Catalogue Raisonné* represents it imperfectly. It may be seen better on a larger scale in Pettigrew's *History of Mummies*, Plate III. Rosellini gives two subjects from tombs where the shrines are of light open work.—*Mon. Civ.* tav. cxxvii. A more substantially constructed one may be compared. *Ib.* cxxviii.

[‡] I am indebted again to Mr. Birch for the following rendering of the inscription:—" Oh Osiris Mentu-Sebau, justified, son of the

top, referring almost certainly to the same individual as the large papyrus from the granite coffin, indicates that the canopy had been used in the funeral obsequies of the personage for whom the sarcophagus had been provided; and it would seem to have been left in the upper chamber, when the mummy, which it had probably overshadowed in the procession, was carried below to the prepared abode.

The history of the sepulchre whose details I have thus attempted to describe, may, with no great difficulty be surmised. Most of the painted tombs in its vicinity in the same hill, whose decorations and inscriptions specify their age, date from the time of the great dynasties of Thebes, and there is every reason to believe from its position, that this one also had been excavated and used at the same period. Indeed the tomb immediately adjoining, whose entrance I discovered first in the area, which must, to all appearance, have been cut with equal reference to both, was sealed, as we have seen, with a cartouch bearing the name of Amunoph III. (about 1400 B.C.): and in all reasonable probability this indication of age may be fairly held as of common application to the two. Morever, this conclusion is

lady of the house, the Sistrum-bearer Rut pi mentu, son of Menkar ra [Mencheres] justified! Him who is attached to the embalming, thou hast come to; he has prepared thy bones; he who is over the hill [Necropolis] has washed thy flesh; he comes to thee under the . . . of the God, . . . : the place of punishment of the Great God, thy mother Nu [the firmament] has placed thee within her. Thou failest not [to be] there for ever."

corroborated by the style of the mutilated statue, the characteristic mummification of the rifled bodies, the construction of the broken coffins, and the other sepulchral adjuncts of the older burials, of which the later spoilers had preserved the traces.

Whether the original occupants were allowed to sleep on in peace until the time of the last appropriation, or whether their right of property had been occasionally infringed in the interval, or themselves and others also in turn displaced according to a not unusual practice for adding to the revenues of the priestly custodiers or owners of the tombs, can only be conjectured. But twelve or thirteen hundred years had elapsed before possession was so rudely taken, and the forcible and final innovation accomplished which left the tomb in the condition in which I found it. Then, in the first century before our era, a complete and radical change was effected. The older mummies were, as we have seen, cast aside, and their home usurped amid circumstances which are at least significant, if the tenor of history forbids that they should excite surprise. Lapse of time, the supposition of difference and dominance of race will account for much; but still it continues remarkable that the last resting-place, and even the corpses of predecessors, should have been treated with such little respect by people who were quite as emulous to secure for their own mortal remains, by the embalmer's aid, a material immortality, and who were to occupy the very same tomb. But in point of fact, it is not necessary to believe that the rifling and the taking possession were part of the same act, or executed by the same hands. The robbery of the dead which in former pages we have seen to have prevailed from very early times, and especially after the revolution occasioned by the Persian conquest, when Cambyses himself is stated to have violated the sanctity even of royal sepulchres—the occurrence of this kind of robbery and the decay into which the Necropolis, like the city of Thebes, must have been falling, leave no difficulty in supposing that the tomb in question had been some time previously spoiled, and left neglected, when it was appropriated and cleared for its latest tenants, the family of Sebau. Not, however, that in thus so far dissociating the new occupants from disrespect to the old, it follows that the existence of deeper feelings on their part must be assumed, of a different character from the ordinary dictates of decency in such a matter. In fact, it would appear that the sanctity attached to the body was not conscientiously attended to by the custodiers of the dead themselves, the priests, even while the ancient faith flourished under native princes. But in the course of ages, and especially after foreign conquest introduced new psychical elements into the country, although the old temples were frequented, and others dedicated to members of the same pantheon, although funeral customs and observances remained, in essentials at least, not greatly altered, this conformity did not necessarily imply a fixed perpetuation of the ideas which had been the origin of these developments. The Greeks followed the formulas of their ancient faith when all their vitality had exhaled, and the gods, from personal individuality, had vanished into mere symbols. The citizen of Rome, in the midst of a blanker scepticism, also continued the language and rites of the past, and in externals committed himself to the future very much after the fashion of his fathers. The Norse Bærserk was carried to his grave prepared for a doubted Walhalla, and in life he poured out horns of beer to Odin and Thor, to Frigga and Balder, although it might be that, strong in his fierce vigour, he had just defied "the sacred wielder of the hammer, *if such there were*," to come and measure his strength with one who believed only in his own martial prowess.

The operation in Egypt also of any law of development, or change, or degradation of this kind, it is true, is not necessarily to be assumed merely analogically, although such law, wherever intellect is not asleep, would seem to apply especially to religions into which polytheism has introduced a fruitful element of mutability. And even others in which this is wanting, such as Buddhism—originally a system of self-reliant effort, rather than of aid-seeking worship—have hardly shown more permanent fixity.* But in Egypt itself, notwithstanding that close approach to fossilization of mind and manners, which so remarkably characterised its type of

* See M. Müller's *Hist. of Sanskrit Lit.* p. 34, and his brochure *Buddhism.*

civilization, there is distinct reason to believe that the husk and emblems of religion contained and represented no unvarying ideology. Whether, at any period from which monuments exist, it had ever possessed the stern realism of a faith held in unity and simplicity alike by priests and people, may never perhaps be precisely determined; but if any such germinal stage had existed, the evidence rather points to its having passed ere the history of the Nile valley comes within the horizon of our vision. In the more recent times, with which we have here chiefly to do, however much earlier, the world-old struggle between reasonable faith and credulous superstition had resulted in an esoteric and exoteric partition of creed — had produced in this case a philosophico-mystical scheme for the *illuminati*, a congeries of ancient practices, and probably meaningless conceptions for the mass.

But even if in the later days religious customs, such as those connected with the burial of the dead, had lost something of their original significance, it is remarkable to observe, while changes have unquestionably to be noted, how much of their identity, were it only in great part ceremonially, was perpetuated through so many ages. Mummification, although, judging by the remains, it cannot well have been followed to the same extent, was still the honourable fashion of disposing of the dead, and chapters of the Ritual (itself a thing of growth), written on a papyrus scroll, deposited by their side, were, for persons of consequence, the prescribed accompaniment. Coffins of simpler construction, with different or no decoration, and generally a less elaborate entombment, characterise the later Ptolemaic and Roman age. The actual divergences, as between this and other and earlier epochs, it is impossible, as has been already remarked, to state with accuracy, in the absence of sufficiently extensive observations. But on gathering up the stray threads of evidence, it would appear that as far as the Necropolis of Thebes is concerned, those deposits of tools or weapons, of household or personal objects, which have been so constantly found with the older interments, are not met with (except to a small extent as regards the more ordinary personal ornaments and such like), with burials of later time. Of more directly religious accompaniments, if the distinction may be drawn, none are so invariable among the sepulchral furniture of the older periods, as boxes of the small clay or stone figures shaped like swathed mummies, and tablets of wood or pottery painted with effigies in colours or gold, of the gods such as Horus, Anubis, Osiris, with whom the dead had chiefly to do, and inscribed with corresponding invocations. Likewise, not to mention specific varieties, there are rarely wanting the doll-like statuettes of Athor or other deities, the hawks of Horus, and the black-painted jackal of Anubis. In later days it would seem that a very small part of this paraphernalia was employed. The clay figures, the tablets, the statuettes, there is reason to believe, from the results of the few known observations, and the imperfect crumbs of intelligence to be gleaned from the more experienced excavating *fellaheen*, are not, or very rarely, discovered with deposits whose other features, such as the shape and character of the coffins, inferentially refer them to the period in question.

The tomb which these pages describe offers in this respect a curious example both of contrast and resemblance. With the early occupants, objects such as have been enumerated, were duly placed, as the rifled vestiges testified. With the new possessors were none of the invariable *shabti*, as the small figures were called, nor any correlative in place of them; neither were there tablets, or wooden effigies of gods, or their emblems. But although the old tutelar deities of the dead were not present in this species of personality, they had their place in the four animals (a change perhaps itself not devoid of significance), at the head of the granite sarcophagus, and in the groups inlaid on the mummy delineated in the foregoing plate. These generic coincidences carry on the wooft of the ancient system: the precise force of the divergences could only be a matter of doubtful speculation.

The presence and the nature of the two papyri fortunately determine the date of the burial in the tomb which is our more immediate subject, and also the social position of the family whose remains it sheltered. The general as well as the philological bearings of those papyri will be illustrated by Mr. Birch, in an introduction to facsimiles of them now in course of preparation; and for a valuable exposition, such as his name guarantees, I refer to that forthcoming publication. But, with ever ready kindness, he has furnished me with the following facts, derived from a preliminary examination, which have a direct relation to the occupants of the tomb.

"The scroll from the granite sarcophagus was written for Sebau, the person, no doubt, on whose breast it lay. He is designated as guardian or keeper of the royal *khemu*, and of the *mahau* \* of the king. He also had charge of the royal horses. According to the usual genealogical references in such documents, it is mentioned that he was the son of Menkara or Mycerinus, who was captain of soldiers in Southern Annu or Hermonthis, lord *repa-pa*, nomarch, governor of the city, holder of some other office, the meaning of which has not been made out, and priest of the local deity Mentu, or Mars, lord of Southern Annu or Hermonthis. The mother of Sebau was called Ta . . . pa Mentu, which combination, containing in it also the name of the god to which her husband ministered, suggests that she derived her origin from the same city, and that the whole family was one of high consideration in the district. Sebau was born on the 28th of the month Athyr, in the thirteenth year of the reign of Ptolemy Philopater III., or Dionysos. He passed the age of fifty-nine, and entered upon his sixtieth year by a month and fourteen days. He died in the twenty-first year of Cæsar (Augustus), and appears to have

---

\* Who the *khemu* and *mahau* were is still somewhat uncertain,—perhaps certain classes of workmen or public servants.

been embalmed from the 10th to the 26th of the month Epiphi: on the 10th of Epiphi the embalmment undoubtedly commenced. He appears, in fact, to have been born B.C. 68, and to have died B.C. 9.

"The ritual inscribed on the papyrus prepared for him is not an extract of the great Funeral Ritual, but compiled from other sources, having, indeed, many ideas in common with the former, and turning upon the exit and future life of the soul. It ends with the *Shai en sen sen* or 'Book of the Lamentations of Isis.' Throughout it consists of a bi-lingual version. The columns are headed by appropriate vignettes representing the embalmment, and deities connected therewith. Beneath there is the hieratic text, and in a lower part of the page the demotic or enchorial translation. This papyrus, therefore, as also the other from the same tomb, which proves to be that of the wife of the functionary Sebau, are most valuable additional keys to the decipherment and translation of demotic literature.

"The second scroll here mentioned is smaller than the first. The lady whom it describes, and who doubtless bore it in the tomb, was Tabai, daughter of a lord, *repa*, and nomarch, *ha*, who also held the office of priest of Mentu, lord of Hermonthis, 'one very great amongst mortals,' as the phrase runs, and named Kalusheri or Calasiris.* Her mother's name was

* The name of Calasiris is already known from two other rituals, one in the British Museum, the other belonging to Lady Tennyson. This appellation, indeed, may have been assumed by many Egyptians,

Aaiut, and she was married to Mentu Sebau, keeper of the *mahau* of the king, and son of Menkara, as stated in his own papyrus before quoted. The genealogy of the husband and wife will therefore stand thus: —

Menkara ┬ Ta ... pa Mentu  =  Kalusheri ┬ Aaiut
Mentu Sebau                              Tabai

As it does not appear they had any children, the line would end here.

"Tabai was born on the 26th of the month Pashons in the nineteenth year of Ptolemy (Dionysos). She reached fifty-four years of age, and died on the 29th of Mesore in the twenty-first year of Cæsar (Augustus), being about a month after her husband. Calculating from these dates, it follows that she was born B.C. 63 and died B.C. 9. A large part of her papyrus, in which these facts are stated, is filled with repetitions of the names, titles, and genealogy of the deceased and her family, the earlier portion only containing a few ideas about the embalming. At the end is an abridged version of the *Shai en sen sen*, or 'Book of the Lamentations of Isis,' as is also the case in the papyrus of Sebau. There is, likewise, a bi-lingual version, the demotic translation of the hieratic accompanying it throughout."

Although the date at which he lived and the status

as it is the designation of the class of soldiers supposed to be so called from their dress or uniform, the *calasiris* tunic; and it is found as a man's name in the *Æthiopus* of Heliodorus.

of the principal personage as well as other personal particulars can thus be ascertained by means of the papyrus scrolls, it cannot be otherwise than hypothetically decided what, if any, connection had subsisted between all those who in this tomb were so closely associated in death. There is no difficulty in supposing the occupants of the sarcophagus and of the five panelled cases to have been related by family ties, as is, indeed, proved to have been the fact in one instance. But between him who reposed in state in the former, and the man, for instance, who had no more handsome coffin than the plain box like a workhouse shell, there appears a broad line of separation; nor does it seem that their juxtaposition can be easily accounted for except by some such conjecture as supposing the domestic or other personal dependence of the one upon the other. That the chief of the group, the granite sarcophagus, was among the last deposited, I think is more than probable. The planks and rollers, even a chip of coarse pottery, holding the residue of the cement which had been used to fasten down the lid, all left lying on the spot, would indicate that no considerable rearrangement had subsequently been made.

Having witnessed vicissitudes like these, and after having experienced for nearly two millennia a repose denied to so many of its kind, changes still more uncontemplated by the old designers await this sepulchre. For fully three thousand years it has been dedicated to the departed. It may shortly begin a new episode as a dwelling for the living. While I was at work in the neighbourhood I prohibited its occupation, with a view to further excavations close at hand, on a future occasion; but I had not cleared the doorway of the tomb adjoining more than two days when possession of it was sought, and the simple operations commenced for converting it into a habitation. So, on this spot, as elsewhere throughout the Necropolis, the past and the present will be blended in a manner almost emblematic, as well as visibly demonstrative, of the decadence which here divides them; and life, no longer fruitful of the works of old, will be content to repose beside the symbols of that actual death which typifies its degradation.

> "Und du flickst zwischen der Vergangenheit
> Erhaben Trümmer
> Für dein Bedürfniss
> Eine Hutte, O Mensch!
> Geniessest über Gräbern." — Göthe, *Der Wanderer*.

## CHAP. V.

### A BURIAL-PLACE OF THE POOR.

AN interment of a very different order — where the living had done little more than follow the mere necessity of burying their dead out of their sight, was the subject of exploration about the same time as the costly sepulchre described in the last chapter. In the comparatively flat tract of the Necropolis at the foot of the hills, and particularly in that part of it between El Shekh Abd-el-Goorneh and El Drahaboo-Neggeh, which lies at the opening of the valley of El Assasseef, there are many hillocks of rock now very generally drifted over with sand, and distinguishable only as the not very marked culminations of the undulating surface. While the actually level spaces between these had been filled with pit-tombs, or with others of greater pomp, where the receptacles opened from large sunk areas — those protruding crags themselves were bored with horizontally tunnelled or chambered sepulchres.

At a point, as at many others, about three hundred yards to the east of the house in which I lived, the presence of one of those excrescent rocks was indicated by a slight elevation and corresponding gradient. On passing it one day with a shrewd *fellah*, whom I had promoted to the rank of overseer of a working party, he accidentally mentioned that, many years before, when digging with some others on their own account, they had come upon three mummy-cases in the sand where a depression still showed some evidence of their work. An untimely visit of the Nazer, or some other official, had caused them to desist, and as the mummies in the cases had been entirely undecorated and yielded nothing for their pains, they had not thought it worth while to resume the search. On a subsequent occasion, circumstances gave me reason to speculate that if by accident any tomb in that immediate neighbourhood had escaped rifling before the deposit of the three coffins, their presence was some sort of guarantee that the place had not been disturbed for many long years, and accordingly it seemed to encourage a trial.

In a couple of days a band of some five-and-twenty made a considerable impression at the selected point; and when the removal of a large mass of sand and stones had carried down the funnel-like hole which they dug, to a depth of about twelve feet below the present surface, four mummy-cases, lying side by side in the rubble, verified the report of the previous yield. Day after day for more than two weeks this trench was enlarged and deepened; and constantly coffins, singly or in groups, were brought to light. Some rested on, or nearly on, the rock; and while it could not be said that any were placed in formal tiers, they occurred at different depths from eight to fifteen feet, and sometimes in several rows. The characteristic circumstance, however, was the apparent absence of systematic arrangement of so large a number of such objects. In an irregular space whose area might be estimated at forty feet by twenty, more than eighty coffins were exhumed from the desert *débris*, as well as four coarse oblong jars, containing sawdust and sodden shreds of linen, which had no doubt performed a part in the process of mummification of some of the bodies.

Of the coffins rather less than one third were of the familiar form in the shape of a swathed mummy; and of these, while some were perfectly plain and also mouldering, a few were handsome, in excellent preservation, and covered inside with religious paintings, and outside with columns of hieroglyphics, of a style chiefly referrible to the period of the three great Diospolitan Dynasties. Indeed on one of them were ovals bearing the name and prenomen of Amunoph I. of the Eighteenth Dynasty (about B.C. 1500). But in almost no case did they appear, as it were, to belong to their occupants. In only three did these last fit their receptacles in point of size with reasonable accuracy, or correspond with them in any degree in the finish and style of the wrappages. In all the others the discrepancy was marked. There were many instances of the bodies of young persons in coffins much too large for them; and in others the bodies lay with an inappropriateness that showed a want of identity with their receptacles; while the rudeness of the bandages and the coarseness of the embalming process, which had generally destroyed the tissues, were similarly inharmonious. For example, in one of those coffins, on which the painting both inside and outside was so well executed, bright, and perfect, that I brought it to this country as an excellent specimen of its type, the contained mummy is little more than a bundle of rags.

By far the greater number of the bodies in this burial-place were encased in mere shells of roughly smoothed deal, fastened with wooden pegs, and tapering like a large truncated wedge from one end to the other. They varied in size, but not always so as accurately to accord with that of their occupants, who were of all ages. In a few were planks which had been sides of painted cases; and one of small dimensions had a lid which, having formerly belonged to a decorated coffin of full size, was pared down to the proper measure, the carved human face having been cut off, and, curiously enough, placed inside at the shoulder of the dead.

Two mummies had no protection but their coarse linen bandages; another had outside of these a tightly bound covering of long palm branches laced together by cords of the fibre of the same tree; and another in a similar basket-work was also, it might be supposed as an after-thought, crushed into an old painted coffin.

The less refined of the processes by means of natron had been those employed for the embalmment of all the bodies, a few of which (I may say five) more carefully prepared than the rest, were also more elaborately bandaged. But otherwise there was nothing to distinguish them from the majority, and they were without any accompaniment or ornament, as was the case with all their neighbours except eighteen out of the whole number. The objects which had been deposited with these, who were mostly, if not all, children and young girls, were of the humblest kind, as will be seen by a statement of the simple details, in as many instances as will serve to note any special characteristics.

There was a child some four or five years old, with toy-like bracelets on the wrists, each consisting of a single string of very small blue beads. Another of equally tender age had a similar ornament on the right arm and its fellow round the left ankle. Another a little more advanced from infancy bore the same kind of armlet, and round the neck a common cord, on which was strung a single large bead of a red, vitreous substance. On the neck of a mummy of somewhat larger growth still, a coarse cord of the same description had attached to it a tightly rolled ball of osier fabric, like undressed papyrus, which looked of the nature of the amulets against the evil eye, worn in the country now. A plain cord merely knotted at intervals occurred as a necklace upon another, whose wrists were encircled by two similar cords, one of which was threaded through a small figure in pottery of Pthah, and the other through a similar effigy of the same god, along with the emblem known as the eye of Horus.* There was another instance of a cord necklace, from which depended four tiny representatives of the cat-headed goddess Athor; and yet another with two figures of Pthah and an eye of Horus. The mummy which bore these last has been already mentioned as having by its side the carved face cut from the lid of its coffin; and lying beneath it there were also two pairs of thin brown leather shoes. Nor was this the only example of such accompaniments, which, indeed, with some classes of Egyptian interments, were, in one form or other, undoubtedly common.† Under the head of another mummy, which was committed to its rest without one more of its earthly possessions, was a single small ankle boot, made to lace up in front. A

SHOE OF REED AND STRAW PLAIT — ELEVEN INCHES LONG.

youth also had been sent on his last pilgrimage with only a pair of straw-plaited shoes by his side — not

* For Ritual reference to it, see Rev. Archéol. N. S. vol. i. p. 92.

† Referring to fifteen pairs in his collection, Passalacqua observes,— "Ils étaient placés par paire aux côtés de plusieurs momies de Thèbes et de Memphis." — *Catalogue*, p. 153.

sandals, which are most frequently found, for although there is no *upper*, as the term is, a ridge nearly two inches high surrounds the sole, except at the toe, which tapers to a sharp point. And so it would seem, that that half-vanished custom which can in one shape or other be traced through so many ages and races, and which like most popular beliefs had a religious origin, was not foreign to the wisdom of the Egyptians; and that in those ancient days, when friends departed on a journey more enduring and not less solemn than the new path of life which marriage opens, the old shoes, which, to invoke good luck[*], are now in some parts of the country thrown after a wedding, were then another sort of viaticum after a death.

In this burial-place there were a few other examples of the presence of shoes. In one a pair were under the head of a mummy, which was otherwise marked by the presence of a small, coarsely-cut, glazed limestone scarabæus, tied like a ring by a twist of plain cord on the fourth finger of the left hand. This very common emblem and ornament — for the scarabæus was both, occurred in only two other instances. In one, it was fastened round the left wrist; and in the other it was secured, as in the first case, on the fourth finger of the left hand of a mummy, which bore also a necklace of small blue beads intermixed with shells like

---

[*] " And home agayne hitherward, quick as a bee,
　　Now *for good lucke* cast an old shooe after mee."

Works of John Heywoode, 1598, quoted in Brand's *Popular Antiqs.* vol. iii. p. 169.

cowries, and a knotted cord rolled three times round the left arm above the elbow. This, it may be remarked, is exactly the position where the modern *fellaheen* carry their knives, or sometimes a small leather scroll containing a text of the Koran as a charm. Our own folklore recognises the efficacy of knotted cords; and at no distant date spaewives, in the north of Scotland, confided them to their clients, as safeguards against harm, and especially to fishermen as guarantees of success. Indeed, in the whole armoury of the sorcerer's art which, in geological phrase, has generally been made up of the detritus of old religions, there is no more potent spell applicable to every phase of human affairs than casting knots; and its efficacy is or has been acknowledged even in very distant countries, such as Greece, the islands of the Archipelago, and elsewhere in the East.*

In our day and region, the simplicity of Christian rites hardly admits of such marked gradations in the conditions of actual interment, that, independently of monuments, and after the lapse of years, they would be indicative of definite variations in taste, or rank, or feeling. The doom of dust to dust would not have been impeded; and there would hardly be a vestige of ceremonial trappings sufficient to challenge the ultimate equality. But among the Egyptians the inequalities of life were, from the peculiarities of custom and climate, so to say, stereotyped in death,

* In Dalyell's *Darker Superstitions of Scotland*, pp. 306—310, many curious examples are collected.

and carried down until they confront us even now. Nor are these the only breaches in uniformity which their graves present. There are likewise the divergences of locality and of age; but running through all, there is still the one obvious classifying distinction, — the difference in rank or wealth. From the great king imbedded in his vast pyramid, as at Memphis, or deep in the heart of a rocky mountain, as at Thebes, reposing in a sarcophagus of alabaster, surrounded by we know not what accompaniments in the halls of his splendid sepulchre, and adorned with we know not what jewels, if we may conjecture how rich they were from the beauty of those in the coffin of a princess recently discovered by M. Mariette, with his former good fortune, — from an embodiment like this of royal status, there were, not merely in tombs, but in individual personality and all its adjuncts, infinite descending grades, down to such an exemplification of poverty as was manifested in the burial-place which this chapter describes. In ancient times at least, bodies of the humbler classes were, at Thebes, deposited in large catacombs, in which they have been found more or less carefully mummied and bandaged, although not usually coffined, and piled together to the number, it is said, of hundreds. These were accompanied in many instances by such tools, implements, and appliances as form so interesting a feature in our collections, and which, according as they were observed beside respective mummies, were not unreasonably supposed to define the trade or profession which these had followed in life.* But although the dead which are at present under our notice had no direct indicators pointing specifically or inferentially to their worldly position, the patched coffins, coarse cerements, and huddled burial, all seemed to show that small consideration had been their portion as well in life as in death. There could be no doubt

"Hoc miseræ plebi stabat commune sepulchrum." †

As affording some means of estimating how and when they came to their resting-place, it may be well to glance at the circumstances under which they lay.

It has already been stated that the chief object in excavating in the neighbourhood of such a deposit, was the implied possibility that there might be a tomb close at hand which had escaped at least recent rifling. Perceiving that the constant occurrence of the coffins was leading the trench away from the covered protruding rock in which a doorway or two might be looked for, I stuck a palm branch in the sand where the elevation naturally showed that the scarp should be expected, as a mark for the men in the bottom of the excavation, defining the direction in which they were steadily to work. In two days thereafter the point was reached; and the same landslip which brought down the branch disclosed the opening of a tomb precisely above which it had been planted. Of course this exact contiguity was mere accident;

* Passalacqua, *Catalogue Raisonné*, Notes, *passim*.
† Horace, *Sat.* i. 8.

but as, on a former occasion elsewhere, a chance shot of the same kind had happened to go equally straight to the mark, the younger *fellaheen* were rather confirmed in a floating notion that Frankish lore included some method of determining the hidden sites of tombs; and this they associated with the compass, level, or thermometer, which they saw from time to time employed. The old hands were much too astute, and far too familiar with both failures and successes to believe in the existence of any royal road, except that very universally accredited one of revelation by dreams. But I remember how the former idea seemed to fall quite naturally from the local Kasheff, a functionary whose powers another chapter will mention; for during a visit of the most tedious length, which respectful civility, according to Eastern fashion, requires, he asked of a certain excavation in progress, where "the instruments" showed that the entrance was to be found.

In the present case "the instruments" would have divined to very little purpose; for when the doorway was cleared it was seen that but a little of the original building which had protected it remained, and that the interior presented only a confusion of large stones and rubbish on the floor, without even a trace of burial vestiges. The tomb was of the common shape of this class.* The doorway opened into the side of an oblong rock chamber, some twenty feet in

---

* See above, p. 56.

length, from the back wall of which a tunnel nearly twice as long, the repository for the mummies, ran in at right angles. The outer vault had been, as is usual, plastered and painted, but the plaster had everywhere disappeared from the walls, except at one corner near the roof, where it bore in bright hues the coloured fragment of a cornice or border, the head of a human figure, a bundle of bows and another of axes. In the complete scene these no doubt formed part of a group of weapons, similar to that on the wall of a well-known tomb near the top of El Shekh Abd-el-Goorneh, whose more perfect condition has preserved several interesting military details, as well as the fact that its possessor had been an officer of rank. It is in every way likely that this sepulchre had belonged to some owner of the same grade, to the members of which many monuments in the Necropolis belonged; and, as to age, the style of the remnant of the painting points to the period of the Eighteenth or Nineteenth Dynasties, whence so large a proportion of the decorated Theban tombs descend.

It hardly bears distinctly upon the question that, in course of the excavations outside, the crushed and broken portion of a roll of hieroglyphic papyrus was found among the drift sand, for the probability tends in favour of its having come there from the early rifling of some neighbouring tomb, rather than from the interior of this. But it must be said that its character would well harmonise with the latter. When unfolded, under the direction of my friend Mr. Birch, the ready aid of whose philological learning I have again the pleasure to acknowledge, he conceived the execution of the scroll would refer it to the time of the Eighteenth Dynasty; and the opening portion was sufficiently entire to enable him to determine the station of the person who had borne it. His name was Usr or Sesr, and he held the post of "royal auditor, chief military governor, in the whole earth governor of the Nome" or district. His father, who had been a similar functionary, was named Hatu, and his mother, Ta aa matu. If his titles had not been preserved, his importance would in some degree have been guaranteed by the size and extent of the papyrus. For even in the greatly mutilated remnants Mr. Birch has traced portions of the text of Chapters 7, 13, 14, 23, 24, 25, 27, 28, 41, 43, 53, 99, 102 and 125, of the Ritual of the Dead.

Exteriorly, this tomb was adjusted in the usual manner, as already described in a former page.* A rectangular area had been chiselled into the slope of the crag, until a perpendicular scarp about five and twenty feet long was formed, sufficiently deep for a doorway to be cut into its face. Above the scarp, and flush with it, there remained about two feet of coarse building, in continuation, as it were, of the elevation of the front of the tomb; and I mention this here because, imbedded in the building, and stretching very nearly its entire length, were two rows of clay cones,

---

* See above, p. 78 compared with p. 54.

impressed with a hieroglyphic subject on the ends turned to the light. Cones, of which a specimen is given in the woodcut, have been constantly found in

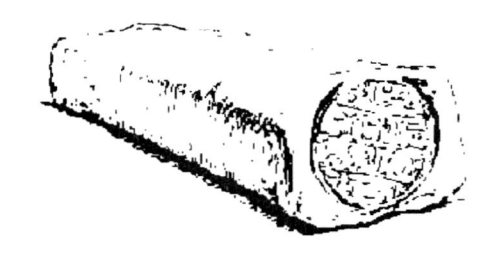

STAMPED BRICK CONE — ELEVEN INCHES LONG.

the sand about the entrances of tombs. They are usually from ten to fifteen inches long, tapering often to a point at one end, and presenting at the other a surface some three or four inches in diameter, on which is embossed a religious group, or a short hieroglyphic text of invocation, or such like, containing the name and status of the deceased person to whom it refers. They had been called the seals with which the closed and plastered entrances of sepulchres had been secured; but it was pointed out, that as the figures they bore were in relief and not in intaglio, they must have received rather than were calculated to transmit an impression. Of the great number in existence, it does not appear that any before had, in observed instances, been met with in any definite position, as they were merely dug up among the *débris*, with little clue to their probable destination. But the mode of their occurrence here would seem to show distinctly, what might be inferred from corresponding discoveries at

Warka, in Babylonia\*, that while their inscriptions or figures may have had, as being connected with burial, a religious significance, and their presence an undeterminable memorial meaning, their direct purpose was ornamental, like an inserted entablature or frieze. In the present case their number was nearly ninety, all stamped with the same impression. What that was, I regret, I cannot now say, without the risk of mistake; for although I selected three specimens, and carefully marked them as they were packed in the same case with several others of the like kind, the distinguishing papers rubbed off in course of the long journey from Thebes. Curiously enough, this was almost the only instance in which such an accident happened in many large packages containing several hundred objects.

It was in the outer court, as it may be called, which these cones overlooked, that the great proportion of the coffins were crowded together. Some stretched out into the sand beyond the limits of the rock-cut enclosure; but what may be the full extent occupied by those burials I do not know, as my design was at once fulfilled and frustrated when the entrance to the empty tomb was discovered. After that there was no sufficient object to warrant a special disturbance of any more of the humble sleepers, in addition to those who had come under examination in course of the search. One thing, however, was evident, that, whatever their numbers, they must have been laid to

---

\* Birch's *History of Ancient Pottery*, vol. i. p. 25.

their rest after the great day of Thebes had passed, when the Necropolis was falling into neglect, and the readily encroaching sand of the desert was drifting in among the tombs. The one before which they lay, some of them even within a few inches of its doorway, had already been reduced to little more than a mere cavern. If we conjecture as to the hands which placed them there, we shall not be led to suppose that those of relatives or friends had thus shuffled them in pell-mell together. It is more likely that, as Egyptian sepulchral arrangements were, at all times, under the care of a regular official class, the proper functionaries, having received their payment, charged themselves in cases like the present with the disposal of the mummies, and buried the poorer sort in groups or masses at a time. In this way from their stores, or from the wrecks of rifled sepulchres, they turned old coffins to account for a younger generation.

## CHAP. VI.

### EXCAVATIONS AMONG TOMBS OF VARIOUS GRADES.

It has already been explained why disappointment should be such a frequent result of excavation among the sepulchres of ancient Egypt; and in setting down here some of the instances in my own experience where the blanks were not quite so complete, it would hardly be of interest to give details of mere operations, lengthened or even exciting while in progress, which ended vexatiously. Neither shall I do more than select a few examples which may tend to illustrate the character of tombs of various kinds, and the state in which they are generally found. If before proceeding I allude to one attempt where the failure was utter and complete, it is only on account of the importance of the locality.

From all times the Tombs of the Kings have been the central point of interest in the Theban Necropolis. Their extraordinary character challenged this prominent attention alike when the earlier Greek travellers preserved in their books memorials of their visits, or their more demonstrative countrymen scratched proofs of their admiration which still endure on the painted corridors, — as when the narrative of Bruce and his successors, the detailed labours of the French Commission, and the successful researches of Belzoni, attracted the notice of a later generation. As mere objects of curiosity, these splendid sepulchres were not likely to lose their charm, but since historical results have been so diligently sought from Egypt, their importance has been enhanced as links in the chain of dynastic records. Accordingly, all the scientific missions, and various individual excavators, have made the valleys which contain these monuments the subject of more or less special research. Nor was there wanting a confirmatory inducement to do so. Diodorus Siculus had recorded the circumstance learned by a preceding writer from the Egyptian priests, that their registers contained a list of forty-seven royal tombs[*], and Strabo had mentioned that "*about* forty,"[†] existed beyond the Memnonium, no doubt also founding upon some previous statement, as the number accessible in his own day was apparently not quite half so many. Again, the Eighteenth, Nineteenth, and Twentieth Dynasties, which were Theban, and each of which and no other is represented among these sepulchres, consisted together of some five-and-thirty kings, while in the Bab el-Molook all the presently known entrances, whether of completed tombs or not, are twenty-one. And if to these are added the four

---

[*] Diod. Sic. lib. i. c. 4.  [†] Strabo, *Geog*. lib. xvii.

in the more distant "Western Valley," we have still no more than twenty-five.

It may not be necessary to assume the precise accuracy of the figures handed down by Diodorus, as it would not be difficult to suppose them erroneous as a matter of fact, like so many Egyptian details preserved by Greek media, or as referring to genealogical catalogues of the various Theban Dynasties, rather than to the actual existence of so many individual tombs of the characteristic magnificent design. Nor is it an indispensable sequence, with reference to the lists of the three Dynasties in question, that a tomb for each king is to be expected in those valleys. For, in the first place, dimly perceptible revolutionary movements and foreign usurpation took place, which might well account for certain of the royal line not finding a resting-place among their race. Then, again, there were princes who seized the results of the sepulchral labours of predecessors; and one of the tombs gives proof of three appropriations.[*] And, finally, as among the known catacombs in those two gorges none are referrible to the first kings of the Eighteenth Dynasty, it is not improbable that only the later ones had changed the place of sepulture, and that the earlier were buried with less pomp, befitting their less brilliant sovereignties, nearer their capital. These may perhaps have had their tombs in that, the older, district of the Necropolis called El Drah-aboo-Neggeh, where

---

[*] Wilkinson, *Handbook*, p. 360.

funeral traces have been found of members of a former Theban Dynasty.* But allowing for all these and other contingencies, enough remains to encourage the belief that in or near those desolate and death-like ravines there exist "the eternal homes," as their own phrase was, of more Pharaohs than are now disclosed.

As for the Bab el-Molook, so thoroughly has it been searched that I could not detect very many reasonably suggestive spots which did not bear marks of previous attempts. In the Western Valley, from its remoter position as well as greater extent, less has been done, and in it and the approach to it there was ample field but vaguer guidance for selection. I commenced at the former (the Bab el-Molook) with two detachments of *fellaheen* of about twenty each. One after the other the experimental trenches proved fruitless, and the daily ride over the mountains came to be a round of laborious duty unrelieved by interest. But one afternoon when I was engaged nearer home superintending a working party in El Assasseef, a messenger came hasting over the desert from the overseer at Bab el-Molook, with the announcement, which if occasion should arise he had orders immediately to make, that he believed they were approaching the entrance to a tomb. And so it really seemed, as I found on reaching the valley.

The rock above the openings of the royal tombs

* See above, p. 105, for reference to this discovery.

has usually been rough chiselled to produce an even face in which the doorways were cut; and it was the sudden disclosure of the upper part of a perpendicular scarp like this, not many yards from the great sepulchre of Sethi I., discovered by Belzoni, which encouraged the good hope that the track this time was right. Down against the rock the excavation was pursued, and the smooth surface still continued. Nay, farther, a long palm stick, kept for such exploratory purposes, when thrust into the sand to a much greater depth, met with no obstruction, and even turned inwards, penetrating, as was assumed, the entrance of the tunnel. Expectation was great, and the *fellaheen* needed no stimulus beyond their own excitement to work with vigour. But from the constant reflux of the sand nearly two days more were anxiously spent before certainty was gained; and then the collapse was complete. The perpendicular scarp, which bore so deceptive a resemblance to artificial hewing, had been produced by a natural cleavage, which, as if to make the snare more perfect, terminated in a rift trending inwards at an acute angle, where the unconscious palm probe supposed that it had found a door.

The remaining points in Bab el-Molook were speedily and quite as unsatisfactorily, if much more easily, disposed of, and the next part of the plan came on for trial — a search in the Western Valley, where the prospect of success has generally been considered more promising. But on the very evening I had directed the men to move there, I unfortunately broke down seriously. This I owed to the long rides over the desert under a sun, powerful even in mid-winter, the concentrated heat of the ravine where the works were in progress, combined with the additional fatigue of superintending at the same time other gangs in different parts of the Necropolis. But I only mention here a circumstance so entirely personal to explain why, for that season, I was obliged thereafter to be content with the hope of having sufficient strength to finish excavations within easier reach, and was compelled, with a reluctance equal to the disappointment, to forego the opportunity of testing those points which I had marked out in and near the Western Valley. There and thereabout it is undoubtedly most likely that any royal tombs of the series in question, yet to be disclosed, have their place. As for the Bab el-Molook, having dug at I believe every available spot it presented, not bearing evidences of previous search, I feel reasonably confident that no more sepulchres except those already known, exist within its proper limits.

Next in importance to the royal burial-places, and in certain respects more valuable ethnographically than the larger proportion of them, are those tombs of much more moderate dimensions, whose small outer chambers are covered with paintings which afford, at least in outline, so many panoramic vistas of life and manners. From the prominent position which the greater number of these occupied, and the inviting accessibility of their doorways, which with hardly any concealment penetrate the acutely angled talus of the crags, they, least of all, had a chance of safely keeping down to our day the trust which had been committed to them. In searching, therefore, among the sites where they are most usually placed, for entrances which the accumulated drift of years might have shrouded, the hope had to be limited to finding, not the funeral or votive contents, but walls which might have received and preserved any of those decorative records so singularly illustrative of contemporary social history. Sometimes these frescoes are wanting altogether; sometimes they have been greatly damaged; and frequently they are mere repetitions of such stereotyped and perfectly known subjects, as to offer nothing of novelty and little of interest. Of the first contingency I had instances in several parts of the Necropolis; of the second a case in El Assasseef; and of the third, two in El Drah-aboo-Neggeh.

A tomb which I opened about half-way up El Shekh Abd-el-Goorneh, was also to some extent within the last category, as garden and agricultural scenes of the same generic kind as those represented in it are not infrequent. But there was a precision in some of the details, and a brilliancy of colouring, in consequence of protection from exposure, which made the uncovering of these pictures very acceptable. It was the more so as the data on the subject, of houses, their size and construction, are not, as has been previously adverted to, so full or satisfactory as the nature of the case requires. On the left-hand side of the door on

## PICTURE OF AN EGYPTIAN HOUSE AND GARDEN. 147

entering the tomb, the home retirement of a wealthy Egyptian is portrayed, of the time of Thothmes I., about 1500 years B.C. In the foreground is a high wall with a large gateway, and behind this, overtopping it by two thirds of its height, stands a house as represented by a square tower capped by a row of semicircular cornice stones, like some still existing on the temple-palace of Medinet Haboo. In this building are two windows, one not exactly over the other but higher than the level of its top, and showing two storeys above the wall,—if, indeed, this be the intention, considering the kind, or rather absence, of perspective. Farther in the rear sits what may be presumed to be the master with his wife, in a shaded arbour. Before them a servant stands with fruit from vines and fig and other trees, which fill up the space between them and a pond, from which a gardener is drawing water in two jars or buckets slung from either end of a wooden yoke on his shoulders.

On the other side of the doorway all the ordinary labours of the husbandman are set forth, from sowing to threshing out the grain under the feet of oxen; but similar groups are of such constant occurrence, that in these there was nothing remarkable except the very creditable execution of the animals.

Almost at the top of the same hill of Shekh Abd-el-Goorneh, and behind what, with reference to the plain of Thebes, may be called its front elevation, I came, while digging among open tombs of the description to which reference has just been made, upon one concealed by the sand, in a condition very unusual in this class. It seemed never to have been used, or if ever used, it was in process of being completely readapted and remodelled. In the inner tunnel chips from the final hewing still lay, and the outer chamber, which measured some twenty feet square, was only in course of being prepared for decoration. The smoothly-plastered wall had as yet received no colouring; but to the left of the entrance spaces were draughted off by horizontal black lines, and at one corner a series of squares were formed upon these by other perpendicular lines. Upon these squares, in their character of graduated scale, the outline of two upright figures was traced according to the manner of drawing observed in similar unfinished works in the Bab el-Molook, the ceiling of the temple at Ombos, and a few other places.* As such instances of the elements of composition are instructive from their bearing on Egyptian conventionalisms and canons of proportion, I wished to make a careful transcript of those in this tomb; and in directing the sand to be more fully cleared out for the purpose, very strict orders were added that care should be taken not to touch the walls. But on returning a few hours thereafter, I actually found that the plaster on which the figures were drawn had been wilfully scratched across and across with such pains that they were utterly defaced. That this had been done from fanatical com-

* A series of several may be seen on a large scale in Lepsius's *Denkmäler*.

pliance with the texts of the Koran against graven images, I could not believe; for there has on these grounds been no modern raid against the monuments, and I knew none of the Goorneh men to whom credit could be given for enough religious rigour to impel an unusual attention to the stricter injunctions of this kind. In fact the motive must have been either mischief or malice, most probably the former; but the perpetrator could not be discovered, and sturdy denial was on all hands volunteered. The overseer of the party, whose own repute was involved, strongly urged that, as seven of the men were known to have had their turn of work inside, each should be well bastinadoed, and then the guilty one would be certain to have his due. This ingenious plan, however, had too little of fair play to recommend it, and retributive justice had to content herself unappeased.

Other tombs of the same general formation as the class just described, but much less carefully elaborated, are found in similar positions. They are merely low, rough hewn, horizontal tunnels, from twenty to forty feet long, expanding in the rock into spaces sufficiently large for the mummies, or leading each into a more regularly formed chamber. These are particularly prevalent in the craggy range which sweeps up from El Assasseef to the temple of Der el-Bahrée. In that district I made several quite unsuccessful excavations; and the object in persevering was locally supposed to be the hope of finding a subterranean passage leading through the mountain to the Bab el-Molook, which native speculation insists must be there. I came, however, upon one of those plain tunnel tombs with its contents unrifled. But they were very meagre, and consisted merely of four coffins of the ordinary Egyptian shape, coarsely finished and entirely undecorated, lying wedged together on the floor of a small crypt, some thirty feet from the outer air. The mummies were the subjects of as little adornment as their cases; and the only memorial adjunct among them were four coarse pottery figures of the genii of the Amenti, fastened to the bandages of the shoulders of one.

Another tomb of similar character, which may be worth describing, was found in one of the rocky undulations in front, and not far from the foot of El Shekh Abd-el-Goorneh. Several brick cones [*] were dug up near the entrance, which itself showed other signs of previous exploring; but presently the outline of mummies seemed to break against the dim light which the clearing of the doorway allowed to penetrate into the interior. In instances where there was any prospect of finding a deposit in such a condition as to render an examination of it in its integrity desirable, a very necessary rule, both for this purpose and to guard against the risks from fingers of doubtful reliance in such circumstances, was to enter the tomb before the workmen were permitted to do so, or effect any disturbance, and as soon as possible after the

---

[*] See p. 137.

lapse of a reasonable time allowed some fresh air to permeate. At no time was this an agreeable duty, and on this occasion it happened to be peculiarly unpleasant. Former searchers had dragged the mummies from the inner recesses forward towards the light, the better to examine and rifle them, and so, in crawling in, the way lay over these, involving an undesirable proximity with their broken fragments and torn bandages, from which the pungent impalpable dust of the embalming substances rose with blinding and stifling effect. The tomb was simply a tunnel about four feet high, first descending slightly for forty feet, and then rising correspondingly for twenty feet more, as it expanded somewhat in width and height. It had contained several mummies, probably from twelve to fifteen, and they had all been subjected to rough overhauling. A few were quite dismembered, but generally the outline of the swathings was left perfectly entire, as they were merely ripped up across the throat and down the breast, where ornaments had been expected. It did not seem probable that all had been coffined, although portions of some painted cases were strewed about.

The rifling must have taken place in times when ordinary relics had not their marketable value for native diggers, otherwise none would have been left unheeded as they were and scattered among the bodies in the inner part of the vault. Of such objects there must have been several of wood; but their precise character could not be determined, in consequence of the shrivelled condition of the vestiges, produced most likely by the exposure to air after the tomb was first opened. The tough material, however, of a semicircular head-rest or pillow of the common form, though considerably shrunken, had preserved it tolerably well. Less subject to atmospheric or other decaying influence, there were six clay jars with wide mouths and rounded bottoms, each with capacity for holding about a gallon. They were then empty; but when deposited it is not unlikely, from analogous observations, that they contained, some the sweet water of the Nile or potables of richer body, and some, corn or other elements of sustenance. With them may be classed a small stand, also of unglazed pottery, like a plate, six inches in diameter, on a fixed pedestal as many inches high. On such stands, I believe, bread cakes and fruit, which more than two millennia had not consumed, have been found; and in this tomb a few berries and figs were picked up. Only one more waif it seems necessary to mention, a beautiful scarabæus of lapis lazuli, which was raked out from among the scraps near the entrance where its first finder had probably dropped his prize.

Tombs of another and very numerous class are those in the flats at the foot of the mountains, and which consist of well-like shafts with one or more small chambers branching from the bottom. In the Necropolis of Geezeh, and that of Sakkara, they are sometimes of very great depth,—sixty or eighty feet,—as well as of considerable size, having large vaults entering from their sides at the lower levels, and smaller sepulchral crypts at higher elevations. From such the Hebrew prophet could with perfect verbal accuracy have taken his picture: "whose graves are set in the sides of the pit, and her company is round about her grave."* At Thebes I know of none uncomplicated with other designs, which possess so great dimensions. Very large shafts occur in some of the vast subterranean sepulchres, like that of the high priest Petamunap in El Assasseef; but in the simple well-tombs penetrating direct from the surface, the rock cuttings vary from eight to twenty feet in depth, by four to six square. Originally these appear to have been covered with small structures of crude brick, the basements of which are still found; and no doubt plaster and paint gave these chapelries the gay appearance which some of the wall pictures illustrate, and which Egyptian architectural taste enjoyed.

Very many of these shafts I opened and emptied of the sand, in every part of the Necropolis; but they had all previously been more or less completely deprived of their contents, some by decay, some by more active agency. Several of the deeper ones were found to be penetrable by the percolating moisture from the annual overflow of the Nile, which left their floors covered with sodden masses, in which whatever perishable substances may have been present were reduced to pulp. And so it appeared, as has sometimes also been observable at Sakkara, that the old engineers

* Ezekiel xxxii. 23.

had occasionally failed in that foresight regarding the relative changes in the level of the Nile and of the valley which they have been thought to possess. Or, perhaps they did not care to avoid so distant a contingency as such an increase of the gradually accumulating alluvium and corresponding rise of the bed of the river, as would bring the effects of the inundation to bear upon repositories in other respects so conservative.

A large field of those pit-tombs lies behind the Rameseseum, or Memnonium, as it is more popularly called, in great part covered by the mouldering brick vestiges of a town. This had been built over them and occupied in the later days when the religion of old Thebes had given place to Christianity, which monastically flourished in an eminent degree on the same soil, and when the humble emblem of the new faith, the cross, frequently found among these ruins, overshadowed the haughtier symbols of Amun-Ra. Several explorations which I made beneath the crumbling old houses, showed that searchers had done their work even before the foundation of this ancient and long-deserted town. They had broken the mummy-cases, and left the fragments with such other of the sepulchral garniture as they did not prize. From these heaps I sometimes recovered various objects, — in one instance a well-worn mason's mallet, used, perhaps, in hewing out the tomb. But generally the products were merely the usual wooden funeral effigies, as the hawks of Horus, stone vases with the heads of the four genii of the Amenti (Hades), under whose guardianship the contained viscera were placed, — and small painted chests filled with the little figures known as *shabti*. The extremely rude manufacture of figures of this class has often been matter for surprise; but in one of the cases here referred to, it was the more remarkable by reason of direct contrast showing that their imperfections were no criterion either of poverty or artistic inefficiency. A boxful of these images, amounting to more than sixty, each about two inches high, had hardly more finish of contour than as many pellets of brown unbaked clay; and yet in the tomb from which they came, were pieces of a highly decorated mummy-case, and portion of a neatly constructed hawk, covered with stucco like a picture frame, and gilded.

The object contemplated by the deposit of figures of this sort has been variously surmised, but conjecture on the subject is almost entirely hypothetical, and no sufficient elucidation can be gleaned from the texts of the Ritual.* The statuettes themselves are of all sizes from two to six inches in height and of different materials, some being of unbaked clay, some of glazed and coloured pottery of high finish, and some of wood overlaid with painted stucco or bituminous pitch. Their shape is that of a swathed mummy, and the

* Their presence with the dead is provided for in the sixth chapter of the Ritual, but with what view it is not according to the nature of that document exactly to specify.—See *Rituel Funéraire*, par De Rougé, p. v., of which only the first *livraison* has as yet appeared.

imprinted or painted inscriptions which the better descriptions of them bear usually contain the name, with an invoked beatification, of the deceased person with whom each batch of them had been placed. Mr. Birch has supposed that they, or at all events a certain kind of them, "are generally of a late period, probably of the age of Roman dominion." * In my own experience I have found various descriptions of them and the boxes for them always among vestiges of earlier time: and they occurred in great quantity in the tomb of Sethi I. when discovered by Belzoni.† Indeed, as far as the vague data locally procurable warrant an opinion, I am disposed to think that the practice of employing them had almost or altogether passed, and that they did not usually form part of Romano-Egyptian interments.

I may mention another half-rifled well-tomb, which was covered by a heap of sand almost within the enclosed yard of a *fellah's* house, at the foot of El Shekh Abd-el-Goorneh, as from it I procured a curious relic. This was a miniature coffin about twelve inches long, of neat proportions and execution, as shown in the accompanying woodcut. On a black ground the lineaments of the face are picked out in red, and the bands of hieroglyphics, as well as the figures of the deities on the sides, although crushed out of shape by the limited space, stand out distinctly, being painted of the same red colour. Inside is a roughly outlined lay figure of wood, if it may be so called, like the swathed

---

* *History of Ancient Pottery*, i. 29.     † Belzoni's *Researches*, p. 235.

corpse, but it seems as if it might have been intended as a nucleus to be rolled in bandages to make the mortuary resemblance more complete, as there is

MINIATURE COFFIN — TWELVE INCHES HIGH.

ample spare space around it in its receptacle; and the whole has the look of an imitative toy, if so lugubrious a plaything can be conceived. Corresponding objects, which have been sometimes found of pottery, have been supposed to be undertakers' models, and this one is sufficiently well finished and precise to warrant any such conjecture with regard to it. But I have procured other specimens of smaller size as well in clay as in wood, and altogether so coarse and unshapely that it would be difficult to imagine any tradesman keeping them beside him, or producing them, as patterns of form, or style, or workmanship. Again, the size and appearance of the present example recall the account given by Herodotus of the curious custom which he states to have been in use after the banquets of wealthy Egyptians. "A servant carries round to the several guests a coffin, in which there is a wooden image of a corpse carved and painted to resemble nature as nearly as possible, about a cubit* or two cubits in length. As he shows it to each guest in turn, the servant says: 'Gaze here, and drink and be merry; for when you die such you will be.'"† But whether this dainty little mummy-case had ever performed a part in those not very lively episodes in good men's feasts, or had been among the trade requisites of a dealer in the trappings of woe — or whether the presence of it and others with the dead, had, independently, some ceremonial significance, the motive for the deposit of them, as of certain other sepulchral paraphernalia, must remain purely conjectural, unless some future documentary discovery shall afford a precisely explanatory comment on such observances.

About a couple of hundred yards nearer the outskirts of El Assasseef, a few *fellah* dealers in relics, digging in partnership and by secret spells, as their manner is, came upon another of the numerous well-tombs in that locality, with more of its ancient contents left by previous visitors than it is usual now to find. They had almost finished their search before

---

* The Greek cubit was a little more than eighteen inches.
† Rawlinson's *Herodotus*, lib. ii. c. 78.

I chanced to hear of it, and although I was in time to see the last of the objects handed up from the depths, and to secure them along with some of the others not previously sold, which a friend, himself a collector, kindly resigned to me,—it was impossible to make out with accuracy, as it always is in such cases, what had been the state of matters in the burial chamber when entrance was gained. It appeared, however, from the planks which I saw, that there had been at least one large outer coffin of the kind which may be described as a plain rectangular sarcophagus. This had been broken up by the earlier riflers, who always went straight to the mummy in search of valuables; and the body, as well as the painted cartonage which probably surrounded it, had been destroyed. But there were left for the new explorers, besides the more external relics, two scarabæi which, according to the usual course, must have been in connexion with the wrappages of the deceased. The first, of large size, being two and a half inches long, is well moulded out of fine clay incorporated with a bright blue pigment, which gives it a perfect resemblance to lapis lazuli; the other, which is much smaller, is of glazed limestone, having a head of the goddess Athor cut in the back, and on the obverse a cartouch enclosing the hieroglyphic characters, the sun, the castle, and the beetle—the prenomen of Thothmes III. of the Eighteenth Dynasty, but also of the fourth king of the Twenty-first, nearly five hundred years later.

The earlier spoilers, most likely, had also reduced to the fragments which were found, the fellow of the large vase here represented, which was brought up almost entire, and is now very nearly in its original condition, notwithstanding some damage sustained in its long voyage to England. Standing about two feet high by fifteen inches in greatest diameter, its form is that of a nearly cylindrical amphora, with spherical bottom and somewhat contracted mouth, near which two pairs of small handles are attached. The bottom,

PAINTED VASE — TWO FEET HIGH.

from the spring of the bulge, is painted in conventional wedge-shaped bands, like the lotus flowers of the frescoes; and then round the upper part of the jar, on a light ground, certain of the funeral deities,—

> "Osiris, Isis, Orus and their train
> With monstrous shapes, . . . .
>             disguised in brutish forms
> Rather than human —"

are portrayed in bright colours. One of the scenes which is best preserved, and which may be seen in the woodcut, appears to represent the deceased person under the guidance of Anubis, offering the usual lotus flower on an altar before the ibis-headed Thoth. This vase is the only one of the kind I remember ever to have seen; but it does not offer much of special interest, beyond adding another to the endless modes in which religious representations were associated with the dead. The painted subjects are of the same nature as those so common on sepulchral stelæ, whether of stone or of wood; and two of the latter material, for example, from, or from near the same tomb, have nearly similar groups in gilding as the vignettes to the prayers with which they are inscribed.

The same uncertainty as to precise locality which applies to these last-named tablets, is attached to a gaudily-coloured image of the goddess Athor which I bought from the same diggers, and to two wooden dolls, about twelve inches high, with legs and arms jointed in the fashion most in request among denizens of modern nurseries. The most characteristic of the two is here copied; and in looking at it, or such like, we are apt to be reminded that a glance at what are really trivial objects quickens that sense of the reality of life in the past, which a survey of more splendid vestiges may often do little more than awaken. Many such playthings procured from the tombs call up

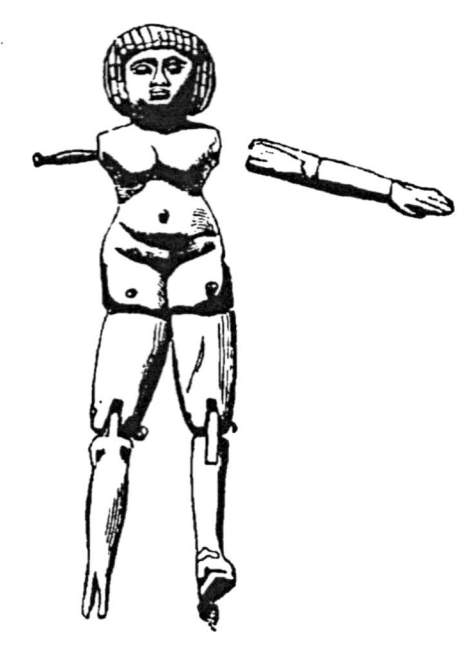

WOODEN DOLL—ONE-FOURTH ACTUAL SIZE.

before us the children of ancient Egypt; and that their toys should be identical with some now in use, need be in no way surprising. Another instance of this similarity is a neat little stool in my collection, measuring two and a half inches in length by one and a half in height, which is quite like a piece of furniture from a German toy-house.

The reason why there is some doubt as to the exact position of the tomb or tombs whence the statuette of Athor and the dolls were procured was this—that the finders stated themselves to have discovered some relics about the same time in a shaft in the immediate neighbourhood. Besides, as they were habitual traffickers, by no means prone to supply correct specifications of their wares, there was an equal chance that objects not seen to be produced from the particular tomb in question, either by my friend or myself, might have been formerly in their possession, and procured from some other source.

But there was another series of interesting relics, without doubt referrible to this spot, as they were recovered after I had reached it, and were brought to the upper air in my own presence. They form the greater part of the outfit necessary for a hunter or sportsman — being a walking-stick, three clubs, three bows, and some twenty arrows. The stick, about four and a half feet long and perfectly straight, is simply the prepared and barked branch of a hard-wooded tree. It is topped by a short natural fork, formed where a somewhat smaller bough had sprayed off, the two having been lopped within about a couple of inches of their junction. The use of this kind of head seems to have been a very prevalent fashion, for in the sculptures, when a man is represented with a stick, he grasps it about a foot from the top, which almost universally terminates thus. Some illustration of the clubs may perhaps also be recognised on the walls of several tombs. In scenes * from out-door life, a sportsman is occasionally depicted gliding in a light boat among the reeds, and knocking down water-fowl as they rise, with bent sticks, which he throws with force and dexterity. The

---

* Several are given by Wilkinson. *Anct. Egypts.* vol. i. pp. 235, *et seq.*

present clubs, although corresponding to those by curves at one end, are probably too unwieldy (as they are nearly three feet long) to have been the missile regularly used; and if this may have been their occasional duty, their general destination was most likely to answer the purposes in any way of an ordinary hand weapon, like the *neboot* of Nubia, a short stout cudgel now in very popular demand there. The arrows are of light reed tipped with long tapering points of hard wood, having projecting notches to keep them in the wound. Others with flint heads, or with tips of bronze, have been met with, but such as the above are better adapted for the use of the hunter and especially the fowler. At one time Egyptian arrows of all kinds were so uncommon, that Belzoni thought it necessary to mention he had only discovered one in the whole of his excavations[*]; but although they are rare, a few bundles have since been procured.

Two of the bows are, each, about five feet long, round and smooth, and bending slightly towards either end, which tapers to a sharp point. Of the third there is only one half, but I have little doubt that the other was also in the tomb, for that in my possession bears crisply the marks of the ancient cutting where notches had been purposely made to break the weapon in the middle. If it were thus originally deposited, as seems most likely, it comes down to us as a monument of singular expressiveness. We may not be warranted in

[*] *Researches*, p. 172.

assuming from its presence, as in analogous cases elsewhere has been done, that it testified to beliefs for the future in which the actual life of mortality is quenched in the hope for rest or in still higher aspirations. But we can have no difficulty in recognising the appropriateness of the symbolism, whereby, "when the silver cord is loosed," the bow is snapped and laid beside the dead, in mute token that his merely earthly pleasures and pursuits are over. Beneath the soil of our own land similar evidences have been disclosed of a feeling as instinctively natural as it is eminently human. In the tumular graves of the early islanders, a bronze sword broken in twain is sometimes found with the mouldering bones or inurned ashes of him who was wont, as we may believe, to wield it.*

Returning to the well-tombs, the relics from one of which have occupied attention for the last few pages, I may refer to yet another species of them, if indeed it be necessary to draw so marked a distinction in what is merely a matter of size. These last are to be found chiefly, and in great number, in the valley stretching from the temple of Der el-Medeeneeh towards that of Medinet Haboo. They, like the others, are, or have been, marked by erections of crude brick, the low arches of some of which still remain: and these covered † the

---

\* Several instances are specified in Wilson's *Archæology of Scotland*, p. 265. Others might be added.

† In some cases the brick erections no doubt constituted in themselves the tomb, without any subterraneous repository. Examples of this description occurred on the island of Philœ, the excavation of

small shafts, which are not more than five or six feet deep, and lead each to a single little chamber at the bottom. I opened several of these with hardly any success, sometimes finding no single vestige whatever among the disintegrated brick and sand with which they were filled, sometimes disinterring rude platters or bowl-shaped jars of equally coarse pottery, and on one occasion turning up a large heavy leather sandal* along with a sort of double cruse of clay, being two small vases baked together on the same stand. But although the graves in this locality were so unproductive, and generally are of such limited dimensions, they have in former times yielded interesting relics; and indeed an ascertained stray case of this sort quite recently occurred. About eighteen months ago my friend and fellow-traveller for two years in Egypt, the Rev. W. F. Hood, chanced to be in the valley when a fellah had come upon a tomb in which were deposited portions of agricultural produce. He was able to secure a sheaf of papyrus plant, and a short-handled wooden corn-fork, as we would call it, of which the prongs are formed from two spraying branches: along with these there had been jars containing various kinds of grain.

While on the subject of well-tombs, I am induced to

which Lord Henry Scott and the Rev. H. Stobart kindly superintended, at the cost of considerable trouble, from the peculiar circumstances which led to the search. The interments there were found to be of the most meagre character, the mummies, whose swathings were inexpensively simple, being accompanied only here and there by a coarse scarabæus, or a rude wooden head-rest.

* See above, p. 130.

refer to certain of this type which during a former season I investigated at Geezeh. It would be out of place to enlarge upon the specialties of that Necropolis, but, as is very generally known, its most characteristic features are the Pyramids, and other sepulchres of the highest antiquity which even Egypt has monumentally to offer. Among them there is one class of very substantial costly construction and prominent appearance; and of these a marked group of several rows occurs from two to three hundred yards from the south-east corner of the Great Pyramid. They consist each of an oblong rectangular mausoleum, generally some sixty feet long by twenty broad, and six or eight high. They are plainly but admirably built of massive blocks. How they may have terminated as to superstructure, is somewhat uncertain, as they are all now truncated; and in the flat tops of each the square casing of a shaft near either end lies more or less uncovered, except by the overflowing sand. From this obvious dilapidation, boding little chance of reward for the labour of raising the debris out of one of the shafts, there does not appear to have been any attempt to do so in later years. I was inclined, however, to undertake the work (which was very considerable with no other appliance than two small baskets pulled up hand over hand by relays of Arabs), from a desire of seeing what might be the arrangement beneath. I had also the hope that although any more moveable relics might have long before been carried off, or have perished, there might be, in a tomb of such pretension, a stone sarcophagus or other sculptured object, illustrative of the early period to which, most probably, belongs this group of mausolea, on the exterior of none of which are any noticeable inscriptions.

When the selected shaft, which measured about nine feet square, was emptied to the depth of fourteen feet, a cylindrical jar, twenty-two inches high, and with circular bottom, was found in the sand, containing the crumbling bones of a very small child, and scaly metallic traces, as of anklets or armlets. The time of its deposit cannot well be surmised, but it stood as a guarantee that the lower depths had not for long been molested. But several days passed, and many more yards had to be cleared ere they were reached; and the tape-line ran out fifty-five feet from the surface, before the hoes of the workmen struck on the rock bottom, and a built-up doorway was disclosed in the side of the shaft. I was then let down by the ropes, and found, indeed, that the doorway was secured by carefully squared blocks of stone, but that, as had been expected, an early hand had displaced three or four of them, and formed an aperture rather more than two feet square.

This was the first Egyptian tomb I had ever opened, and the anxiety was natural, speedily and personally to ascertain the result. I certainly had the common prudence to wait some time, and see that a candle on the end of a stick would burn inside before crawling forward. But I shall not easily forget the heat and stifling solidity (for that was the sensation) of air not sufficiently renewed after having been penned up, probably, for several hundred years in the heart of the rock. It was a practical lesson to moderate impatience on future occasions, the more especially as the interior, when gained, was utterly destitute of any contents whatever. Not a shred or fragment had been left by the spoiler or by time. The chamber itself, which I afterwards measured, was ten feet by eight feet six, and nearly seven feet high. A large trough, seven feet two inches long by three feet four broad, and three feet six deep, was cut in the floor to the right of the entrance, and in this no doubt a body had reposed as in a sarcophagus. When I came to examine it, however, it contained only a thick layer of fine silt, which, in the course of years, had filtered in after heavy rains; or it may be, that, reduced to the utter insignificance of this impalpable powder, was all earthly that remained of the personage for whose rest so enduring a home had been prepared.

Two other well-tombs at Geezeh, which I shall describe, were on a very different scale. Following a friendly suggestion of Sir Gardner Wilkinson's, given one day on the spot, I had been digging in a tempting sand-hill standing about two hundred feet north of the Sphinx, and so nearly on the same parallel with reference to the Second Pyramid, that it looked as if it might cover a corresponding colossus. Experimental trenches, however, sunk in various parts of the mound, forbade this hope, as they either disclosed the rough natural rock, or the entrances of empty tombs in such positions as to leave me no room to doubt that the Sphinx is solitary as ever, and had no twin brother. This, I fear, may disappoint Dr. Lepsius, who set his heart upon a pair leading up to a temple with the pyramid behind, warmly adding, "I cannot deny that this connexion would be most satisfactory to me."[*]

While at work in this neighbourhood, I caused a few of the men to excavate in a small level space about twenty yards to the north of the mound in question, and there the two tombs referred to were met with, forming together as it were one structure. In dimensions, shape, and details, they were quite similar, and an account of the first opened, which may be distinguished as No. I., will equally apply to both, except as regards the deposit. At the bottom of a shaft of rude rubble work, built in the desert drift, two feet ten inches square, and six feet four inches deep, a small chamber, three feet eight long, two feet ten broad, and two feet six high, with similar walls and spanned by large stones, projected on one side. Within this cell the burial, which altogether wanted the preservative specialties of Egyptian sepulture, had been effected; and in it there lay a mouldering skull near the centre, surrounded by, or rather in the midst of, other bones of the frame, and having on either side an article of unusual shape, of common baked clay. Of one of these objects little more than one half remained; the other was nearly perfect, and may be described as a

---

[*] *Letters from Egypt*, p. 66.

cylinder compressed towards the middle like a modern dice-box, but open at both ends. Its height is about ten inches, and greatest diameter four inches. Both were lying horizontally, and they contained nothing but the sand, with which, intermixed with small stones, the whole tomb was filled. It throws little light on the reason of their presence that nearly identical *shapes* occur occasionally in the wall sculptures*, as tables or stands in connexion with offerings to the gods, and that two somewhat similar objects, but more definitely of this last character, are now in the British Museum.

Besides these cylinders, and a fragment of a still coarser platter, turned up near the bottom of the shaft, and retaining traces of burnt or black adipocere matter, there were no other vestiges, except those of the body; while in the corresponding grave, No. II., nothing whatever was met with save only a few bones in the last stage of decomposition. This last tomb, as has been already mentioned, formed, it may be said, part of one structure with the former. The sides of their shafts were parallel, and the chamber of the one was built so as to meet the chamber of the other, from which it was separated only by the thickness of the wall, which served as a partition between them.† Their plan will be readily seen by the accompanying section, as also the position of the deposit.

* Examples may be seen in Rosellini. *Mon. del Culto*, tav. iv. and xxxi.

† I gave the details of those tombs at the time, when I opened them, in the *Proceedings of the S. A. Scot.*, vol. ii. p. 274.

As to the probable period and relative circumstances of these interments, it is difficult to offer a satisfactory

SECTION OF TOMBS AT GEEZEH.

conjecture. They furnish none of the usual data from which it is possible to determine the respective epochs of Egyptian remains, and no analogous case has been previously noted. Their situation in the centre of a very ancient necropolis would afford a certain presumption in favour of their own high antiquity. But in addition to this there would be no evidence derivable from their inartistic construction, or from the fact that the bodies had not been subjected to any preservative process, as both these circumstances might be simply indicative of poverty without reference to age. But if this last point must, therefore, remain indeterminate, it is worthy of notice that not only had there been no mummification, but the bodies, so far as the position of the bones and the shape of the cells warranted a judgment, must each have been crumpled into some bent posture, or, not improbably, dismembered. If this surmise be correct, and it does not seem easy to avoid it, the departure from all previously observed Egyptian practice is so much wider than mere absence of mummification, that the question suggests itself whether strangers may not have been buried in these graves. Herodotus[*], for example, mentions that one of the Libyan tribes, almost or quite on the confines of Lower Egypt, the Nasamones, "interred their dead in a sitting attitude, watching when one is about to expire, that they may raise him up, and he may not die on his back." A custom did actually exist likewise in Assyria of crushing or otherwise disposing of bodies into limited spaces; and Mr. Layard found many examples at Nimroud and Kalah-Sherghat.[†] But archæology is now so familiar with remarkable coincidences of primitive practices among races scattered all over the globe, that it hesitates to assume, on that account, inferential connexions more close than the occasional uniformity of development under the operation of common psychical and physical conditions. And with regard to this particular method of inhumation, very much the same system is shown, by the contents of primeval cists, to have prevailed largely among certain of the aboriginal populations of Western Europe, while it is followed at the present day by savage South American tribes.[‡]

[*] *Herod.* lib. iv. c. 190.

[†] *Nineveh and its Remains*, vol. i. p. 253, and vol. ii. p. 58.

[‡] North American might also be added, as the Carib Indians have the same practice. Hodgson's *Letters*, ap. Akerman's *Arch. Index*, p. 5. For Europe it is unnecessary to give special references, as archæological literature teems with examples.

The skull which was recovered from one of the two tombs, I had hoped to have turned to account, as in some measure elucidatory of the difficulty, by affording an element of comparison with reference both to the heads of mummies and to general craniographic characteristics. With this view I stored it in a wicker basket, which was deposited within the ropes of my tent as a place of perfect security, where harm was not expected from exposure in a climate conservative rather than destructive. But I had forgotten the hungry prowlers of the edge of the desert—the jackals, which were constantly running about; the more cautious hyenas, whose tracks were sometimes seen; the wolves, which occasionally showed themselves; as well as their brethren the dogs from the nearest village, whose appearance and habits were hardly more civilized. And one morning I found the basket overturned, with the skull gnawed into rejected fragments. Nor, in the soporific air of the desert, had I heard the teeth horribly at work on their melancholy morsel, although where I lay I was only separated from the spot by a space of six feet and two folds of cloth. And so, unfortunately, this last vestige of the old denizen of the Necropolis, roused from its quiet subsidence into nothingness, met the fate to which the dying philosopher besought his friends to resign his body, to show in what little regard he held the tabernacle when the spirit had fled.

"Non tumulum curo, sepelit natura relictos."

## CHAP. VII.

### ON THE THEORIES EXPLANATORY OF EGYPTIAN SEPULTURE.

The sepulchral rites of the Egyptians having been so elaborate and peculiar, and the correlative vestiges being in every way so remarkable, it is not surprising that the strongest interest has constantly been felt in investigations which might tend to explain whence these customs arose. Nor does the interest centre alone in the desire for an elucidation of the growth and meaning of a very curious series of facts. It embraces also the idea, sometimes perhaps too rigidly conceived, that from the nature of these facts, any just exposition of the causes and motives which produced them would concurrently represent the psychological status of this extraordinary people in relation to the most important topics which can awaken the mental life, and exert an influence on any section of mankind.

In such a case there are obviously two channels from which enlightenment might be sought. The one would be any distinct statement of the objects contemplated by given details of procedure handed down from the Egyptians themselves, directly by writers of their own, or indirectly, with reasonable authority; and this, if existing fully, might be so conclusive of itself as to render application elsewhere unnecessary. The other source, an alternative, and, we may add, a doubtful one, would be a discriminating induction from the facts themselves as to their origin and bearings. The former of those channels is, in reality, as we shall presently revert to, most indistinct, from its not including any sufficiently articulate expository definitions; and recourse has, therefore, been had to the latter, not only to piece out deficiencies and afford intimations to be read in conjunction with such aids as the former offers, but also to give independent results. But of these and such like endeavours, it might be difficult to point to any in which the principles of the inductive method, though professedly or at least tacitly appealed to, are not gravely misapplied. Nor is it in archæological and historical inquiries affecting Egypt alone that springs of causations are inferred, which are called inductions or even discoveries, but which are simply entitled to no higher name than guesses. I hope for another and a more special opportunity to go into the question in its connexion with general archæology, as to the elements on which the inductive process may, in such researches, be brought to bear with true gain, and without misleading by the evolving of mere conjectural uncertainties. But as in this work Egyptian sepulchral rites are the subject, it will be proper that any remarks here should be restricted to their reference to these.

In the first place, it may be premised that there are two distinct classes of facts respecting which such vestiges as are alluded to might be interrogated, namely, the practices which they reveal, and the causes, or motives, which called these forth. How completely the one falls within the dominion of induction need not be pointed out; the other can only find a place there in certain favourable cases, where experience and analogy can be appealed to for aid, and even then, with not more than approximate propriety, varying ever in degree according to individual circumstances. For example, when we see certain primæval relics scattered over Western Europe, from which we can infer a given stage of barbaric life, and when we find existing races in the same rude phase of manners burying with the dead man his worldly weapons, from the belief that he would again require them beyond the grave,—then on the occurrence of spear or arrow heads in the ancient European tumuli, we know, not only what was the practice, but have some justification for assuming what was its cause.* But in the case of any sepulchral

* I give this as a good illustration; but although it is as favourable an one as can be found of what induction may do in this department, even it includes an element of uncertainty, and shows how little results so arrived at can be depended upon in this field. For, as well as weapons being buried by rude tribes from the reasons stated in the text, we also know there are examples of the practice being followed by others alike on memorial, honorary and symbolical grounds; and it

custom (for instance, that central one, mummification) in use among a highly civilised and speculatively reflective people, like the Egyptians, we are on very different ground. As to the practice, *that*, its concomitants and influence, can, as above, be comprehended, and much more thoroughly from the ampler aids. But as to the motive, if specific contemporary definition be absent, while experience is silent and analogy fails, where do we stand? If we say, what *has been* said, as we shall presently see, that this careful preservation of the body *must* have arisen from a belief in its resurrection, or because its integrity was necessary to the soul's accomplishing its destiny, or on account of comprehensive sanitary regulations, or from any one other assumed efficient principle, it cannot be too clearly pointed out that such modes of leaping from effect to hypothetical cause can hardly be allowed rank, even according to their relative intrinsic probability.

I am not here alluding to the abstract difficulties attending definitions of Necessary Connexion which Hume discussed[*], and which philosophers have since found to be one of their most fruitful topics; but speaking of causation in this matter in the intelligible sense of its implying the reflective or other originative processes which have occasioned given acts or works, I am referring to the vague and worse than uninstructive manner in which this ex-

may thus be seen what ample space there is in which to go astray in attributing psychical developments or religious tenets to races on secondary inferential evidence.

[*] *Essays*, vol. ii. p. 63.

planatory instrument can be employed. In investigating the products of the constructive labour, or other such traces of any of the lower animals, let the practice (that is, the habits), of the worker be therefrom known, and consideration being had to extraneous conditions, a knowledge of the motive follows as of course. Whether the inquirer starts with the supposition that the animal was adapted for the circumstances in which it was placed, or that the circumstances begot its special modifications, he feels equally sure that, once having ascertained its procedure, he can, from his confidence that that depends directly on the necessities of its life, define, *ipso facto*, the moving spring, subject to a possibility of error from incorrect observation or inference, and subordinate, of course, to a misconception of the primary cosmical relations of the particular animal.* But with regard to many of the works of man, instead of so direct a vista between the character of the execution and the nature of the impulse, there lies a labyrinth of infinite involvement. It is true that he too proceeds according to the requirements of his position, but the range of his perceptive, and the play of his moral faculties, combined, on the one hand, with the more or less potent executive capacity which he can wield, and, on the

* The fact that there are some forms of animals of elementary organization, and but "slightly adapted to special purposes of life," would hardly offer a technical exception, as they occupy their anomalous position because very little is as yet known of them. — Phillips's *Life on the Earth*, p. 28.

other, with the influences of his imaginative element, not only add to the complexity of his operations, but proclaim the variety of the motives whence these might have originated as well as their possibly composite character. The physical or external circumstances in which he is placed, are more than a mere area on which he performs: they are less than the sole formative principle according to which he acts. Soul and body together in inexplicable communion constitute his individual manhood, not merely soul acting on body, not merely body exclusively determining the intuitions of soul.[*] Such in like manner are his relations to the outer world and in the mass. The material conditions which surround him so far mould his procedure and his progress, bending even the growth of his mental faculties; but the latter with their diverse outgrowths, whether practical or mystical, co-ordinately assert so far a directing guidance on the influence of the former. Their relative operation too has been, and is, ever changing, with the developments which they themselves produce.

Hence the possible fallacy of arriving by a short cut, and selecting one as being a somewhat probable

[*] If the inquiry were intended to be fully pursued with reference to the disputed ground in metaphysical systems, the phraseology in this and preceding sentences ought to be more technical and properly philosophical; but it is hoped that the idea designed to be conveyed in its direct signification may be sufficiently intelligible. I am also aware that the terms of the proposition stated in the text include the battle-fields of idealism and materialism, of sensational and intuitional systems, but the object is not to endeavour here to enter into its various extended relations.

causation to account for certain special practices, such as we have at present in view; and hence, also, it seems to me, the weakness of many of the formally constructed systems of wider scope put forth as elucidatory of human progression. An able writer, for example, following Positivist rules, may bespeak assent to his method by asking whether it will not be admitted that "if we were acquainted with the whole of the antecedents, and with all the laws of their movements, we could with unerring certainty predict the whole of their immediate results."* And supposing this granted (although requiring even then on the grounds above stated, that the term shall not mean merely physical "antecedents"), the proposition which looks so fair, is, in reality, a mere play of words. For, from his own point of view, it is because he can *not* know *all* the antecedents that the propounder would fail in determining the just measure of their respective operation in the past, still more in defining their formative influence on a future, which, as it is to grow out of them, must offer new combinations, to which deductions from experience, which has no cognisance of their like, cannot, therefore, be logically applicable. But it may be said there are fundamental laws universally and eternally controlling. And while this is not to be denied, it is necessary to bear in mind their character, and that between them and ultimate phenomena come chains of intervening operations. All are equally and in a loose sense rightly called laws; but they will, as

* Buckle's *Hist. of Civilization in England,* vol. i. p. 17.

we believe, be more accurately apprehended as modes of procedure, as the accommodating channels through which the divers energetic forces are manifested, begotten by the action of more primary dynamic agencies, one and all converging into, or rather emerging from, the central unity of the Divine originative will.

Take an example even from the purely physical world, where that series of peculiarly variant, namely, the psychical, elements are wanting. It is usual to speak generally of the laws of vegetable growth as an intelligible idea; but is it possible to apprehend the complexity of their application to the kingdom over which they rule? They are to be conceived of as circles within circles of forces, touched at every point of their circumference by others, all being mutually deflected in relative degrees. One fixed axis they have, the principle of life, but it is the conditions which surround it that constitute the laws of growth\*; and these conditions being the phenomena produced by the harmonious conflict of all cosmical energies, from the widest to the purely local, involve such specialties in the concatenation of laws as no mere general propositions can do more than crudely overtake. And man, possessing not only a physical but a moral and intellectual life, is the subject in his own race of agencies, some

---

\* I am here simply referring to the abstract fact of plants having this relation to their surroundings, not adopting and being unable to adopt as an illustration Mr. Darwin's developmental or assimilative hypothesis, however valuable I may consider some sections of it within greatly restricted limits.

identical, many nobler, all apt to be more complicated because more composite, but illustrated in a certain imperfect way by the *aggregate* history and aspect of the vegetable world around him.

Admitting, then, the efficiency of such laws, or rather modes of progression in human affairs, their very nature, since it is the effect of their operation to produce infinite shades of development, must be like in some measure to the fecundated germ in the phenomenon of parthenogenesis,—their very nature must be to include provisions unfolding themselves only as growth requires, and adjusting themselves with ever varying capacity to the ever varying circumstances which their own endless complexity evolves. To assume that they, and the changeful elements on which they work, can in this sense be adequately apprehended, as is necessary on the principle of knowing "all the antecedents," would be to assume the possession of an omniscient faculty. And failing any pretension to this, is it implied that reliance on broad generic ordinances will give the key; that a few general propositions will answer the purpose, deduced, it may be correctly, from some of the mere primary facts lying on the surface, as, for example, that the fruits of labour must supply, in surplus, the necessaries of life ere the higher civilization can flourish; that a remote inland country would not be a diffusive commercial centre; that a Plato would not arise among the painted Britons, or a Newton among the Kamchadales, whose arithmetical perceptions are limited to the number of their fingers? The probable accuracy of results thence derived we might, in a certain, although in an imperfect, degree, appreciate, if we consider what would be the success of the gunner whose grasp of the conditions affecting projectiles was limited to knowing that, with his piece at a given angle, a given charge would, in a given state of atmosphere, propel a given weight to a given distance, but who was not in a position to estimate precisely the effects of the infinite grades of change possible in each of these circumstances in relation to the whole and to each other. The dependence to be placed in his aim, is some measure of the dependence to which formulated systems of the character in question would be entitled, although, with this difference, that in his case we should have some hope that his shot would proceed in the right direction, while, as to their arguments, we should want even this assurance. Wherever we turn among expounders of the more dogmatic principles of historic interpretation, we generally meet with portions of this element of weakness, however diverse their methods. For example, in Vico and Montesquieu, and partially in Herder and Voltaire, but especially in Comte and his followers it presents itself. And when, with reference to human affairs, these guides are content to deal only in wide sweeping circles, determining from such what is natural law, what cause, what effect, and what will be future result\*, the expressions, except when applied

---

\* With reference to the application of such systems to the future, their irrelevancy, even in comparatively narrow spheres, follows, as

in a few narrow foci, want all necessary approach to logical precision. More or less ingenious in vague hypothetical bearing they may be; more or less founded on perceptive grasp; and the systems with which they are interwoven may, here and there, be in like degree more or less instructive, by fixing attention on certain mutual relations of things which some merely historic narratives often overlook. But we cannot, in their full proportions, concede to them more determinate claims; while we have often to complain of their so looking at the facts of ethnography or history, as to rest the eye only on those which will compress into a few preconceived axiomatic moulds. Aided by the records of his acts, and by observation of them, as well as by deductions from his nature, we may conceive much that is accurate as to the general framework along which the career of man as a physical, moral, reasonable being entwines. But the key to human phenomena is not simply the direct application of a few

---

above, from the very elements of their construction. They share with other inductions that inapplicability on the grandest scale of all, deduced from the argument involved in the Theory of Probabilities, which is thus summed up by De Morgan:—"Experience can never on sound principles be held as foretelling all that is to come. The order of things, the laws of nature, and all those phrases by which we try to make the past command the future, will be understood by a person who admits the principles of which I treat as of limited application, not giving the highest degree of probability to more than a definite and limited continuance of those things which appear to us most stable. No finite experience whatsoever can justify us in saying that the future shall coincide with the past in all time to come, or that there is any probability for such a conclusion."—*Essay on Probabilities*, p. 128.

*quasi*-mathematical formulæ. Results of approximate reality are to be expected only at the hands of inquirers whose grasp, strengthened by an appreciation, in their proper place, of general principles, will not pass over the effects of that individuality for which nature, in all its parts, shows provision, and those aggregates of individuality, equally provided for, which constitute race.

I have thus summarily entered upon a somewhat abstract discussion, not in the light of a digression, but from the consideration that special points of the nature here in question can be best apprehended when general propositions, on which they constantly impinge, are kept in mind. Returning, then, to our immediate field of inquiry, it may be said that there are few subjects in which the licence of inference has been more largely employed, with the semblance of induction, and demanding a corresponding authority, than in discussing the psychological and similar questions suggested by the sepulchral rites of the ancient Egyptians. Take, as a specific example, an instance originating in one of the first elementary conditions which, *inter se*, can distinguish sepulchres or indeed any other works, — the inequality in their size. The rock-cut tombs of the kings at Thebes differ from each other in the extent of their excavations; not less do the pyramids in the great Necropolis of the district of Geezeh vary as to the area which they cover. With regard to the former, Champollion, at an early stage in the researches which his genius did so much to illustrate, pointing out that their respective dimensions had relation to the reigns of their royal occupants, averred, somewhat cursorily, that a glance at the size of the one would indicate what had been the duration of the other.* Further investigation does not substantiate the existence of any such definite ratio, although, as there is every reason to believe that the monarchs' tombs were prepared in their lifetime, it was natural that their respective elaboration should be influenced by individual, or periods of national, magnificence; and it does so happen that there were certain coincidences between long reigns, and great prosperity, as synonymous at least with power and architectural luxury. But an equivalent to the suggestion of Champollion, loosely referrible in this way to the royal Theban tombs, as it might also, for aught we know, be in like degree to the pyramids, has been applied to these last absolutely as a chronometric criterion by Lepsius, whose very distinguished labours in Egyptian antiquities render it surprising to find among them so singularly unsubstantial an addition. Adverting to the structure of these massive monuments, whereby the bulk might be increased by layer after layer enwrapping an original nucleus, he insists that such progressive enlargements proceeded *pari passu* with the length of the reign of the king who, in his lifetime, was thus creating a memorial of it. The mode in which this occurred is stated to have been, that each royal builder, estimating his own prospects of longevity, conducted his plan accordingly, and that,

* *Lettres écrites d'Égypte et de Nubie*, p. 246.

when failing strength foretold him his end drew nigh, the outlines of the growing pyramid were kept in correspondent approach to completion.* And this is alleged to have been the guiding principle which determined the size, as if the relations betwen life and death were commonly regulated by so nicely graduated a scale,—as if the duration of the former were invariably to be estimated according to present vigour, which was always sapped only by a gradual and forewarning decay,—as if mortal man either could or would arrive at a reasonably just conclusion as to the length of days in store for him. Yet, in the present case, it would be necessary to assume this, not only to give validity to the alleged general rule, but, prominently, with a view to the special circumstance of the close juxtaposition of many of the pyramids, particularly the smaller ones.† The builders of these would require to be supposed to have possessed enough prescience to know the given and very limited term of life awaiting them, or they would not have selected sites whereon any considerable expansion of their tombs would have been impossible, by reason of the close proximity of similar monuments.

---

\* Lepsius's *Letters from Egypt*, p. 65, and his paper *Ueber den Bau der Pyramiden*.

† Those who may not have seen the field of pyramids at Geezeh will find their relative positions in the plan affixed to Wilkinson's *Map of Thebes*, and inserted on a smaller scale in his *Handbook for Egypt*, 1858, p. 165. The same careful observer has pointed to their mutual proximity as an objection to Dr. Lepsius's hypothesis. Note to Rawlinson's *Herodotus*, vol. ii. p. 203.

## BURIAL RITES AND RELIGIOUS IDEAS.

This illustration* of the kind of results that have been produced by unsatisfactory explanatory processes has been dwelt upon, because it happens to be of tangible outline and, being connected with prominent features of detail, has a bearing on the treatment sometimes directed to the scheme and scope of Egyptian sepulture generally, which we are endeavouring to consider.

That a connexion subsisted between burial practices and rites on the one hand and religious conceptions on the other, might, on common grounds, be predicated, while, in the case in question, it is certified by specific evidence. But what were the exact points of contact, what the constructive operation of each upon the other, and the influence of external conditions on both, are problems which, although this has not been customary, it would be more instructive, and certainly more correct, to admit as inextricably involved from containing many contingent elements. The idea entertained by the Egyptians themselves upon the subject has not come down to us in any distinctly recorded statement. If it had, there would not the less have remained a necessity to consider the point

---

* It has also an additional interest, as since the promulgation of the hypothesis it has had a tendency to exert a kind of fascination, probably from having a *prima facie* resemblance to a rational explanation, so far, of these old mysteries the pyramids. It seems frequently to reappear axiomatically in useful books both in this country and on the continent; *e.g.* Stanley's *Sinai and Palestine*, p. xliii.; and Duncker's *Geschichte des Alterthums*, vol. i. p. 14, whose condensed care, historical insight, and well-balanced subdivision, entitle it to high rank.

of view in which we might be placed, according to the nature of any such record. Its character might be of a kind only to authenticate the import attributed at a given time to certain customs and forms, and it might by no means retain remembrance of the actual conditions under which they came into being. For, dogmatic interpretations of such practices, subsequently created or worked out by ingenious systemists, might be far from exhibiting the actual influences and development of thought under which they primarily originated. But we do not possess at present any direct exposition even of the nature of dogmatic interpretations, which might show the significance attached to sepulchral conditions and define their psychological bearings, were it only at particular periods. Herodotus[*] and Diodorus[†], who describe with some minuteness the burial customs of the Egyptians, have not added to their pictures a key which might explain the native conceptions then bound up therewith.[‡] And the hieroglyphic

---

[*] Lib. ii. c. 85, 90.        [†] Lib. i. c. 7.

[‡] A passage of Baron Bunsen's might seem to intimate (*Egypt's Place*, vol. iv. p. 641) that Herodotus had preserved explanations of this kind on one point. He says, "the real meaning of the celebrated passage in Herodotus *about the reasons* why the Egyptians bestowed so much care on the preservation of the body," &c. His reference is "*Herod.* lib. ii. c. 135," but chapter 135 of Book II. is devoted to an entirely different subject, namely, the alleged wealth of Rhodopis; nor, in any of the chapters of Book II., descriptive of funeral customs, can I find any allusion to "reasons" as above, offered by Herodotus, if that be the meaning. The context would seem to show that Baron Bunsen had in view Herodotus' statement as to the Egyptian belief in metempsychosis, which occurs in chapter 122 as a substantive fact,

literature, as already said, has as yet failed to yield any definite aid of this kind. Of the great result of death, the soul's futurity, it does, indeed, largely treat, but only through the channel of a most mystical ritualistic apparatus; and as yet there has not come to light any document of an expository character, professing to offer in terms a direct statement of the scheme of belief*, if, in fact, such were to be expected, considering the developmental as well as subtle character of the tenets which ever flourished in the valley of the Nile. Enough, indeed, has already become manifest to show that the central point in the creed of this ancient race was belief in the soul's immortality, coupled with the ennobling adjunct of personal responsibility in the matter of its future fate, according to a code of morals, conventional in only a few of its details, but of eternal validity in its general precepts.† But the connexion between spirit and matter, or rather the light in which the body was viewed in relation to the futurity of the soul, does not appear to be, with any clearness, set forth. Even were such

---

interposed in a narrative of regal succession, and having no indicated reference to "preservation of the body," or to any other burial custom. However the two things may have been connected, they are not connected by Herodotus.

\* A species of commentary has been found attached to the seventeenth chapter of the Ritual, which is an important one; but the commentary is hardly a shade less mystical than the text. It is the subject of two ingenious papers by De Rougé.—*Rev. Archéol.* N. S. vol. i.

† See passage from the Ritual in which the soul of the deceased is made to disavow having violated in life a given series of duties. Translated by Birch, ap. Bunsen's *Egypt's Place*, vol. iv. p. 644.

a topic dealt with, except in the plainest terms, or in the most elementary manner, it would not have been surprising that the utmost obscurity should enwrap it, not only from its inherent nature, especially when reflected by a national genius of the most mystical type, but also from the esoteric modes of expression likely to be, and in existing cases, actually employed, as well as from the peculiar character of the medium of utterance itself, if that were the hieroglyphic writing. The ingenuity of Champollion and Young did indeed find the key to this extraordinary script, and the labours of the former, extended by a few devoted scholars, with Birch, Lepsius, Brugsch, and De Rougé at their head, have brought the application of it to a remarkable degree of certainty, in texts embodying plain narrative or direct statement. But from the large figurative and symbolic element, and from the number of homophonous characters allowing room for intricate shades of expression, the dubiety that might attach to interpretations of passages containing metaphysical subtleties is not to be overlooked.*

In considering any renderings of religious writings, I believe it is necessary to keep steadily in view the existence of these sources of probable misconception. The great sacred repertory, the Ritual of the Dead, has, besides, a special atmosphere of haze around it,

* Mr. Sharpe puts this in a strong light by saying, "there are peculiarities (in the hieroglyphic writing) which must often have made the reading doubtful to the most learned of the priests."—*Egyptian Hieroglyphics*, p. 8.

arising from its nature, as before alluded to. It is not what would, in fact, be its necessary complement — a creed, a confession, a canon, or an exposition, but a formulary of prayers and injunctions, incorporated with a narrative of mystical events in the unseen world. And therefore, in its various sections, it is mandatory as to acts, allusive as to doctrines, now figurative in its references, now emblematic as to style — in short, anything but precise.\* Besides, it is, on the one hand, a production of cumulative growth, and, on the other, is probably an incomplete embodiment even in the most comprehensive existing copy — that now at Turin, which consists of one hundred and sixty-five chapters.† On all these grounds there would apply to it with marked force an observation of Coleridge, as to the strange medley of doctrines that might be educed by " taking any moral or religious

---

\* Those who are interested in this most extraordinary product of early religious conceptions, will look forward with impatience to the publication of an interpretation of the entire text by Mr. Birch, which has been for some time in type. This " colossal performance," as Baron Bunsen has, from its laboriousness, termed it (*Egypt's Place*, vol. iv. p. 660), will for the first time present a deciphering of the Ritual in its fullest attainable integrity. Hitherto its tenor has been chiefly known, first from the few notes of Champollion; subsequently by analyses of portions of it by Birch in various publications; by researches of Lepsius, including the preface to his *Todtenbuch;* and from the careful *Études* of De Rougé, in the *Revue Archéologique*, now in course of being reprinted, subject to revisal, as the introduction to facsimile lithographs of a hieratic copy of the Ritual in the Louvre.

† This is the copy published in lithograph by Lepsius as *Das Todtenbuch der Ægypter:* Leipzig 1842.

book and interpreting every phrase in its literal sense, as conveying and designed to convey a metaphysical verity or historical fact." Its mechanical ordinances are of course distinct enough so far as they go, such as specifying given funeral invocations, enjoining certain texts and prayers to be painted on the coffin, as well as certain amulets to accompany the dead; and the great central truth round which they all revolve, the spirit's imperishable being, is also plain. But the conditions affecting its immortality with reference to the body with which it had been associated, are not more but less intelligibly expounded than the mysterious cycle of trials, which led from death to futurity, and the conception of the ultimate status in that futurity. There are passages which point to the beatification of the soul after death under the designation of Osiris\*, and run parallel to something like the Brahmanical dogma of absorption into the divine essence. There are other sections which preserve strongly the personality of the deceased, in which it is said, "there are given to him bread and drink, and slices of flesh off the table of the sun; when he peregrinates the fields of the blest, corn and barley are given to him, for he is as provided as he was upon earth."† Of these latter texts, again, there are the discrepant views, that they embody a mere crude materialistic conception of beatitude, like the Norse

---

\* Cf. Rosellini, *Mon. Civ.* vol. iii. p. 472.
† Birch's *Hieroglyphs*, p. 272.

Walhalla, if not with its endless perpetuation of the enjoyments of prowess and carousal; or, on the other hand, that they are simply indicative of the individualisation of the soul, and that in its consciousness of divine life it "continued to have an organ (body) as Osiris has [according to the Ritual] his body in the sun."*

Another and very perplexing element is infused by the remarkable statement of Herodotus that, according to Egyptian belief, the soul of man at death entered into the body of a new born animal, thence passed on from one into another until it circled through the forms of all the inhabitants of earth, water and air, and reverted to humanity, being born again after a cycle of transmigration of three thousand years.† There are very palpable obstacles in the way of reconciling a tenet such as this with those intimations derivable from hieroglyphic sources, which point to divine judgment as the sequence of death, with, on the one hand, the reward of the good in the mansions of light, and, on the other, the relegation of the wicked to punishments in the darkness of hell. A judicious writer has almost understated the case in saying, that we are only imperfectly in a position to specify the place which the doctrine of metempsychosis occupied in the circle of Egyptian conceptions as to the future life.‡ Another has ingeniously bridged over the difficulty, by suggesting that the doom of transmigration

---

\* Bunsen's *Egypt's Place*, vol. iv. p. 664.
† Herod. lib. ii. c. 123.
‡ Duncker, *Geschichte des Alterthums*, vol. i. p. 73, 2nd ed.

was not held to apply to the spirits of the just, nor yet to those of the utterly wicked, but to those of less deadly transgressors, who were thus sent back to the earth as a penalty and a probation.* But it is to be observed that, on the one side, the existing ritualistic formularies do not seem to make provisions corresponding to this idea, and that, on the other, the statement of Herodotus, whatever its significance, demands from the connexion in which it stands, an application of the transmigration of the soul as universal as its attribute of immortality.

In view of these and other seeming incongruities, a preliminary question may be offered for consideration. In investigating and comparing the apparent evidences of ancient Egyptian religious beliefs, which have been handed down either in a direct or inferential shape, are we on the right track in referring them all to a standard of uniformity, and requiring that they shall all harmonise one with the other, and link together with the logical appositeness of parts of one integral conception? In the first place we do not even know whether, as an initial assurance of unity, the elementary scheme of the Egyptian religion, in its typical form, came into being under an authoritative code even as homogeneous as the Veda, much less the Koran; but there seems no reason to doubt that, with whatever rigidity it may have retained many outlines, its history, ideologically, was developmental. Meta-

---

* Wilkinson's *Account*, vol. ii. p. 380.

physical speculation of its kind was active, certainly, alongside of it. Specific declarations, as well as the universal tradition of antiquity, testify the importance relatively, the considerable scope, and the ingenuity of Egyptian philosophy. Where its germinal growths may have been grafted on the sacred stem cannot be defined, or how far they continued to flourish separately. But with a learned priesthood ministering under the shadow of a system whose traces show that it had been the subject of, and therefore possessed capacity for, mutation, it can hardly be questioned that new forms of thought would from time to time be introduced, not perhaps so much into the externals of worship\*, as into the opinions entertained in the shape of doctrinal mysteries. It is not therefore difficult to conceive that the Ritual, especially since it was not a substantive creation, but (as there is reason to believe it was,) a thing of growth, or rather an agglomeration of various documents†, should contain allusions of diverse or even apparently inconsistent character. And still less difficult would it be to suppose this, if the combined subtlety and mysticism of the old Egyptian intellect be kept in remembrance as manifested subsequently, for example, in the Christian gnostic heresies, where, on the one hand distinctions, and on the other parallelisms and identities

---

\* Throughout the long period illustrated by the monuments these were singularly stable.

† See De Rougé, *Études sur le Rituel — Rev. Archéol.* Fév. 1860, p. 70; and Lepsius, *Das Todtenbuch;* Vorwort, pp. 4, *seq.*

were maintained, which the modern European mind can hardly even apprehend.

Further, when in what may be called extraneous narrative, passages like that already referred to in Herodotus present themselves, stating in general terms that certain speculative dogmas were Egyptian beliefs, the reflection ought to arise,—were these fundamental constituents of the religion, or more recent products of exegesis, and if the latter, were they universally accredited articles, or the tenets of philosophic schools? Suppose the circumstances reversed, and that the subject to be considered were the import of similar remarks recorded by Egyptian travellers in Greece. It may be that the analogy between the religious systems and conditions of the two countries is not exact, but it is close enough to make it an admissible illustration of the position in question. Let us imagine, then, that in Greece about the beginning of the fourth century B.C., after, not as in Egypt a millennium or two, but after three or four hundred years of native intellectual life and metaphysical evolution, when the speculations of various philosophies had infiltrated, expanded, and even absorbed some of the early religious elements which show themselves in comparative simplicity, for example, in the poems of Homer—let us imagine that, at this period, foreign writers, without placing us in any special point of view, were to have left observations that the Greeks believed certain given dogmas, we might well, without or with only scanty collateral guidance, be puzzled to determine the force of the testimony.

In fact it may be said with regard to the details of Egyptian religious conceptions, their realism or symbolism, their growth, their respective chronology, and relative authority, that the data at present existing are at once heterogeneous and incomplete. And while it cannot be a satisfactory process to endeavour forcibly to fuse them into unity, neither can it be a reliable one, in the absence of definite insight, to determine the significance of points of departure between them, that is, between various allusions *inter se* in the native rituals, narrative statements of indefinite application by early foreign writers, and more elaborate disquisitions by somewhat later authors who were likely either as commentators, or as interpreting according to the spirit of their own age, to impart to tenets which they expounded the colour of the newer philosophies under whose influence they lived and thought. The facts of the *cultus* do indeed stand out, for the most part, with considerable distinctness, but some of even the more important fundamental principles with which it was interwoven, are by no means to be asserted with certainty, much more the growth and actual systems of creed, and such relations of belief to practice, as nothing but precise contemporary definitions could with accuracy unfold.

With reference to the particular case of the metempsychosis, there can be no doubt that some such speculations had flourished in Egypt. The statement of Herodotus is itself sufficiently circumstantial to verify the fact. Ritualistic allusions, presently to be referred to, are stated to point to it. And wall-paintings in the tombs have often been indicated as confirmatory. The evidence of these last, however, is not so clear. The prominent group, which is commonly appealed to as an instance, and indeed the only one of an approximately direct nature which I can remember or discover any reference to, is the subject in the tomb of King Rameses VI. at Thebes.* In it a file of nine human figures, presumed to be coming up for judgment, appear mounting as many steps of a dais on which Osiris is seated. Before the god stands a balance, whose use is illustrated by other frescoes and vignettes of papyri, in which the heart of the deceased is weighed against the emblem of truth; and on an upper line turned away from the throne, a pig, supposed to contain a judged human soul, is seen in a boat in charge of two monkeys, sent off, as it has been inferred, on the way back to earth. Now, with regard to this picture, the suggestion might arise that as the Ritual adverts to the souls of the justified dead assuming in some mystic manner the shapes of certain animals so as to elude various ordeals that lay before them in the unseen world on their way to ultimate beatitude,—does not the pig, referring it may be to a condemned or probationary soul, represent a transformation in the spiritual and not in the material

---

* Wilkinson ap. Rawlinson's *Herodotus*, vol. ii. p. 197. The subject is given in his *Ancient Egypts*. 2nd series, Pl. 89. Rosellini publishes it in colours, *Mon. del Cult.* tav. lxvi. Between these copies, however, there are very great discrepancies.

world? If, however, the scene really exhibits the dogma of metempsychosis in the Pythagorean sense, it is to be remarked that it connects the transmigration with judgment, which Herodotus has not intimated. In two obscurely mystical chapters of the Ritual, again, Mr. Birch considers it to be implied that "the soul revisited the mummy, and if this decayed, then immediately transmigrated."* In point of fact, the present state of knowledge must render any attempt vain to define the actual scope of Egyptian conceptions on this subject. But in the ritualistic association of the career of the soul, and the preservation of the body (possibly for some limited time), we seem to see one of those cases of the hierarchical intertwining of a religious idea with an important custom, and so imparting a sacred value to a priestly function. If we are to consider that the custom, I mean mummification, was actually originated by the idea, we have not yet the materials to follow the process, and evolve the reasoning whereby the preservation of the body was considered to be essential to the fate of the soul.

We certainly cannot be content with the common explanation of the connexion between the two things which Rosellini, although by no means the originator of it, specially elaborated. The notion which he worked out was, that it was held to be essential the body should endure as long as the transmigration of the soul lasted, and that with reference

---

* See Birch's Article, *Mummy — English Cyclopædia.*

to the ultimate destiny of the latter, it was necessary the former should be preserved from the possibility of decay for the three thousand years.* But even supposing that the ground was quite clear for the reception of this hypothesis, the facts, if looked at in any other than their simpler relations, refuse to come within it. For example, only a small proportion of the mummies, being those embalmed by the more costly substances, were calculated to continue intact for the lengthened period required. With a vast mass of the others, the effect of the preservative processes was not such as to prevent their destruction within a very much shorter interval. In various stages of disintegration down to the merest residuum of dust mingling with the wrappages, they have constantly been found; and as this eventual result could not remain unknown to the ancients themselves, are we to suppose that the future hopes of vast numbers were thus carelessly doomed, as they would have been if the preservation of the body in the alleged relation to a transmigration of three thousand years were a sacred, fundamental, and even originative necessity? In the same point of view would fall to be discussed the undoubted reappropriation of the tombs, even in very ancient times, which quite militates against the probability of that inviolable perpetuation of the body for so long a period being of such vital consequence. Indeed, I have some doubt whether all the Egyptian

* *Mon. Civ.* vol. iii. p. 308.

dead were really embalmed; and of those that were, I am induced to believe that in course of the sepulchral adjustments as to space, a large number were found to have mouldered away as above stated, or were constantly subjected to circumstances of more active demolition, after a lapse of time by no means inordinately long, and thus were cleared away. For, looking to the case of Thebes, it does not seem possible to do otherwise than arrive at one or other or all of these suppositions. The extent of the Necropolis, great as it is, could not well be made to represent more than an area measuring three miles by half a mile. Of this it need hardly be here pointed out, how considerable a proportion is occupied by tombs in which the space employed bears an extravagant relation to that actually required by the few bodies for which each was designed; while there are, on the other hand, only a very few subterraneans which, from the mummies having been piled in them in tiers, may be said to stand for a larger area than the surface measurement they represent. But making every kind of allowance, it would be an extreme calculation to assume that more ground was occupied than would be represented by a single layer of bodies covering what has already been called the ultimate area of the Necropolis, or three miles by one half. Now the population of Thebes at the various stages of its existence we do not know, but as its site was nearly as large as that of modern London[*], the

---

[*] See Chap. I. p. 30.

number of souls it contained, although by no means to be calculated in the same ratio, must have been very great; but whether the maximum within the city, its suburbs, and neighbourhood, is to be estimated at 250,000, 500,000, or 1,000,000, it would be impossible to determine.* If the first be assumed, the burial space above indicated would provide for the wants of not more than six hundred years, if the last, for only one hundred and fifty, supposing all the dead to have been embalmed, and all the mummies to have maintained their position. It might of course be said, that the windings of some neighbouring unsuspected ravines may contain undiscovered grottoes with legions of the ancient dead, which would materially increase the data for calculating the area of occupation. But to counterbalance this contingency, it might be pointed out, that as a not inconsiderable portion of even the assumed space of three miles by one half, is filled with tombs referrible to the seventh century B.C.,† *that* would require to be limited with reference to the long preceding ages over which Theban sepulture must have been spread. It cannot, however, be necessary to avow that from a computation like this, in which each element can be only approxi-

---

\* The inhabitants of ancient Syracuse had been stated at 1,200,000; but Niebuhr, pointing out that "statements of population in antiquity were monstrously exaggerated," estimates the reality in this case at 200,000.—*Lect. Anct. Ethnog.* vol. ii. p. 261.

† The tombs dating under the Twenty-sixth Dynasty, which occupy the greater part of the large valley of El Assasseef. See Chap. II. p. 50.

mative, it could not be proposed to deduce an argument of the nature of an arithmetical result. The figures are placed in juxtaposition merely to help to bring out, that allowing for the possibility of much error they, in a vague way, represent circumstances corroborative of the other facts which show that, while the higher ranks, from what has ever been a common desire for sepulchral perpetuation, succeeded more or less in achieving it, the evidence is against the existence of a fundamental *general* principle enjoining the lengthened inviolability of the body and attaching it to the alleged transmigration period of three thousand years.

The same objections, as is evident, apply with increased force against a corresponding inference, that the cause of the Egyptian embalmment of the body was an assumed belief in its resurrection or rejunction with the soul at the end of the cycle of wandering. In its merely inductive aspect this inference had the additional weakness of being bound up with reasoning which revolved in a circle; for, in what is perhaps the earliest historical connecting of the two things, in a sermon of St. Augustine's, the starting point is at the other side, and he attributes to the Egyptians a belief in the resurrection, *because* they so carefully preserved the corpses of the dead, and made them as lasting as brass.* That conceptions as to metempsychosis had

* "Egyptii soli credunt resurrectionem, quia diligenter curant cadavera mortuorum: morem enim habent siccare corpora, et quasi ænea reddere."—*Serm*. ccclxi. *De Resurrect. Mort.* ap. Rosellini, *Mon. Civ.* vol. iii. p. 305. The Peruvians, before the Spanish conquest,

existed among them, appears, as already said, to be beyond question, although we may know nothing of the origination of these, and little as to the position they occupied with relation to the public faith, or the manner in which they may have become intertwined with sepulchral usages. And so in like manner is it with regard to ideas the same people may have held as to some future connexion between the soul and its earthly body, or at least *a* body. Some recent researches go to show from allusions in the Ritual, that such a topic likewise had been among their speculations. For example, the title of the eighty-ninth chapter is rendered by De Rougé, "Chapter of reuniting the soul to its body in *Ker neter*" (the ordinary place of sojourn of the dead).* Still, all the difficulties al-

---

applied the desiccating properties of the cold, dry air of their mountains to shrivel, or, as it were, mummify bodies; and Prescott (*Conq. of Peru*, vol. i. p. 83) states that "a belief in the resurrection of the body led them to preserve it." From the imperfect examination of the Spanish authorities which circumstances have as yet allowed me, I have not been able to find the exact grounds on which this belief is asserted to have been held by the Peruvians, but I have strong suspicions that the foundation was merely a modified induction by some of the early Spaniards familiar with the Christian doctrine, and very much the same in kind as that of St. Augustine mentioned above. This is the more probable, because the alleged causation-link, at all events, appears to be broken by the fact, that the preservative method in question was by no means the only manner in which the Peruvians disposed of the dead. See for examples Desjardins, *Le Pérou avant la Conquête Espagnole*, pp. 168, *et seq.*: Paris 1858.

* *Études sur le Rituel*—*Rev. Archéol.* vol. i. N. S. p. 85. Birch appears to understand this chapter as referring to the soul revisiting the mummy. See above, p. 200.

ready pointed out as attaching to ritualistic passages and interpretations of them come here broadly into play. Whether the actual significance of the very mystical chapters (three), in which the body is the subject, has been made out, may well be considered uncertain, and it remains to be determined whether any portion of them can be supposed to point to ideas as to resurrection. If so such tenets could only be reconciled, by some extraordinary paradox, to the main scope of much of the Ritual, or must be recognised as an admitted inconsistency, explicable only from the heterogeneous character of that compilation. Moreover, to those at least who held the transmigration dogma set forth by Herodotus, a resuscitation doctrine could not be rendered compatible; for, according to them, the soul was eminently independent of one individual human body, and after the lapse of three thousand years was born anew in another. In fact, the Egyptian mind, dealing with the great question of futurity, had doubtless evolved various phases of thought upon the subject, and it dwelt strongly on that link between soul and body which gives to man his earthly personality, and nearly everywhere has attached some degree of sacredness to his mortal part. But unless the force of such speculations, and somewhat of their history be sufficiently known, it is delusive to fix upon any one of them, and declare it to have been the cause of a custom with which it may have a certain accordance, but only some of the facts of which harmonise with it. That the type of national genius from which such speculations arose, had great influence on the growth of sepulchral procedure is sufficiently certain; but except on the clearest contemporary evidence, to describe this procedure as having been caused by one or other of the specific ideas in question, or to attribute specific ideas from our own inductions, is an unsound method of dealing with the subject.

If from explanations of this strange mortuary practice, mummification, founded on the allegation of an origin in given religious behests, we turn to others which fix attention rather on physical causes, we may observe that they are accompanied by facts whose efficiency (so far) there is no difficulty in recognising. Among these there is the primary one, that the sand of the desert does, under certain conditions, contain the preservative salts,—natron, nitre and alum,—best calculated to arrest decay in animal tissues[*]; and it is possible to conceive of circumstances in which bodies, unwittingly deposited in it, might have been found to show the action of the antiseptic properties of its constituents. Then again, the geological characteristics of a large part of the country tended to discourage interment in the alluvial soil, as once a year it became a sodden mass, and pointed rather to excavation in the soft rock which, covered slightly or not at all by drifting sand, bounds the cultivable valley. And so these two physical circumstances reacted on each other. For, vault burial once contemplated, considerations of

---

[*] Gliddon's *Otia Egyptiaca*, p. 60, note.

suitability and decorum would encourage the application of embalming processes. But when it is added that this is all which is necessary to account for the peculiarity of Egyptian sepulture, a little reflection will show that the proposition only eludes a difficulty by offering an incomplete and inaccurate conception of the matter. The physical circumstances in question were only predisposing conditions: the determining causes must have been moral. For, in the former, there was no irreversible necessity requiring that the body must be disposed of in one method, and no other. It is true that the scarcity of fuel in a country without any great command of timber was against the use of the pyre on a considerable scale. But why might not the ancient Egyptians have raised mounds of earth or sand, and simply interred their dead like the modern inhabitants; or, as in some Italian cities, deposited them in daily masses, accompanied by quicklime, in a well to be closed till its turn came round again in twelve months; or, like the Parsees, placed them on the tops of towers to be dealt with by the elements and by birds of prey? That they did not do so, and followed another method not actually more inevitable, shows that, in the main physical conditions, we have not before us all the originative causes. What the others were which must have supplied the formative element would be still to seek. Whether they may have taken shape from some special reforming or innovating effort, like that which Solon is stated to have applied to sepulchral usages in

P

Attica*, is not at present to be ascertained, or whether, as is more likely, they were the product of gradual growth, and of phases of thought and circumstances, the action of which upon each other could not now be traced.

But if the precise links of the causation which produced the practice in question, may, as in the case of so many customs both ancient and modern, be incapable of full demonstration on account of their possible involution, there is reason to hope that subsequent philological research may place in a clearer light the special aspects in which the sacredness so universally attached to sepulchral rites was, at certain periods, viewed in Egypt. The phenomenon, so to say, may come to be better known, and its influence more exactly appreciated; but even then it may be necessary not to forget what now it ought to be essential to remember, that a determination to explain likewise the reason of its existence, might be a much more unscientific procedure than to acknowledge the absence of sufficient light on the subject.† A suggestion of Dugald Stewart's has, in certain walks, no doubt, its value, that "in examining

---

* Cicero, *De Leg*. ii. 26.

† There is a good illustrative remark of Schlegel's, as applied to history, which, if he had himself always borne it in mind in practice, would not have been detrimental to his *Philosophy of History*, where it occurs (p. 71). "Extremely hazardous is the desire to explain everything, and to supply whatever appears a gap. For in this propensity lies the first cause and germ of all those violent and arbitrary hypothesis which perplex and pervert the science of history far more than the open avowal of our ignorance or the uncertainty of our knowledge."

the history of mankind, as well as in examining the phenomena of the material world, when we cannot trace the process by which an event has been produced, it is often of importance to be able to show how it may have been produced by natural causes."* But (and especially with regard to the former field), placing little reliance on the ultimate validity of results so obtained, chiefly for the reason which the same writer has subsequently stated, that the real channel of progression has not been always that which seems the most natural, I believe we should view with more than suspicion the application of this method to details in ethnographic archæology, unless when put forth carefully and avowedly in its provisional aspect. From a strong feeling that something beyond this, namely, an unscientific commingling of hasty deductive attempts of this kind with imperfect inductions, has still too large a place in many branches of archæological literature, I have in this chapter, above and subsequently, followed some lines of argument, which may be considered too minute, and also tedious, especially as they are, and necessarily, not always constructive. But whether these in themselves may be found to be right or wrong, I have proceeded on the conviction that archæological and ethnographic investigations of all kinds can only be satisfactorily conducted when the closest attention to rules of evidence is maintained — when inferences are restrained within the due bounds which facts warrant — when, in short, the conjectural

---

* Stewart's *Memoirs of Smith, Robertson and Reid*, pp. 48 and 53.

leaven is entirely expelled, which, during the time of its most active operation, produced in Egyptian research the extravagances of Kircher, or in our native antiquities the fantasies of Stukely or Vallancey.

There is another remarkable feature in Egyptian sepulchres — the deposit of various articles in the tombs — regarding which it would be of considerable interest if we could ascertain, in like manner, what were the ideas associated with it at certain epochs, as well as what were the motives which primarily led to it. On the former point there may, as in the previous case, be some hope of eventual elucidation; the latter, similarly, is most likely to remain uncertain or obscure. It is true that as to the sepulchral objects of an obviously religious character, such as effigies or emblems of deities, and tablets inscribed with prayers or litanies, there might hardly, in one sense, be room to speculate respecting a thing so natural as their deposit in the tombs of a people of whose religious worship they were important constituents. Still the fact that other races imbued with idolatrous polytheism did not always follow the same custom, will recall that special conditions must have developed it, and that it may have had a distinct significance as well as an apparent congruity. But in the case of certain other seemingly sacred accompaniments of the dead, the small clay figures like miniature mummies, which have been already mentioned more than once[*], there are no

---

[*] See particularly p. 155, and the reference there to the Ritual.

merely general grounds on which their presence could be accounted for; and wanting the efficient actual ones we want all.

Then, again, as to the numerous relics connected with daily life, occupations and manners, which the tombs contained, there is a choice of fairly warrantable inferences applicable to them, but each is equally uncertain, and all may be wrong, as must readily be admitted, if, for no other reason, from the very fact that the power of alternative selection presents itself. For example, various instruments or tools of certain crafts being found associated with given bodies may reasonably be supposed to indicate what had been the occupation or profession in life of the dead. But if we ask why were these relics of their earthly career deposited by their side, is the reply, guided by analogies elsewhere, to be that they had reference symbolically to activities continued beyond the grave; or, shall it be the very reverse, that they were laid beside their owners as a token that work was over; or, more simple still, that they were merely a kind of memorial accompaniment? And questions of this description assume a wider scope when considered along with the circumstance, that the contents of tombs were much more multifarious than implements indicative of special personal pursuits. They included those very numerous objects whose great variety has already been mentioned. And with what views were these committed to the sepulchre? The conceptions entertained on the subject when the practice was in full activity, may perhaps, as before stated in the case of mummification, come to be known from some distinct descriptive record : the originative motives which produced the beginnings of the custom may never be brought into clearer relief than necessarily imperfect inductions can accomplish. But supposing it once in existence, in however simple a form, springing from one or other of those conceptive sources, above adverted to, whence similar practices arose among so many different races,—supposing it once in existence it is natural to imagine that it would attain a considerable development where burial took place in dry and decorated vaults. That a part of this development was interlinked with religious ideas, or regulative ceremonialism, is more than probable, although in what precise manner present information fails to define; but looking to the various facts it seems also most likely that a large proportion was merely conventional, embodying growth or changes of fashion in its local, temporary, and even individual relations. In two previous chapters\* I have adverted to those points, and it will be unnecessary to go over the same ground here, as it could only be repeated, that besides the absence as yet of direct contemporary information, there is a want of a sufficient series of accurate sepulchral observations to enable facts to be duly classified with reference to their place, date, or special bearings.

In naming the second of these particulars, date, the difficulty is of course recalled that adjustment in that

---

\* Chapters III. and IV. at pp. 72 and 116.

respect would, over a considerable chronological area, have, as yet, been relative rather than absolute. Earlier than the Eighteenth Dynasty, about 1500 B.C., the measure of time by the lists of regal succession is in a high degree uncertain; and it implies no grudging acknowledgment of the great learning and ingenuity distinguishing some of the formulated schemes educed from them, if it be said that the most elaborate began to crumble ere well completed. It is as yet too true that with regard to the earlier Egyptian epochs, a remark applied by Bolingbroke to certain chronological systems in his day, has not lost its force: "They are so many enchanted castles; they appear to be something, they are nothing but appearances; like them too dissolve the charm and they vanish from the sight." *
All hope of veritable Egyptian *fasti* must centre in the discovery of papyri or similar native monuments, containing distinct chronological notations according to astronomical or other absolute data.† Till then we must be content with approximate symbols.

And indeed with regard to ancient Egypt generally, we can hardly decide at first sight whether most to admire the amount of knowledge which research and ingenuity have recovered, or most to regret that imperfect and in some sort provisional character of many of the results, which is incident to all studies and

* *Letters on the Study of History*, p. 9.
† The principle of following such existing indications is, so far, well exemplified in Mr. Poole's *Horæ Ægyptiacæ*, and in his article *Egypt*, in the last edition of the *Encyclopædia Britannica*.

especially to those depending on discoveries alike of data as in treatment. More than two thousand books * constitute the substructure and the fabric of the present beacons which throw light along this vista of the past. Worker after worker has built a pharos on the great quicksand of oblivion which lies between it and us, but the solvent influence of advancing inquiry has deprived each in turn of cohesive power, causing it to sink down and leave no trace unless its residuum containing substantial elements could make some addition to the accumulating foundations. And of the guides now above the surface it is naturally the fate that they too, in their present shape, must pass away; and the measure of their utility in the future, if with reference to the past the criterion is different, will be the amount of actual facts which their materials may supply to succeeding labourers possessing the benefit of newer and ampler resources.

* A German writer, three years ago, published a catalogue of books and memoirs in all languages relating to Egypt [*Bibliotheca Ægyptiaca*, von H. Jolowicz: Leipzig 1858.] The number of entries is 2675. Many of those publications are of course ephemeral or trivial, while many relate to special subjects not alluded to in the remark in the text. But when I use there the expression "more than two thousand," it will not of course be understood that these writers, or more than a very small proportion of them, were actual constructive labourers on any considerable scale.

## CHAP. VIII.

### THE SEPULCHRAL EVIDENCE ON EARLY METALLURGIC PRACTICE.

It has been customary to suppose that the absence of iron relics among the innumerable spoils from the older tombs of Egypt was sufficiently accounted for by the natural tendency of that metal to decomposition, especially liable to be hastened by the action of the nitrous soil or sand of the country. The fact, however, should be observed, that in a large proportion of cases the objects which have been found in tombs never were or could be in contact with the soil or the sand which might, and did, drift up the doorways, and into the outer chambers, or filled the shafts, but it by no means always reached the sepulchral deposit, even in instances where this had long previously been rifled and neglected. Then, again, as to the question of natural decomposition, the disclosures in the unrifled tomb of Sebau, described in a former chapter, show that exclusion from air in the rock sepulchres of a land where rain has at all times been considered a prodigy, is quite as efficient in preventing decay in objects of iron, as it has long been known to be in the case of substances much more prone to destruction. The hasps and nails of the massive door which guarded the inner repositories were little, if at all, the worse for their lengthened service: and in the funeral canopy from the same sepulchre, two small staples in the rear, which had probably been necessary to fasten it to its base, two sockets for the pillars in front, and two long nails (which secured the cornice) shaped precisely like those now in use, are all of iron, still as lustrous and pliant as on the day they left the forge. Therefore, as two thousand years have made literally no appreciable impression upon them, there appears no reason why, under similar circumstances, they might not have endured for a period immeasurably longer.*

On these grounds, in conjunction with others presently to be referred to, I venture to think that if any objects of iron had been deposited in most of the tombs whose contents fill our museums, they would have been found, and that the absence of such must be explained from some other cause than decomposition. This circumstance leads directly to the inquiry so frequently pursued, as to what position the ancient

---

* The date of the deposit in the tomb in question is fixed by the papyri which accompanied two of the most important of the occupants, and show them to have died about the commencement of the period of Roman rule, during the reign of Augustus, that is to say, about nineteen hundred years ago. See Chapter IV.

Egyptians occupied in relation to working in iron. The frescoes have been looked to for evidence on the subject, and have been held to speak decisively as to the free use of that metal; but I confess that I cannot regard their intimations as so entirely unequivocal as to amount to proof of so broad a proposition, although they certainly point to more than a strong probability of contemporaneous acquaintance with iron. The question is simply, how far the employment of given colours is specifically significant of the materials composing the objects represented. I think it will not be doubted by those familiar with the wall paintings collectively, that no such canon will hold as of universal application. On the other hand, it would be too much to say that in colouring no regard was paid to verisimilitude. So far to the contrary, in depicting ordinary animate beings, approximate fidelity was generally the regulative principle *, determined indeed, as it were, by necessity, since any considerable violation would have produced palpable monstrosities. Such, however, are to be found, even in addition to the case of the anthropomorphic deities, conventionally tinted blue and green, whose divinity, it might be said, removed them from the earthly standard, and warranted their being symbolically portrayed.

* It is hardly necessary to remark that this refers to scenic subjects or actual portraiture; for, in coloured hieroglyphic texts, where animals occur, any such natural rule was but indifferently attended to, and, in fact, would seem to have had no hold whatever.

But when the objects were inanimate, when in actual fact they would have been capable in their reality of receiving almost any hue, then in representing such objects, or even trees and other members of the vegetable world, there is ample proof to show that a liberal licence was taken, and colours were used conformably to the decorative idea present to the artists' minds — an idea defined partly by the inelastic trammels which shackled Egyptian art, partly by the limited range of colours which they seem in the main only to have adopted. Moreover, with regard to the two very pigments which enter chiefly into the present inquiry, red and blue, they were among the few most commonly employed, and there are numerous instances of their very indeterminate use. Nor are such wanting among the very subjects from which evidence is adduced in the matter before us. For example, the fact has been cited that, in some of the early tombs around the pyramids of Geezeh, there is a well known group representing a man about to slaughter or cut up the carcase of an animal; and it has been pointed out that the man appears in the act of sharpening a red knife on a blue object similar in shape to the modern *steel*, whose material, as prescribed by that name, the colour is held to indicate. But I have remarked, in one of these same tombs, the identical subject, in which, however, the steel is red and the knife blue: and the idea suggests itself from the transposition, whether the colours might not have been used for the sake of contrast, more clearly to define the two objects, rather than as rigidly descriptive.*

Another element of uncertainty arises from the circumstance that in decorative hieroglyphic texts objects of bronze are usually coloured *green*, but Champollion, in stating this as a general rule, adds justly, that many such characters are painted indifferently green, blue, and red.†

Again, in the representations of Egyptian armour at the later date of the Eighteenth Dynasty, preserved on the walls of a crypt in the tomb of Rameses III., at Thebes, similar indications of vagueness are manifest with regard to some of the objects. In a group of swords the blades are alternately red and green; in a group of spears the tips are alternately red and blue; the blades of long knives are blue, of short curved ones also blue; the blades of axes are blue; and of two identical scabbards on each side of a panel, certain portions of one are blue, while precisely the same parts of the other are bright green. Much in the details of those groups would indicate mere contrasted or decorative colouring, but at the same time it is difficult to conceive that the use of blue just at certain of the critical points where iron might be expected, was

---

* Rosellini, assuming the use of certain metals, throws over altogether the special significance of colour in the matter in an incidental passage: — "Per questo colore (rosso) eran soliti gli Egiziani distinguere più frequentemente il rame *ed anche il ferro*, sebbene qualche figura di strumento che sembra dover essere stato di rame di giallo la colorissero." — *Mon. Civ.* vol. ii. p. 293.

† *Grammaire Égyptienne*, p. 10.

altogether accidental. On the other hand considerable difficulty, independently of criticism on these paintings themselves, lies in the way of a literal interpretation of this blue. Read thus, it would for instance imply that, although spear heads were either of bronze or iron, it was the practice to make the axes of iron; while the few actual examples* that have been recovered are all of bronze. And equally, this literalism would indicate iron as the constant material for the curved knives, whilst elsewhere these weapons appear painted red in the hands of soldiers. One more corresponding instance from another tomb may be mentioned, where of two sculptors at work, one holds a chisel of yellowish brown, the other a similar tool of blueish tint.†

Although, then, the paintings cannot, it would appear, be regarded as sufficiently precise to afford a certain, and in themselves unimpeachable guide, the occasional adoption of the colour blue to depict certain objects which we might expect to be of iron, may be allowed to bear a generic import, as so far showing that the artist knew of a metal whose tint was such as to warrant the use of blue in representing metallic objects. Even this, however, under the circumstances, would be straining this evidence alone, fully up to, if not beyond its strictly admissible force; and it is in collateral considerations that the principal

---

* Not more, I believe, than three or four have been preserved. One of the best is given in the folio *Illustrations of D'Athanasi's Collection*, by Visconti.

† The subject is copied by Rosellini.—*Mon. Civ. tav.* xlviii.

guide is to be sought. Among these we should first naturally turn to the hieroglyphic texts for precise intimations, but, as it happens, they offer only a dubious aid.

The character shaped like a sack, or inverted cowl, and known conventionally as a crucible, being found in positions where metal would seem to be implied, and being accompanied by three dots or balls, the usual determinative of the names not solely of metals but of gems and other valuable mineral substances — was interpreted by Champollion to mean iron.* Subsequent research has met with authority for attributing to it also the signification of *wood* and *cloud*†, so that, in fact, its precise import is decidedly uncertain. One reason of this may perhaps be surmised to be that the Egyptian word might have been descriptive of some quality rather than a radical designation, and so might have been applied to different substances naturally, or, on the other hand, non-naturally, by the figurative interchange so common to Eastern tongues, and which forms a specific feature in hieroglyphic expression. The small number of cases where the character in question occurs, presents another difficulty in the way of its precise elucidation; for, as Rosellini states, with truth, it is found as rarely in the inscriptions as actual objects of iron are found among the vestiges.‡ The remarkable wall sculptures embodying annals of Thothmes III.,

* *Grammaire Égyptienne*, p. 90.
† Hieroglyphic Appendix, Bunsen's *Egypt's Place*, vol. i. p. 533.
‡ *Mon. Civ.* vol. ii. p. 301.

chiefly descriptive of his conquests and his spoils*, contain a few examples of texts in which it occurs more prominently than perhaps in any other known monument. But here also the rendering does not become quite sufficiently specific, although it has a strong verisimilitude when, among the metallic and other articles of tribute brought by a conquered nation, there are twice enumerated "forty bricks," or pigs, and on one occasion "two bricks," of the substance which the crucible character signifies. If this be iron, the latter quantity especially might seem inappropriately small, but it would not be incompatible were the metal supposed to be rare or little employed: while the fact is also corroborative that it is stated to come from a people called the Asi, whose name fairly indicates their Asiatic home, a region whence we shall find reason to believe that its ampler diffusion subsequently proceeded.

But while waiting for more distinctly literal hieroglyphic evidence †, it may be said that anything of the

---

* Translated by Birch. *Archæologia*, vol. xxxv.

† It is very greatly to be desired that the hieroglyphic mode of expressing the names of certain metals and relative details were most carefully investigated. Besides the comparative uncertainty as to iron, there is still greater doubt as to another metal, tin, whose place in the primeval world renders any fact connected with it of even greater importance. It has been supposed, that a group read *Khesbet*, expresses it in hieroglyphic texts; but quicksilver and the stone lapis lazuli have also been conceived to be the meaning; and Mr. Birch has thrown out the ingenious suggestion, that Khesbet might possibly be identified with the κυάνος of Homer and Hesiod. (*Sur une Patère Égyptienne*, p. 50; *Mém*. Soc. Ant. de France, vol. xxiv.) It is true that this would not bring us much nearer a definition,

kind which we now provisionally possess on the subject of iron, offers on the one hand indications of its infrequency, and on the other of diminutive quantity. To this point also the other proofs converge; and in discussing the general result of them all, any difficulty that can arise is not as to whether the Egyptians in the days, say of the great Diospolitan Dynasties (from 1500 to 1100 B.C.), were acquainted with iron, but as to what extent they employed it. For, independently of directer evidence, or rather pending and supplementary to such, we may point to allusions in the Pentateuch\* and the Book of Job referring to its correspondingly early use in countries with which the Egyptians had intercourse; and it is not likely that a people so skilled in art-manufacture, and so capable of forming an estimate of any metallurgic process, were ignorant of this. Access to the ore would not, if desired, have been wanting, for the north of Africa is in various places richly productive of it. In Egypt itself, Sir Gardner Wilkinson, after a lengthened acquaintance with the

---

as κύανος is itself, in Homer at all events, a most doubtful term, and probably meant several substances, if the weight of evidence is in favour of its standing generically for some deep-coloured enamelling pigment (Gladstone's *Homer*, vol. iii. p. 498); and I have only adverted here to the difficulties connected with tin hieroglyphically to illustrate those equally applicable to iron.

\* It is needless to say, however, that these are few, in comparison with the references to copper or its alloys. Movers has made the estimate thus:—" Während der Pentateuch gegen vierzigmal Kupfer erwähnt, gedenken die ältesten Bestandtheile desselben nur zweimal des Eisens."—*Das Phönizische Alterthum*, t. iii. ab. 1, p. 67.

characteristics of the country, has observed only one iron mine that had been anciently worked.* In Ethiopia the metal is extremely abundant; and one of the Jesuit missionaries at Khartoum, Dr. Knoblicher, found, during an expedition on the White Nile, savages almost under the equator who turned the mineral treasures of their country so far to account that they were excellent artificers in iron.† Still further south, Captains Burton and Speke were astonished to encounter in their recent expedition, as narrated to the Geographical Society, tribes, in the lowest stage of barbarism, manufacturing and employing the same metal. Again, in the north (but such instances are merely illustrative), the spurs of the Atlas hide similar wealth, which, as existing traces show, was sought in early times ‡; and here also the rude indigenous race, the Kabyles, are skilled metallurgists.§ Indeed, the whole continent of Africa may be said in this respect to exhibit a similar state of things; and, in the remote south central regions, the presence of iron, and its use by native savages, are facts among the valuable observations of Dr. Livingstone.‖

But while a variety of circumstances will not permit it to be disputed that the Egyptians were cognisant of

* *Ancient Egyptians*, 1st Series, vol. iii. p. 246.
† Taylor's *Journey to Central Africa*, pp. 352—354. More full accounts of the iron-working in those regions, where a race called the Djours possess considerable skill, are given in Petherick's *Soudan*, p. 396.
‡ Blakesley's *Four Months in Algeria*, p. 249.
§ Daumas, *Kabylie*, p. 46.
‖ See particularly his letter from River Shiré, Nov. 4th, 1859, read at British Assoc., Oxford 1860.

some of the properties of iron at a very early period, whether by priority of discovery, so as to have been themselves the teachers of this art (as of so many others), to the West and North, or whether as learners, we shall probably never know, although I suspect the latter — still the evidence appears to me to show that, for all practical purposes, the ore, as far as they were concerned, might never have been smelted, and that up to, and even beyond the period when Thebes was in its zenith, they could have used it only in very small proportion. To see this, we may in the first instance glance at the absence of iron relics among the innumerable antiquities recovered, which acquires a new significance from the perfect preservation in which the nails and hasps remained in the funeral canopy and the door of the tomb of Sebau. One or two objects have indeed been met with connected with very ancient vestiges, but under circumstances far from conclusive as to their origin. A piece of wrought iron, as is well known, was brought to light by Colonel Howard Vyse's researches, in an inner joint of the stones near the mouth of one of the air channels of the great Pyramid.* Although the various professional gentlemen engaged as engineers, or otherwise, in inspecting the work have certified their belief that the fragment was coeval with the structure, it is no disrespect to them to say that, occurring as it did in so very critical a position, in a building which had been the subject of constant quarrying and attempts at viola-

* Vyse's *Pyramids of Geezeh*, vol. i. p. 276.

tion, mere constructive circumstantial evidence of antiquity is too dubious to be conclusive. Another object, to which an exactly parallel difficulty is attached, was a cutting instrument, of the shape of a modern sickle, found by Belzoni among a group of sphinxes at Karnak. For, although the sickle was under a sphinx, the sphinxes themselves were lying in an "irregular and confused manner, as if hidden in a hurry,"[*] and so the evidence as to age halts again. No other article of iron, he leads us to infer, ever came under his notice; and Dathanasi not less plainly declares that, "after eighteen years of laborious research, and after having opened so many tombs in Thebes and in Abydus, I have not met with the most trifling article of iron-ware of Egyptian origin."[†] A very few relics of iron have been brought from Egypt at all, nearly the whole of them belonging certainly to what is called late time in the archæology of the Nile Valley, such as keys, one of which I possess; and I believe it is the case that there is no recorded personal observation of the finding of any iron objects under circumstances, or in connexion with other remains, which would satisfactorily prove their having been contemporaneous with remains of the older date in question. For example, Colonel Vyse, in a note illustrative of the fragment in the Pyramid, intimates that the Duke of Northumberland was stated to have brought an iron weapon from Egypt. But the Duke of Northumberland informs me that he knows of

---

[*] Belzoni's *Narrative*, p. 162.
[†] Dathanasi's *Account of Researches*, p. 67.

no such object, and that although when in the country pieces of iron were brought to him by *fellaheen* at times (as has also been my own experience), he never met with any bearing indications of date, and as they therefore had no value he never secured any. Again, in Rawlinson's *Herodotus**, an iron knife is mentioned by Sir Gardner Wilkinson as in his possession; but I learn from him that although he bought it at Thebes, there were no means of ascertaining where or how it had been found, and that, as it is exactly like sacrificial knives used by the Romans, it may very possibly be Romano-Egyptian. Further, in Passalacqua's *Catalogue*†, two arrow heads, and certain small objects (number not specified), supposed to be connected with surgery, are stated to be of iron; but his notes, which give some details of the finding of nearly every other article he possessed, are perfectly silent as to these arrow heads, and give only such cursory reference to the other specimens as to afford no data for conjecturing the date of the mummies with which they are said to have been found. Cailliaud ‡ likewise mentions incidentally having met with bracelets of bronze, and sometimes of iron, in excavations at Goorneh; but there is no specification of circumstances by which the age of the mummies, which the latter might have accompanied, may be inferred.

But in forming a judgment on this subject I would rather rely, not on the negative evidence of what the

* Vol. ii. p. 141.   † *Cat. Rais.* pp. 27, 154.
‡ *Voyage à Meroë*, vol. i. p. 259.

tombs may as yet have failed to offer, but on the more positive testimony deducible from what they have produced. Looking in the light of illustrative circumstances to the harvest that has been gathered from them it is not easy to see from it that there was room, for the use of iron. Applied to nearly every practical purpose it is bronze we meet with. Do we turn to arms, the variety preserved is certainly not great, nor the specimens numerous, but they are all of bronze. The daggers we have are of this metal, fabricated with such skill as to rival steel in the elasticity which they retain to this hour. The arrow tips are nearly all of the same, when not of stone or of reed. The axes offer no exception; and in my collection is the central portion of a shield of doubtful and probably late period, also, as was indeed to be expected, of bronze. Nor is it at all different with metallic objects of every kind applied to the ordinary purposes of life. I procured at Thebes a carpenter's saw, chisel, and piercer, of bronze; and similar tools, always of the same material, are familiar in most museums. A much rarer relic, likewise in my collection,—a needle duly provided with an eye—is of the same metal; as are also a pair of tweezers, whose spring is perfectly efficient, and a knife of a common type, found together, and supposed to be surgical instruments. Fish-hooks, as well as specimens of the objects just mentioned, are likewise to be seen in the British Museum; and every collection offers examples of a like nature, of one kind or other.

Descending from refined to the roughest operative purposes, there is even a specimen of a chisel of bronze, found among chips or quarry rubble at Thebes\*; and it is remarkable that Agatharchides, an official under Philometor and Euergetes II., in the second century B.C., of whose writings some fragments are preserved by Photius, mentions that bronze wedges were occasionally discovered in ancient gold mines in Egypt. Various other common appliances, I say nothing of those of an artistic nature, are of this substance; and some in which metal might not unnaturally be looked for, are altogether of wood. For instance, this was the case with the hoe, as various specimens, of which I have one, show. Whether the ploughshare was similarly unprotected, as indeed the tractable nature of the soil deposited by the Nile might have allowed, or whether it was shod, and with what, there is no evidence. In mere constructive carpentry no metal of any kind appears from the relics to have been employed, and the necessary junctions were accomplished by dovetailing, mortice-work, or wooden pins instead of nails. A remarkable example, where the assistance of metal might naturally have been looked for, but where it was not the less excluded, is in the only known chariot †, that discovered at Thebes in course

---

\* Wilkinson's *Ancient Egyptians*, pop. ed., vol. ii. p. 156.

† I have not had an opportunity of examining it; but this circumstance in its construction is incidentally mentioned in the notice of it in Murray's *Handbook for North Italy*. In the life of H. Salt, a handsome chair, discovered at Thebes, inlaid with ivory and ebony, is

of explorations instituted by Rosellini, and termed by him a "*Scythic* car,"* but on no grounds adequate to counteract the *primâ-facie* probability of its native character, and the concurrent testimony deducible from its general fabric as compared with the sculptured representations of more elaborate vehicles.

If, then, we have regard in the first place to the prominent absence of iron among the vestiges which remain to us, and if, thereafter, by applying to those a kind of exhaustive process, we find that for, it may be said, every purpose bronze was employed—from the coarse quarry wedge to the fine-edged knife, from the pliant saw and elastic dagger to the rigid chisel;—when we find this, it is impossible not to conclude that we must recognise bronze as the then great staple, and as that alone which it is necessary to take into account in the question of economic metallurgy. As for iron, there is practically, in this relation, hardly, as has been already said, a vacant place for it; and when Rosellini, in the noble monument which his industry and research have raised, insists that it *must* have been used by the ancient Egyptians, because without it they could not have cut and sculptured their adamantine granite†, he was not probably aware that within the close range of modern history a people

---

described as "put together entirely with wooden pegs instead of nails or other fastening."—*Life of Salt*, vol. ii. p. 186.

\* *Mon. Civ.* vol. iii. p. 263.

† Sharpe, *Hist. of Egypt*, 3rd edition, vol. i. p. 17, assumes the same supposititious necessity to be conclusive.

had existed in another continent, the Mexicans, who, with implements only of bronze, were constantly performing perfectly similar tasks, and were graving even on emeralds with the highest finish.*

It is the more desirable to endeavour to form a fair estimate of the position occupied by the ancient Egyptians in relation to iron-working, from the illustrative guidance which the subject is capable of reflecting on archæological fields of far wider extent than that to which the special inquiry belongs. In dimly exploring the prehistoric ages of all Europe, and not of Europe only, contemporary vestiges afford not the least important aid, and among these metallic relics take a prominent place. Their materials, as ranged under the broad classification of bronze or iron, and the supposed relative capabilities of each, have, as was natural, exerted a considerable influence on the results of speculation. But, in adjusting the hypothetical value of such criteria, it is no useless landmark to keep in view what metallurgically characterised the earliest manifestation of social advancement of which we have any definite knowledge, and to consider that the Egyptians with bronze, so to say, as the instrument of their progress, went far

---

* Humboldt's *Researches*, vol. i. p. 261, *et passim;* Prescott's *Hist. of the Conquest of Mexico*, p. 470. The Peruvians also could perforate emeralds without iron. The pointed leaf of a wild plantain, along with fine sand and water, is stated to have been the boring instrument. (Bollaert's *Researches in South America*.) With such appliances as these, time of course is the one condition of success.

beyond the mere threshold of civilization, both intellectually and practically, attained a highly developed ingenuity, and achieved very great mechanical triumphs.

When and under what influences iron assumed a prominent position among metallic appliances in Egypt is a subject mixed up with several important archæological considerations. The great mass of relics illustrative of social economy which stock our museums, among which, as has been stated, this metal is not found (I believe it may be said without risk — so far as the means exist for judging),—date from that most active period of national power, marked by the reigns of the great Diospolitan Dynasties, more especially the first two, say from 1500 to 1200 B.C., or, at all events, prior to the Persian Conquest in 524. The painted tombs, too, among whose decorations are depicted scenes and circumstances of daily life, are referrible to the same or still earlier epochs; nor can I recall any specimens of this *quasi*-scenic style which are known to be subsequent to the time of Psamittichus I., about 650 years before our era, while of such late examples the few that exist offer no assistance. But when we receive the first direct account of the country from Herodotus, there can be no doubt that iron had largely assumed the place which everywhere has been its lot, as the active operative metallic agent. For although his suggestion, that to the cost of the great Pyramid must be added some enormous sum for the iron tools employed *, is no evidence as to the material of the implements actually used in the construction of a monument even then of high antiquity, it is sufficient to show that this was the metal present to his mind as the obvious instrument, and that there was nothing in prevailing practice to interfere with the assumption.† Nor is this otherwise than perfectly natural, if we reflect on what had already occurred and what was the then existing state of matters in this respect in his own country, Greece, and adjoining regions. When the poems of Homer first break the gloom, though objects of iron are mentioned, bronze is evidently still the staple.‡ But after the lapse of a few centuries, Hesiod describes himself as living in preeminently an age of iron; and as soon as the interrupted stream of Classical literature begins to gather strength, we find first allusions in Herodotus pointing unmistakably to the prevalent use of that metal. Aristotle § also draws an illustration of the principles of caloric from intricate manufacturing processes applied to iron. Moreover, from actual vestiges discovered in tombs, as well as from representations on their walls, it is known to have been used for many purposes in Etruria ‖ at an age synchronous

* Lib. ii. c. 125.
† See Hodgson, *On Ancient Brass, Archæologia Æliana*, vol. i.
‡ Millin, *Minéralogie Homérique*, passim.
§ *Meteor.* lib. iv. c. 6.
‖ Dennis's *Cities and Cemeteries of Etruria*, vol. i. p. 224, and *Berlin Acad. Trans.* ap. Prichard's *Researches*, vol. iii. p. 257. In a paper on *Bronze Swords*, in the proceedings of the Soc. Ant. Scot.

with and even earlier than the days of those later writers. In fact, it would seem that between the epoch of the Homeric poems and the full historic period of Greece, iron had come to be extensively employed there. And I conceive that in like manner, and within about the same interval, if probably with an earlier commencement, the same metal was more or less completely displacing bronze in Egypt. Nor would it be a hasty supposition to conjecture that, both in the one country and in the other, the change was accomplished by influences proceeding from the same source. In the very period we have defined, we know that there existed, in the utmost activity, a most diffusive centre of practical civilization and mechanical skill, having its place on the northern coast of Palestine; for the trade of the Phœnicians is one of the great characteristic rays of the dawn of historic light in Europe. Neither are there wanting various evidences prominently to associate this people and the region they inhabited with early iron-working. When the Hebrews were conquering their future home, the Canaanites, with their "chariots of *iron*," were able successfully to resist the invaders.* When the great Temple of Solomon was designed, one hundred thousand talents of iron were among the materials†, and from Tyre came the craftsman "skilful to work

---

vol. ii. I have already referred to some of the facts in early metallurgy here brought forward. It is right to add that in some respects it is imperfect, as in its allusions to Egypt.

\* Joshua, xvii. 18. † 1 Chronicles, xix. 7.

in gold, in silver, in brass, *in iron*, in stone," *
to engage in or superintend the operations. In the
*Iliad* there is more than one allusion to the metallurgic ingenuity of the Phœnicians, inferentially the
manufacturers of the splendid breastplate of divers
metals presented to Agamemnon.† Further, a classical
tradition‡, referring to the country of the Chalybes,
to the north of Judæa, from which supplies of valuable iron were derived, points to this part of Asia
Minor as a supposed fountain whence flowed early
instruction in processes of working in iron. To the
known frequency and constancy, within the period
in question, of Egyptian intercourse with all parts
of Palestine, both by commerce and conquest, it is
unnecessary to allude.§

In looking to this region for the dissemination, say
within that portion of the world to which our attention
is now directed, as the general question which could
not satisfactorily be discussed here, is, for the present,

* 2 Chronicles, ii. 14.

† *Iliad*, xi. 19. Mr. Gladstone alludes to it with apparent justice as " evidently meant to be understood as Sidonian or Phœnician work." *Homer, and the Homeric Age*, vol. i. p. 189. See also *Odyss.* xv. 112, 117, and xxiii. 863.

‡ Various ancient writers allude to it, as Strabo, Festus Avienus, &c.; and Ammianus Marcellinus embodies it more expressly by adding after the name of the Chalybes, in a description of those parts, " *per quos erutum et domitum est primitus, ferrum,*" lib. xxii. c. 8.

§ For certain special facts as to Asiatic intercourse, see Birch on *The Statistical Tablet of Karnak, Royal Soc. Lit. Transact.* vol. ii. p. 317, and on *Ivory Ornaments at Nimroud*, ib. vol. iii. See on the general topic of communication between Egypt and Asia, references in Grote's *Greece*, vol. iii. p. 427.

reserved; in looking thither, I repeat, for the dissemination of the employment of iron on a considerable scale for ordinary economic purposes, we presuppose nothing as to the localisation of the discovery of the use of this metal, nor yet as to the chronological determination, whether relative or absolute, of any such event, in the aspect of an epochal starting point. I know of no facts in archæology capable of satisfactorily affording distinct definitions like these.* We do indeed find, lying back into the past and over a large tract of the earth, a broad basis of bronze-culture, if this Germanised expression may be allowed, on which an iron-culture has been, as it were, superimposed. But we shall look in vain among actual vestiges for substantial proofs of such hypothetical schemes as Goguet † or his school, paraphrasing the poetic if reasonable picture of Lucre-

---

* With regard to any general proposition, philology also is alike deficient; and even in special relation to individual races, it gives, notwithstanding most attractive promise, but an uncertain sound. The inductions based upon the comparison of the names of metals in various languages, while ingenious and often instructive, can hardly be hoped to be conclusive, or more than collaterally valid, from the not at all fixed laws which would naturally govern the adoption or rejection or modification of the nomenclature of substances. But whatever degree of force may be conceded to the results of such linguistic comparisons in their bearing on the *minuter* conditions of ancient civilizations, it is impossible not to recognise the interest and value of the process generally, as worked, for example, by Pictet (*Origines Indo-Européennes*) and Lassen (*Indische Alterthumskunde*) in relation to general Arian ethnography; by Mommsen (*Römische Geschichte*) in connexion with Italy; or by Gladstone (*Homer, and the Homeric Age*) in reference to Greece, elaborately, but less satisfactorily, from the doubtful hypotheses involved.

† *Origines de Lois*, lib. ii. c. 4.

tius, could minutely set forth, whereby men, led on step by step according to supposed regular gradations of awakening ingenuity, are made to arrive at a knowledge of iron only after a previous probation with more simply fabricated metallic substances.* Theories of human progression running in grooves so smooth have at no time much to recommend them except their simplicity. And in the case of bronze and iron, while the latter is no doubt more difficult of extraction from the crude ore†, the former implies so much skill in the mingling of the alloy and in the discovering and determining the properties of the constituent, tin, which is so sparingly diffused in nature, that it would be difficult to judge which of the two would be expected to be first produced. In fact, there is nothing to fix a relative chronology in the matter of mere discovery, which may have depended on the mineralogical or other physical conditions of the countries ‡ inhabited

*    "Arma antiqua, manus, ungues, dentesque fuerunt,
    Et lapides, et item sylvarum fragmina rami,
    Posterius ferri vis est, ærisque reperta;
    Et prior æris erat quam ferri cognitus usus."
                                     *Lucret.* lib. v. 1282.

† In *Ancient Workers and Artificers in Metal*, by J. Napier, are to be found instructive details of smelting and other processes with reference chiefly to the metallurgy of the Old Testament. It is to be regretted that the writer's practical knowledge was not brought to bear on the subject of early metal working from a more comprehensive point of view.

‡ For instance, it is stated that iron only, bronze rarely or never, is found among early metallic relics in Norway, where the ores of the former are so abundant and rich. Worsaae, *Zur Alterthumskunde des Nordens*, and Wilson's *Archæology of Scotland*, p. 358.

by the pioneers of civilization, or even upon circumstances in this respect accidental. But while we may cease to look for such definite data as would enable us to decide which of these two metals man first wrung from nature, and may even conclude that, from a most remote antiquity, both were in his hands, we do know that in regions where iron was subsequently employed for the great purposes of practical life, bronze had previously occupied the prominent position, and even continued to do so after we have distinct evidence of the co-existence of iron-working. Whether this arose merely from an imperfect appreciation of the capabilities of iron, and a highly developed application of those of bronze*, which made it a matter of less consequence to look elsewhere for the necessary properties, it is impossible to say; or whether the cause was a scanty supply of the former and the difficulty of its production, is equally uncertain. But if, as true children of the iron age, we are disposed to conclude unreservedly in favour of this second supposition, believing that were the substance once known, nothing short of compulsory conditions would prevent men

* It is well worthy of remark to what a pitch skill in its manufacture had arrived. Experiments undertaken in recent times, but not with sufficient minuteness, have failed to produce the hardness, temper, and elasticity which the Ancients attained, unless a case described by Caylus (*Rec. d'Antiq.* vol. i.) may be regarded as an exception, where the result was partially gained by the addition of a small proportion of iron to the alloy. See also Mongez, *Mém. de l'Institut de France*, vol. x. 1803, and Mauduit, *Découvertes dans la Troade*, part II., pp. 120, *et seq.*

from adopting the metal whose very name is to our minds the type of mechanical power—if we are disposed to come unhesitatingly to such a conclusion, it may be well to remember that iron, after all, is the symbol rather than the cause of practical progress. It is true that for more than two thousand years it has presided over the advance of material civilization. But is its reign to be perpetual; or will it in its turn give place to some other body, or some other composition, now, perhaps, neglected, unknown, or but little employed? Even now the possibilities of such important changes are opening into view.*

* See, for example, the remarkable results of experiments by Faraday and Stodart on the alloy of steel with small quantities of platinum, iridium, silver, and other metals. Faraday's *Experimental Researches in Chemistry and Physics*, p. 57.

## CHAP. IX.

#### HOW THE DEMAND FOR EGYPTIAN RELICS HAS BEEN SUPPLIED, AND ITS INFLUENCE ON THE CONDITION OF THE MONUMENTS.

As a natural sequel to the details given in this volume with reference to the tombs of Thebes, the exploration of them, and their contents, it will probably be of interest to describe some characteristics of the mode of dispersion, whether by traffic or otherwise, which has brought and is still bringing so many Egyptian relics into public and private collections.

For the earlier history of the draughts upon the vestiges of ancient Egypt, we should have to look to the times when the granite obelisks were carried off to be reared again in the imperial cities of Rome and Byzantium. It might be traced, too, towards the close of the Middle Ages, when mummy as a drug was so favourite a recipe among the physicians of the period[*], that dealers embalmed their dead contem-

---

[*] Curious particulars as to the place occupied by *mummy* in the old pharmacopœias are given in Pettigrew's *History of Mummies*, pp. 7, *et seq.* Many quaint ideas entertained in former days as to the medicinal properties of substances used in mummification may be found in Greenhill's *Art of Embalming.* Lond. 1705.

poraries to meet the demand which the ransacked tombs could not supply.* But although various sepulchral and other relics may thus have become disseminated, as it were incidentally, it is probable that, except as objects of taste or curiosity, they were not much sought after for themselves until the stimulus to historical and other inquiry, which succeeded the invention of printing, gave them a place and importance in the general activity of research. By the earlier half of the seventeenth century, when Kircher was producing folio after quarto on the mysteries of the hieroglyphics, there is no doubt that very many relics had found their way into Europe. Indeed, as I have already had occasion to point out, a traveller † in Egypt, about the year 1655, describes the Arabs of Sakkara as continually occupied in digging among the tombs of that Necropolis for the purpose of selling the objects which they might discover.

It is probable that the first considerable collection procured systematically in the country itself was formed by the scientific commission which accompanied the Emperor Napoleon's military expedition in 1798, and the results of whose labours are embodied in the massive *Description D'Égypte*, published shortly thereafter by the French Government. A few years later the pursuit was in full progress

* Mummies of more modern manufacture, for purposes of deception, are also known. See Birch's article, *Mummy*, in the *English Cyclopædia*.
† Thevenot's *Voyage au Levant*, p. 431. See above, p. 65.

on an extensive scale; and from that time to this, although in varying degrees, it has never ceased. It was at first, when the field was comparatively new, the possibilities encouraging, and the success considerable, that the efforts were most vigorous, if, unfortunately, not always conducted in the best direction or from the most satisfactory motives. We discover now, with no great pleasure, the method in which some of them were prosecuted, or read of the disputes which arose out of them.

The chief collectors of those times were the consular representatives of England and France, Mr. Salt and Signor Drovetti; and after the disposal of the valuable accumulations gathered by them, to European museums, the transport of Egyptian antiquities in large numbers together became familiar. The example of organising a regular search was soon followed by others, and particularly by Belzoni, when, after a rupture with Salt, for whom he had first been acting, he set to work on his own account. That collisions should have arisen where there were antagonistic interests, and those too of different kinds at work in the same field, was not surprising: and the history of relic-gathering in those days is that of one long *imbroglio*.* There were quarrels and even fights

---

* Besides what may be learned by personal inquiry, some remembrance of those early proceedings is preserved in Hall's *Life and Correspondence of Salt*, 2 vols.; in Belzoni's *Narrative*; in Dathanasi's *Brief Account*; and in various allusions in the Egyptian literature of the time.

between the working parties of rival collectors. There were difficulties from intrigues and counter-intrigues with corrupt local governors. There were disputes between employers and employed as to the terms of service. There were misunderstandings in the communications of sellers and Government buyers in Europe on involved questions of price and public duty. There were even, at least locally, sparks of national ill-feeling aroused, chiefly between English and French, in consequence of the right of property in tombs, or such like, assumed to vest from priority of discovery, being sometimes infringed.

The first energy of these proceedings had somewhat subsided by the year 1828, when the united French and Tuscan commissions, directed by Champollion and Rosellini, began their labours. With the investigation of the monuments and the publication of the results as their chief aim, the securing of such antiquities as the opportunity presented was naturally a part of the undertaking; and the Louvre and the museum at Florence were greatly enriched.* In 1842-45 another scientific expedition, that of Prussia under Lepsius, made large collections in Egypt for the splendid museum at Berlin. In 1851 and succeeding years the Louvre again received most valuable additions through the medium of M. Marriette's discoveries; and quite recently the Egyptian Government

* I do not know if the latter has even yet been properly arranged for exhibition.

has begun the formation of a collection under the agency of the same successful excavator.

But these official operations, as they may be termed, have only been a small proportion of those directed to the same end. Various private persons, such as Passalacqua, Caviglia, and Cailliaud, brought together considerable treasures, by engaging, directly or indirectly, in excavations; and most of these have found their way to the museums of Europe. Other collections, again, were formed by European residents in Cairo and Alexandria, whose tastes or opportunities led them to seize the advantage of their position and secure from the *fellah* diggers, or the class of go-between dealers, any really good relics which then, from a less exhausted source, came more numerously into the local market. Of such collections was the valuable one formed by Dr. Abbott, now, I believe, the property of the city of New York; and there still remain in Egypt a few others of extent and importance.

Underlying all those more systematic enterprises was the regular native traffic. The villagers, particularly at Geezeh, Sakkara, and Thebes, were ever working among the tombs, sometimes in small parties on their own joint account, sometimes under the guidance of employers. Giovanni Dathanasi, who had originally been introduced to the work in Salt's service, resided for eighteen years at Thebes\*, engaged in this manner. And at or near that Necropolis, as well as

---

\* *Brief Account of Researches.*

at Cairo, being the nearest suitable point for the other two above named, there have always been dealers to share in the searches. Either through them, or from the *fellaheen* themselves, a considerable supply of antiquities was forthcoming. These were either absorbed in the accumulations in process of formation in the country, officially or otherwise, or they made their way more directly to public and private collections in Europe, to which, in one way or the other, the stream has constantly been kept up.

Within the last ten or fifteen years the local retailing of relics has received a great additional stimulus, from the increased facilities of communication and other causes having brought so many foreigners to visit the country. Only a few of these may, in continuation of previous pursuits, or with special views, have systematically set about collecting on a considerable scale; but, naturally enough, nearly all have had a tendency to become buyers to some extent, of objects, not only in a peculiar degree characteristic products of the country, but often highly curious in themselves, and sometimes also valuable. At Cairo there are various dealers of different grades to meet this want; and among the tombs of the great Necropolis, at the foot of the Pyramids of Geezeh and Sakkara, the diggers themselves ply the trade. In Upper Egypt Thebes is the chief centre of the traffic. There, likewise, the *fellaheen* search and sell for themselves with practised expertness, and there, also, there are middlemen who, having some command of money and experience in the business, buy of the finders any promising relics that may come to light, particularly in the summer months, when there are no strangers on the river to offer the chances of a ready market. The chief of those speculators has long been a Copt, with all the astuteness of his race, who generally has a hand in the disposal of the best of the relics discovered, either for himself or others. Sometimes his stores, which are hidden away in all kinds of places and in friends' houses, are not inconsiderable, and occasionally objects of value fall in his way. Nor is he apt to depreciate them, or part with them easily. For neatly executed scarabæi, and other ornamental relics, which naturally are the more generally attractive of his wares, he asks and gets extravagant prices. But also he and others are perfectly awake to what may be made of antiquities whose nature may cause them to be sought after on special grounds. For example, twenty, thirty, or forty pounds are readily demanded for an unusually good-looking roll of papyrus. As for the more ordinary Egyptian relics, it is probably the case that they have now a chance of bringing as high or higher prices in Egypt itself than in any other country where they might happen to come to sale.

A demand like this the *fellaheen* have every inducement to meet, as a moderate degree of success pays them amply for their labour. Indeed, at Thebes, they find it worth while to re-empty pit tombs, which they themselves may have opened once or even twice a few years before, in the hope of recovering from among the sand such inferior or minuter objects as they may have formerly thrown aside as valueless, or have overlooked. I have known some of them also make journeys, extending to sixty or eighty miles along the banks of the river to the north or to the south, to pick up at small cost stray ornaments and such like. They count upon finding a few in the hands of less experienced owners at places like El Kab (anciently the city of Eileithyias), where the peasants, in digging earth from the mounds to top-dress their fields, occasionally turn up a relic. If in this way the buyers can extract, for example, a good scarabæus from an ignoramus for a few pence, which at Thebes might bear a value of from one to five pounds, a long journey is well repaid.

But these are merely the incidental operations: reliance for any considerable results are placed upon the chance of efforts in the great Necropolis itself, bringing the searchers upon tombs more or less completely retaining their original contents. Even when these had been partially rifled in earlier ages, as a former chapter points out, for articles chiefly of precious metal, much was often left which has no inconsiderable value for modern diggers. When a piece of good fortune of this kind falls to their lot, they know well how to adopt the precautions necessary, in their view, to make the most of it. Secrecy and mystification are the great points. The former is indeed sufficiently prescribed by the fact that the publication of their success would with tolerable certainty be followed by a visit from some local functionary, which might imply presentation to the visitor of no trifling share of the find, or a compulsory sale at the price fixed by some buyer who had made interest to secure official intervention. The work of excavation, therefore, is, as far as possible, carried on during the night, especially when success is supposed to be near, that the antiquities, if any, may be removed under shelter of the darkness. After this the mystery is carefully kept up, not only that their existence may be concealed from those in authority, but also in the hope of enhancing their value; and it is then certain that, unless under quite exceptional circumstances, no account of them offered by their possessors is entitled to the slightest credit. In the innermost recesses of their tomb-dwellings they usually hide the larger or more important of such relics; and a likely purchaser is conveyed secretly to look at them there. As objects of real interest are sometimes to be met with in this way, I have often, when living at Thebes, gone covertly with the owners to their strange abodes. On one or two occasions so great was the desire for precaution, which had to be humoured, that the visits were made at night, when the neighbours were asleep. The practised guidance of the *fellah* who possessed the relics alone made it easy to pick one's way among the tombs in the dark; and his familiar presence reassured the dogs, which the villagers keep in great numbers.

The manner in which at such times I saw antiquities concealed was very curious. I remember once being rather amazed by the grim midnight companionship which a man had selected for himself. His bed was a low, narrow frame of strong basketwork, covered by a coarse rug: and on throwing back this coverlid, he disclosed a mummy in its case on each side of the bed, and two children's coffins beneath it.

As those precautions are in reality prudent with regard to the more important objects, it is only in accordance with the cunning of the local character that the necessity for them should also be frequently simulated, to give a sort of prestige to the relics to be disposed of. It was no unusual circumstance to find quite inferior specimens hedged round by the most mysterious preliminaries; or a *fellah* might imply that it was of the greatest consequence his possession of some article should be unknown to others, who were in reality his partners in the transaction. There are, in fact, few such tricks which their ingenuity has not turned to account.

It need hardly be said that among these is the concoction of spurious relics. By the ordinary *fellaheen* this can rarely be accomplished more cleverly than to impose only on the quite inexperienced. Their range hardly goes farther than the carving out of soft stone unwieldy imitations of large scarabæi; fastening up scraps of papyrus into the semblance of small untouched rolls; charring handfuls of their last year's crop along with bituminous dust to give the grain the colour of wheat from the tombs; scratching a royal cartouch on an ordinary vase, or executing some of the similar small rogueries within the limits of their slight artistic ability. But there are also less patent deceptions than theirs in the antiquarian market. Among the dealers at Cairo, some of whom it need hardly be said are Europeans and Italians, there are much higher flights. For example, such a thing is known as graving inscriptions, accurately copied from one set of viscera vases, on another that may not have had such an interesting feature, and whose value is accordingly increased fivefold. Bronze figures of deities of the rarer types are also subject to be multiplied with unimpeachable accuracy; and it is quite worth the while of neat-handed dealers to try this, or even to send the originals to Italy, where the art of casting after the antique is so well cultivated. I have known at Cairo some ten or twelve pounds asked as the price of a statuette, about four inches high, of the goddess Selk with her scorpion head-dress, such images of that deity being exceedingly uncommon, as the possessor of the one in question was perfectly aware, claiming for it even the value of being unique. It happened that on the same day I ascertained the existence of other precisely similar figures, likewise for sale, having seen one of them in the hands of another dealer; and some of the circumstances left very little doubt that spurious copies had been produced.

## FORGERY OF BRONZE AND OTHER RELICS.

Even at Thebes, where European ingenuity is not available, this kind of imposition is not altogether unpractised. The Copt, Tadrous, whom I have already mentioned as prominently connected with the traffic in antiquities there, having been by trade a silversmith, has some knowledge of metal work, which he is not averse to turn to account in his antiquarian business, in the way of producing some ill-finished casts. But generally, when he does have bronzes, their origin is of a different kind, although not the less they may not be what they are represented. At Thebes the ordinary statuettes of this metal, although they have been discovered among the ruins of Karnak, are unknown as a product of the tombs. At Geezeh, on the other hand, and especially at Sakkara, they abound. And a few inferior specimens, which there overstock the market, are occasionally consigned to Tadrous, to be sold with the prestige of having been found under the shadow of the Theban temples.

The arch-forger at Thebes does not come much forward in his own person. He is a certain Ali Gamooni, who can turn his hand to most things, being one of those smiths who have never failed, since the days of Vœlund downwards, to vindicate for members of the brotherhood the claim of many-sided ingenuity. Relics of various kinds come within the range of his endeavours; but scarabæi, perhaps, are his greatest success, or at least his chief manufacture. For the coarser descriptions of them he has, as well as chance European purchasers, an outlet in a native market.

They are bought from him to be carried up the river into Nubia, where they are favourite amulets or ornaments, as mothers greatly delight to attach one or two to the girdles of short thongs, which constitute the only article of dress of their children. It sometimes happens, too, that through this very medium those spurious imitations come into the possession of travellers, who may not be likely to suspect the pedigree of objects presenting themselves thus in remote situations and under such unsophisticated circumstances.

But Ali Gamooni is capable of considerably more artistic efforts than the production of merely the inferior kinds of scarabæi to suit the light purses of Nubian mothers. The more elegant and well-finished descriptions are not beyond his range. The material he uses is, for the most part, that which the ancients themselves also largely employed, a close-grained, easily cut limestone, which, after it is graven into shape and lettered, receives a greenish glaze by being baked in a shovel with brass filings. Working in this way some of his copies are singularly good; and as for his examples of the unimportant coarser sorts, which the old Egyptians with little care seem to have produced in the same manner, they are not to be distinguished from antiques. He has now had long practice, for I find in an incidental note that a writer on Egyptian subjects takes credit for having furnished Ali, some twenty years ago (as it would appear), with broken penknives and other appliances to aid his already manifested talent, in the somewhat fantastic hope of flooding the local market with "curiosities," and so saving the monuments from being laid under contribution.* The patron might have been surprised had he learned the growing aptitude of the protege. Not merely a proficient in close imitation, he now aspires to the creative. On the faith of my having been several times in his workshop and having seen the mysteries of his art, he actually came to me one day with a sketch of a group of hieroglyphics, neatly drawn in pencil by himself, to beg advice as to his engraving them on a scarabæus. The text, he said, he had copied accurately from a wall of Medinet Haboo; but he added that, for a cartouch with a king's name, which the original there contained, he had substituted another, which he found to be of uncommon occurrence, with the view of preparing a rarer and therefore more valuable relic; and he wished particularly to ascertain whether there would be any inconsistency between the adopted name and the inscription. What he did in the matter I do not know, or whether this had been his first attempt in so remarkable a field. But the result of a few happy shots in this direction, under favourable circumstances, it is rather startling to contemplate, if we remember that under some of the kings, and particularly Amunoph III.,† the practice was much followed of inscribing large scarabæi with important records. The frontiers of his empire have been defined

* Nott and Gliddon's *Indigenous Races of the Earth*; note by the latter, p. 192.

† Wilkinson in appendix to Rawlinson's *Herodotus*, vol. ii. p. 362.

on the authority of four such relics*, and an incident so important as the first indication of the introduction of a heretical sun-worship has been founded upon one of them.† In fact, the time is fully come when Egyptian antiquities of certain classes must have a further voucher for their authenticity than merely that they have been carried from Egypt.

The draughts on Egyptian vestiges have by no means been limited to the more portable accompaniments of the dead, to which hitherto in this chapter reference has chiefly been made. Statues, inscribed tablets, sculptured slabs from sepulchres and temples, indeed, the sliced-off walls of whole tombs, are among the well known fruits transported to Europe mostly within the last forty years. Of these a certain proportion were the product of the earlier of the private enterprises already mentioned. Not many were, as might be supposed from their nature and size, the subjects of native traffic. Most have owed their removal to the more organised procedure instituted by respective Governments, or by bodies charged with administering the resources of national museums.

In the case of relics of this kind, the circumstances connected with their transference centre not so much in themselves alone or the incidents of traffic, and interest becomes directed rather to their relation to the monuments of which they formed part, and to the

---

* Rosellini, *Mon. Stor.* vol. iii. Part I. p. 260.
† Bunsen's *Egypt's Place*, vol. iii. p. 143.

condition of these. As to the temples, they could not of course have battled unscathed even against the mere wasting revolution of years. But they have often suffered also from the fact that their ancient character as centres of population descended after their sacredness was gone. The mud hovels of later generations thus became crowded in, around, and even upon them, dooming them to all the vile purposes of a *fellah* village, and whatever deterioration that might imply. Occasionally, too, they have been used as quarries on a considerable scale, when materials for buildings of various kinds were required. And some have had long to undergo the hardly less destructive nibbling of *fellaheen* in search of suitable stones to burn into lime. But notwithstanding these and other disadvantages, which shall be presently mentioned, it is hardly necessary to say, with so many pictures, plates, drawings, or photographs in recollection, that a certain number of Egyptian edifices have escaped in extraordinary preservation, considering their great antiquity. Their substantial workmanship has stoutly defied the influence of three thousand years in a climate whose freedom from frost and rain has rendered resistance more easy; their massive proportions cannot well be degraded even by the closest contact with the degenerate products of modern misery; and, if mutilated in part or disfigured in details, they rise up, imposing from their solid strength, amid surrounding desolation, or among the puny parasites that cluster about them.

The tombs, again, being excavated in the living rock,

were saved in a great measure from the chance of being gradually dismembered, or utterly swept away like structural buildings. But although it is true their chambers and passages, deep in the sides of limestone mountains, may last to the end of time, these might still be but as the shadow when the substance was gone; for the more perishable decorations on the walls, which may be regarded as the latter, enjoy no similar immunity. Indeed the deterioration, which in point of fact they have experienced even of late years, is very considerable, as they manifestly show, and as I have been assured by those familiar with them at the period when a voyage up the Nile was only undertaken by the zealous few, and who have seen what they are to-day. They, like the temples, have suffered from the presence in their midst of a lingering population. Inhabited now, as indeed some were centuries ago, dust and smoke and other impurities are accomplishing their work of obliteration in cases where such occupancy, to which all are exposed, exists. The remarkable tomb, known as the Brickmakers', at Goorneh, in which scenes of the most interesting description, illustrative of arts and customs, are depicted with great precision, is by no means the only important one at present subject to these risks.* That under such circumstances the paintings on the walls should grow dim is not surprising; and it may be anticipated with regret, that

* I mention it, as a well-known Eastern traveller has specially deplored its impending fate. Robertson's *Biblical Researches in Palestine*, &c., vol. i. p. 543.

a continuance of this state of things, wherever it prevails, will render them, at no distant date, hopelessly obscure.

The splendid sepulchres of the Kings are not, from their sequestered situation, liable to this sort of treatment; but in them, as everywhere—in temples as in tombs—one great enemy of the sculptures and frescoes has been the very reputation arising from their value. Unlike the usual course, where increasing interest in any object is followed by increasing care, notoriety has in their case been the death-knell of some and the curse of all. It has been their fortune that some of the hosts of visitors, attracted by their fame, instead of bestowing upon them the cheap tribute of respect, have left traces not unworthy of the followers of Attila or of Genseric. Apart from the violation of good taste, the amount of damage which has been inflicted in this manner can scarcely be believed. Whole tableaux, previously uninjured either in outline or in colour, have been sacrificed in the attempt to chip out, perhaps, the head of a figure that excited an ignorant acquisitive desire; elaborate inscriptions have been ruthlessly mutilated to gain possession of one or two of the characters; while here and there are to be found examples of that species of vulgar humour, akin to idiotcy, which exhibits itself in irremediably spoiling a historical document or a work of art for the sake of producing some grotesque effect. But the most glaring offence arises from the pains which so many have taken to secure, if anything, ridicule, or worse, for themselves, by scrawling or chiselling their names in the very midst of the sculptures. So often has this silly and hateful practice been described and reprobated, that I had no intention to allude to it, were it not necessary to say with regret that, up to the last hour within my experience, names seemed to be added in equally objectionable positions to those which already disfigured the monuments. While leaving on ruins so distant, a record of their visit that might possibly be their only epitaph, it did not probably occur to the earlier travellers, like Bruce, to what a disastrous extent it might be in the power of crowds of followers, under an altered state of things, to copy their example without the slightest exercise of discretion. But it is unsatisfactory to find a scientific body recently encouraging this modern folly, by inserting above the entrance of the Great Pyramid at Geezeh a slab bearing their names, which do not the less countenance a mischievous habit because they are composed in hieroglyphics, any more than the act is vindicated by describing it under the classical title *proskunéma*.

Reverting to what has been said as to the mutilations exhibited by the walls of temples and tombs, it need hardly be added that while many are owing directly to foreign visitors, many more have been the work of *fellaheen*. Finding that they could meet with purchasers for a neatly coloured little group of hieroglyphics, or a quaintly sculptured bas-relief head or hand, as the case might be, it mattered little to them at what cost to the monuments such could be riven off.

That the damage inflicted has often been out of all proportion to the smallness of the piece cut out, may be readily believed from their unhandy tools, and still more unhandy application of them.

In connexion with the results thus produced, it is impossible not to notice the mode of action pursued by some of the scientific expeditions, and particularly by that from Prussia under Dr. Lepsius, which spent three years in the country, from 1842 to 1845. It is of course evident that there can be no fixed rule by which to test the propriety of dismantling ancient ruins and transporting the excised fragments to other lands. What in one case would be highly meritorious, would in another be equally reprehensible, the peculiar circumstances of each being the turning-point. Hence an investigator professing to act in the interests of science can only be guided by a sound discretion. That in the exercise of this discretion Dr. Lepsius saw good grounds for some of his proceedings may unfortunately be very true; but there certainly is room for a grave difference of opinion with regard to some of his more prominent operations. Take, for instance, those in the most magnificent tomb in Egypt, that of Sethi I. There, where corridors and halls were in perfect preservation, and all the rock pillars in the latter stood in their original freshness, the Prussian Commission finding them so, are stated to have overthrown a decorated column to secure a portion of it, leaving the remainder a scattered wreck on the floor of the chamber thus done to ruin. Many would not, perhaps, undertake to defend the decision of Champollion, who, twenty years before, neatly cut away two slabs from the projecting jambs of an inner portal in the same sepulchre. The considerate care of others, to whom it was also a treasury of knowledge, will probably be considered more befitting. Sir G. Wilkinson, Mr. Hay, and Mr. Burton, about the same time laboriously examined and sketched the figures on the walls by the dim light of wax candles, rather than injure the paintings with the smoke of torches. Mr. Hay, I believe, before then had also channels made to divert from the tomb any accidental drainage after the rare torrential storms,— a safeguard necessary from the low level, and originally provided by a deep dry well within the entrance, which Belzoni, in gaining admission, had been obliged to fill up.

But not only are the dilapidations caused by Dr. Lepsius of a more violent character than those directed by Champollion, they were also accomplished under a very different order of things. They were executed after numerous visitors from all countries had begun to visit Egypt, chiefly for the sake of those monuments which he was helping to destroy, and at a time when, by increasing facilities of communication, a voyage up the Nile was becoming a matter of so easy achievement that, in such a point of view, to bring the ruins piecemeal to Europe might be deemed as essential as to break off the mouldings from some remarkable Gothic edifice in South Germany, and deposit them in London, or Paris, or Berlin. Nor is it enough to say that the sculptures which Dr. Lepsius removed at such a sacrifice might have been scribbled over, or otherwise ruined by successors like those already alluded to. For, first, the alternative was no inevitable sequence. Second, in so far as the general aspect of the monuments themselves is concerned, it is of little consequence whether they are mutilated by the crowbars of a scientific commission, or by less learned chisels. And finally, since the skill of the draughtsman and modeller has attained such excellence, the presence in our museums of the actual blocks hewn by the old workmen is not so indispensable for purposes of scientific research, that whole buildings of matchless interest must be irremediably defaced to procure them, and that they should be deprived of the chance, probably every year now becoming less remote, of being preserved in their original and peculiar positions, where their value would be tenfold greater. Neither should it be forgotten that this sort of authoritative demolition, by declaring, *ipso facto*, that the ruins are delivered over to perdition, must have largely tended to encourage the destructive faculties of succeeding visitors, and to countenance the wanton carelessness of others. Its general influence can also be well illustrated by a reply of Mohammed Ali, during his energetic government of Egypt. When urged to save the antiquities, he retaliated by saying, "How can I do so, and why should you ask me, since Europeans themselves are their chief enemies?" And thus, although one investigator before named, and then at work, Sir G. Wilkinson, could, and did, intercede for them with, as we have already seen, a good title to be heard, another, M. Champollion, certainly assumed a curiously inconsistent position when he besought\* the Pasha, as he earnestly did, to cherish with religious care those very memorials which he himself had just returned from despoiling.

These considerations seem to show that the propriety of the course pursued by Professor Lepsius was at least highly questionable. It is to be hoped that he saw other reasons which were adequate in themselves and sufficient to satisfy his judgment; for certainly, if he were actuated by no different motive than to bring home tangible fruits of his mission to fill new galleries at Berlin, his well-earned fame and the enlightened liberality of his Government in sending forth the expedition would hardly save both from the verdict in later years of unjustifiable spoliation. His proceedings have frequently been censured severely, and they have sometimes most unfairly been attributed to personal objects. To accusations of this nature, as unjust as they were invidious, he has thought it necessary to allude by repeating that "we made the selection of the monuments not for ourselves, but commissioned by our Government for the Royal Museum, therefore, for the benefit of science and a public eager after knowledge."† Yet this alone would not be enough; the end, we know, cannot always justify the means; and where would this reasoning lead? Archæological collections are no

---

\* *Lettres écrites d'Égypte et de Nubie*, appendix.
† *Letters from Egypt and Ethiopia*, note, p. 41. Horner's ed.

doubt valuable institutions, and so rare is it to see any overweening zeal displayed in their management, that no reasonable man would think of squeamishly conjuring up obstacles to their progress. But there are certain limits to their field of operation: and were they to be conducted on principles of refined cupidity, akin to those which stimulated Aurelian, as some alleged, to sack Palmyra for the purpose of seizing the works of art within its walls, or induced Napoleon to dismantle St. Mark's; were their stores to be augmented at the cost of dilapidating ancient structures in every quarter, without due reference to the circumstances or conditions which might render that course desirable in itself or otherwise—then we should have seed capable of producing all the fruits of a fresh Barbaric irruption, and the world might one day be startled by enormities as glaring as the despatch of an expedition to treat for the removal of the Fountain of Lions from the Alhambra, or to subsidise the Neapolitan authorities for permission to quarry out the choicest vestiges of Pompeii.

As with regard to Dr. Lepsius I can entertain no other feeling than admiration of his learning, and respect for the many evidences of earnestness in pursuit of it which he has shown, it was not from a desire to offer any opinion on the proceedings of his Commission that I have adverted to them here, but from the bearing they have on the general subject of archæological operations. The turn which these have often had a tendency to take has in a great degree depended on the fact that even, or indeed chiefly, when under the auspices of Governments, the economics of a mining speculation rather than the scope of a scientific survey, have been imported by them into the fields of research,—the condition being imposed or implied that for so much expenditure so many tangible returns were expected.

And this view of advancing the interests of science and art, as a grant for such purposes would probably be designated, is not merely a thing of the past. Let us take the latest example (which unfortunately we meet with at home) of excavations carried on in the name of a Government, and we find this idea of procedure acted upon, as well as some proof of the results to which it may be expected to lead. In the recently published account of researches at Carthage, the guiding principle is indicated from time to time.\* At page 288, it is said of an attempt at an interesting point, "satisfied that the results would not be adequate to the expenditure, I limited the period of the experiment, and went in search of a more *profitable* field." What that meant is shown in page 405, where the stopping of another excavation is thus accounted for: "we simply dug with a view to finding objects worthy of removal, and not in order to exhibit ancient architecture." Now at page 444, we shall see the kind of interpretation such a view may receive. Walls of a large edifice were discovered, in which were some slabs with Punic inscriptions; mark what followed. "As

---

\* *Carthage and her Remains,* by N. Davis, 1861.

we were determined to secure every trophy, we were absolutely compelled to demolish the walls in which the inscriptions were embedded. This process of destruction, under other circumstances inexcusable, prevented us from ascertaining the real nature of the building itself. Whether it was a temple or palace, or a sumptuous edifice of a private citizen, will, in all probability, after the havoc we were under the necessity to cause, never be ascertained." *

Again, I repeat that, as in the case of the Prussian Commission in Egypt, I do not allude to these doings at Carthage for the sake of having something unpleasant to say, which I would much rather avoid, but to ask, could I hope to be heard,—if this method of dealing with ancient vestiges is to be recognised as right, above all, when Governments take the field professedly in a representative character as for the benefit of scientific inquiry? That this should be decided is of importance, not now as affecting what has been done in the past, but what may be done in the future. At the present time excavations are in progress in

---

* In the same work (p. 571) occur the following remarks, and as they seem to show the writer's opinion as to the destruction of ancient monuments for the purpose of carrying away fragments of them, they may be transcribed as a strange commentary on the passage quoted above. Referring to the overthrow of a mausoleum, since Sir Grenville Temple's visit, it is said: "In order to secure the bilingual inscription, and to dispose of it to the British Museum, the greater portion of the mausoleum was barbarously pulled to pieces, and reduced to the present shapeless heap of ruins! But the crime (for a crime it was) met with its due reward."

North Africa under the authorisation of the British Government; and although it has always shown itself chary of undertaking such enterprises on any really efficient scale, it is not impossible as interest in all kinds of intelligent research advances, and ancient seats of civilization become more and more accessible—it is not impossible that our own Government, as well as those of other European states, may come to be engaged in furthering such researches. If so, can it be doubted that whenever they appear on a scene where their presence is avowedly as it ought to be, in the interests let us say of education in a wide sense—can it be doubted that the only principle of action worthy of their adoption is archæological elucidation on a broader basis than merely antiquarian rapine? The historic, artistic, ethnographic, or other scientific illustration which the site or ruins under treatment are capable of affording, ought to be the first consideration: the collecting of vestiges ought to be merely the contingent, and not necessary consequence. In the course of the excavations there may or there may not occur relics whose removal may not only be permissible on all reasonable grounds, but a duty to secure their preservation. In a general way, it may be said that all detached objects would come within this category. It might also be supposed to include statues or other sculptures not forming so integral a part of any structure that their removal would involve its actual ruin. But of these it would be understood, from a fair estimate of surrounding circumstances, that the risk of their destruction was such as to make the withdrawing of them from the positions which they decorated be more than counterbalanced by the safety insured for them, especially were they works of high art, which copies or casts might not adequately reproduce. But were it a question of demolishing or fatally dismembering an edifice or monument of any kind, to abstract inscriptions, for example, or ornamental details, then the director of the excavations ought to be very sure of the grounds on which he may propose to proceed. His instructions as to such cases ought to point to care and conservation rather than to recklessness and ruin: his resources ought to enable him to give force to these without loss to the object of his mission. The means of taking thoroughly good casts, drawings, and photographs should be at his disposal; and thus perfect facsimiles could be prepared for museums at home, with photographic or other copies as additional guarantees of accuracy. Of course it is at once to be admitted as an abstract proposition, that the original blocks bearing the ancient touches are preferable to any reproductions however precise. But the question is, not what is absolutely the best within the range of unlimited choice, but what is best relatively to all the circumstances. Now excepting, as I have already implied, works specifically artistic, embodying the loftiest conceptions of genius or extraordinary powers of execution, it may be said with regard to all others of inferior rank, and especially of those whose importance consists in the facts which they testify, that facsimiles, prepared as they now can be prepared, would fulfil every requisite, alike for study and public instruction. If, however, the presence of originals in our museums is nevertheless to be insisted on at the spoliative cost we are now discussing, let it be understood that, were there no other objection, the policy followed would be that best known as killing the bird for the sake of the egg.* To carry off a few fragments, even with the best intentions of aiding the increase of knowledge, we should be unnecessarily dooming to destruction by our act or example historic vestiges which might otherwise become the property always fruitful, in most instances of further enlightenment, and certainly of gratification to each succeeding age. In the case of *half*-explored ruins or cities, to deal recklessly with them thus is even worse; as we distinctly and knowingly cut off the chance of a harvest of instruction to adequate research, by introducing the elements of chaos through impolitic attempts directed only to plucking up, as it were, a few scattered ears by the roots.

It may be said that the insufficient means at the disposal of excavators has led, and might again be likely to lead, to these evils. This may be so. But while such insufficiency may be to be regretted, what should be desired is, that if the means be limited, so likewise

* Already there are some indications of this being avowed in the case of Egyptian remains. Referring to historical slabs removed by Champollion, and to different copies of them, Baron Bunsen remarks that the details preserved in the earlier of these "show that this is another instance of the damage caused by the removal of the monuments."—*Egypt's Place*, vol. iii. p. 130.

shall be the field of operation. Instead of a government issuing what may be called letters of marque for a buccaneering raid over a whole country or a whole site, merely to collect, by abstracting here and there without due regard to consequences, the largest number of trophies, as they have been termed, which the outlay of the money to be spent can produce—instead of this, it would be more to the purpose that when the sum to be expended is decided, such elucidatory work should alone be marked out, within however narrow a compass, as could be accomplished for it thoroughly and well. If, in course of this, opportunities should give rise to considerations as to the removal of relics, whether to our own country or others, then let the decisions be arrived at with reference only to the real interests of knowledge and culture. Let it be seen that the granters of the funds and those charged with the application of them have, above all, not been actuated in forming their judgments by an unworthy acquisitiveness which, not content with the discovering and reproducing of inscribed or sculptured vestiges, demands possession of some of the actual blocks, whatever the ruin,—not because they are required for the necessities of research; but because, being unique or important, they are treasures to be proud of; because, if not clutched, neighbours are supposed to be ready to scramble for them.

As for the monuments of Egypt, it would appear that they may now at length be sheltered from many of the risks to which they have been so long exposed. Six hundred and fifty years ago a traveller in that country, Abd-el-Lateef, condemning, by arguments drawn from reason and philosophy, the ravages which had already commenced, deplores that while "in former times the kings watched with care over the preservation of these precious remains of the past, in these days the reins have been cast loose to men, and nobody has troubled himself to repress their caprices."* Of the present century this could have been said as truly as of the thirteenth, with the unfortunate addition that the rulers in the later age were to be regarded as the most dangerous, because the most sweeping and persevering delinquents, and that too, unhappily, at a time when the progress of discovery was imparting fresh value to the doomed vestiges. But, indeed, it was not probable that their claims would be much considered by a semi-barbarous despotism like that of Mohammed Ali, struggling, as he did, to introduce with rapidity into the country some of the elements of strength and material prosperity. A temple under these circumstances was very likely to go down before a barrack, or become a quarry for a sugar-mill. Many have probably heard of the havoc committed in this way by the authority or consent of the native government; and for those who may desire minuter information on the subject, an energetic writer has drawn up a long catalogue of the doings of this kind attributed to Mohammed Ali, with a zeal which cannot be disputed,

---

* *Relation de l'Égypte*, trad. par S. de Sacy, p. 195.

but with a bitterness almost indicative of personal resentment.*

Under the subsequent governors, such active demolition, as there was less demand for it, was less frequent, but the monuments were always suffering from the minor draughts made upon them, and all the other consequences of complete neglect. On a former occasion, five years ago, when treating of this subject †, it was necessary to express urgently that this state of matters ought not to be allowed to continue, and to hope that the Egyptian Government might be induced to undertake a conservative supervision. What was then said is no longer applicable. It has always been a merit in the various rulers of the country since research among its antiquities began to be actively prosecuted, that they have thrown no obstacles in the way of investigators, and indeed on the contrary have generally granted liberal facilities. But to the credit of the Government of the present Pasha, it has now proposed to assume a protective custody of the monuments. Some of the ruins have been cleared out, and exploratory operations have been instituted. And if

---

* Gliddon's *Appeal to the Antiquaries of Europe*, 1841.

† In a paper of mine on *The Present Condition of the Monuments of Egypt and Nubia*, from which I have extracted some paragraphs in this chapter.—*Archæol. Journal*, vol. xiii. p. 154. It may be proper to state here that in Chapters X. and XI. are two episodes (the description of a religious festival at Cairo, and the account of the conscription) the substance of which I have also taken from letters written when I was last in Egypt, and already printed; the one in the *Literary Gazette*, the other in the *Times*.

an efficient guardianship is now maintained, there will be preserved, for the study of generations to come, some valuable remnants of the labours of a people through whose works are to be traced many of the remotest distinguishable links in the human history of the world.

## CHAP. X.

### THE PRESENT TENANTS OF THE TOMBS.

BESIDES the peculiarities which make up the conditions of life among the rural population of Egypt, or *fellaheen* as they are termed, there is a sprightly docility of disposition exhibited commonly now in their intercourse with strangers, which is apt to beget a sort of personal interest with regard to them, even notwithstanding their loss of nearly all true manliness of character. In natural intelligence and quickness of perception, within certain limits, they may be compared advantageously not only with most races in the same general condition of semi-barbarism as themselves, but also with the peasantry of those countries which, in this respect at least, stand so much higher in the scale. Circumstances have developed various grades of acuteness among them; and while there may not be any of them dull and stolid as a class, even among those who live in the most sequestered situations, the dwellers in those parts of the country where the monuments have formed a centre for external intercourse, have their wits much more keenly (and in like proportion discreditably) sharpened than others. Of these the most prominent types are the villagers in the neighbourhood of the necropolis of Memphis, and those in or around the necropolis of Thebes, who, from the operation of similar causes, have attained the same doubtful superiority. I am not here comparing them, on the one hand, with those inhabitants of the two large cities, who have been brought so much within the circle of European contact, and who, along with a quickened development of action, have had too good an excuse for imbibing most of its worst elements. Nor do I refer, on the other, to the occupants of the remoter towns of considerable size, whose fossilized life, but slightly aroused from the outer world, retains more of its native exclusiveness, in consequence of its more unbroken tenor. But rather I have in view the great mass of the agricultural population who dwell in the villages and scattered hamlets shaded by a few palm trees, which stud the valley of the Nile.

It might naturally be looked for that everywhere throughout a land where the people are as helpless as serfs, and governed by a rule so unscrupulously corrupt in its local administration, astuteness would flourish in so favourable a soil. We should expect that this characteristic, if not absolutely crushed out by the hopelessness of despair (which is foreign to the bulk of all races, and especially Easterns when personal suffering is not continuous), or if not deadened by the heaviness of innate stupidity, would develop itself strongly under such fostering influence as the rampant dishonesty of those endowed with the authority of an executive. But the peasants of Geezeh and Goorneh in particular, have of late years had an additional course of training. Dwelling in the midst of the most remarkable of the remains, they were brought more in contact with European visitors, and with what Lycurgus would have called the moral poison which money brings along with it. They began to find, too, that the tombs around them might yield a source of considerable gain; and, accordingly, they entered on a pursuit distinguished by two prominently demoralizing elements, since it was at once gambling and contraband;—gambling, because success in discovery was exceedingly indefinite and uncertain; contraband, because the governors set over them either professed to prohibit such attempts or seized the fruits. And so they have gone on outwitting or bribing officials, but continuing to search for relics, outwitting each other where possible in the disposal of them, and more peculiarly and chiefly outwitting unwary strangers in their dealings with them.

The constant practice of deceit, all but inevitable, has effected a complete perversion of moral sense, as regards truthfulness or fidelity. So that in various parts of the country, but especially at Goorneh, no statement made by a *fellah* on the simplest question of fact is likely to be correct; and no attestation of it, however solemn, is necessarily accurate, if he has the slightest interest in misleading, conceives any of the extravagant suspicions to which he has too good reason to be prone, or imagines, according to his most tortuous judgment, that giving wrong information might benefit him in any way whatever. It will readily be supposed that by a natural reaction, these Goorneh people would be, from this unprincipled cunning, rather impracticable subjects to deal with in matters of public administration. But as a body of workmen they are not very difficult to manage beyond the necessity for constant watchfulness, since their petty schemes of deception may for the most part be detected; and they are forgiving, good-natured, and docile, trustingly, although I regret to add not always successfully, looking to the stranger for that justice of treatment which they hardly experience, even in name, from the rulers set in authority over them. But, on the other hand, the most ardent professions are scarcely to be repaid with anything like confidence. Honesty among them is, in fact, all but an unknown virtue. I do not mean that thievery, in the common signification of the term, was universal; for I am glad to say that I was never aware of any ordinary piece of property being stolen. But I have had constant reason to be familiar with attempts at cheating and deception in every form which the circumstances permitted. The Cynic in search of a very reduced standard indeed, would certainly not wander among the *fellaheen* of Goorneh in vain. He might, perhaps, find rare instances of fidelity springing from a sentiment of personal gratitude or attachment; but I doubt if he would meet in that community with a single case of honesty arising from principle. Nor is this all. The proverb tells us that we may look for honour even in the relations of thieves among themselves, but that is wanting to the Goorneh men; for they are often treacherous towards each other, the prospect of contingent personal advantage overcoming the ties of complicity, and occasionally of relationship.

In religion they retain little more than the strong fatalism of their faith, and the conventional waiting on providence, which induces a digger among the tombs, if asked as to his success, to return the stereotyped answer, "God will send." The ordinary outward observances they seem completely to neglect, never, so far as I could perceive, visiting the mosk in the neighbouring town of Luxor; and I have no recollection of ever seeing one of them engaged in the prescribed formality of daily prayer, which in many parts of the country is so commonly attended to. To a great extent this laxity is probably owing partly to example, partly to descent; as they, like other villagers on the outskirts of the valley, are in considerable proportion the offspring of nomads who had resigned their wandering life, namely, Arabs of the Desert, who are often not very strict in their devotions. But although they are thus negligent in formal practice, they do not hold in inferior account their name of Muslimeen, which the most squalid or ruffianly follower of the Prophet generally, even yet, regards as a charter of nobility, enabling him, in his heart, to despise alike every grade of *Kafir* (unbeliever). Nor are there wanting instances among them, although these are very rare, where they vindicate their title by one of the highest recognized tests of devotion, the pilgrimage to Mecca. More frequently they make their way to one of those great religious festivals held at Cairo, which so largely minister to the popular religious sentiment, and also to the retention of that archaic individuality of social life, which in the East is slow, even in the most trivial matter, to leave the beaten path of centuries. It happened to me to be in that city during one of the most remarkable of those celebrations, the *Moolid en Nebbée*, or anniversary of the Prophet's birth; which, on that occasion, was thought to be more than usually brilliant for these degenerate days. I will, therefore, shortly describe some general features of a ceremonial which exerts a very strong influence, at all events, on the humbler classes of the community among which it exists.

In accordance with the Muslim method of calculation, which, guided by the moons, brings events of this kind round the whole calendar of the seasons, the jubilee varies its date by nearly three weeks each year. Practically, its celebration, which lasts ten days, is in the hands of the derwishes. That is to say, their singular devotional performances, continued night and day with hardly any intermission, in tents, or booths, at the end of the large square in Cairo, called El Esbekeèh, — are the centre round which those of the faithful are attracted, who come either as spectators, or hawkers of sweetmeats, exhibitors of trained dogs and monkeys, or otherwise as ministrants to the wants of a sort of " holy fair." The zeal and energy with which the derwishes, by means of fresh drafts I presume, carry on their excessively laborious, fanatical service for this lengthened period, is perfectly surprising, and not a little revolting. Their hideous mode of worship is simply disgusting when exhibited with the exaggerated antics of merry-andrews before a crowd, as they howl and gesticulate round an upright post like a maypole, in the open air, or under a canvas booth. And, to me at least, the *zikr*, when so conducted, lost, from its grotesqueness, much of the wild and appalling effect which almost thrills through one when seeing it for the first time performed, with more appropriate accessories, in one of the derwish colleges near old Cairo. There in a small but lofty-domed chapel, as it might be termed, destitute of furniture or decorations, a few interested, and some reverential onlookers range themselves cross-legged along the walls to witness the strange rites of the devotees, who, to the number of thirty or forty, are seated on mats in a circle near the centre of the building. These men are of various classes and of many nations. They have no particular ceremonial costume, and they wear the dress of their daily life,—a workman appearing in his loose blue shirt, a Persian traveller in a flowing furred robe, and even a native Cairene policeman in his incongruous uniform of European cut; but several of the brotherhood, more immediately connected with this college, are distinguished by long, snake-like hair.

Presently the *zikr* is commenced by a prayer to

Allah, sung in low, measured cadence, which, after a short interval, is repeated in louder, but, from their imploring earnestness, still pleasing tones. Then, after a few seconds of absolute stillness, the *shekh*, or head of the order, begins a solemn chant, instantly caught up by the whole circle — *la ila ha ill la'llah* — " there is no deity but God; " and for fully a quarter of an hour these words are repeated in a gradually quickening tone, while the bodies of the chanters oscillate to and fro, keeping time with their rapid utterance. Again there is silence, and a blind minstrel called a *moonshid*, rising from the ground, pours forth, in modulated accents, a hymn rich with glowing imagery, not dissimilar to that employed in the figurative and hyperbolical passages of the Old Testament. He has hardly ceased, when the chant, unvaried in the simplicity of its language, but now accompanied by the softened tones of a reed pipe, once more rings through the mosk; and the position of the derwishes is as yet unchanged. But soon, starting to their feet, they form into a compact ring, marshalled into place by their *shekh*, who keeps in the centre, and the assertion of the omnipotent unity of God is still reiterated. For an hour or more this is continued, the chant slowly degenerating from intensity of excitement into a species of howling groan, in which the one absorbing word *Allah* is alone perceptible, while the oscillating movement is correspondingly increased until every joint is called into action, as the body is pitched backwards and forwards with a violence that would entirely overcome, in a very short period, the equilibrium of an unpractised performer. The *zikr*, nevertheless, goes on apparently with unabated vigour; and casting away their caps or turbans and outer dress, the derwishes still keep to their ranks, and scarcely a symptom of relaxing energy is yet apparent. The long hair of some streaming from their heads, and beating the air at each contorted movement; the rigid, earnest faces of others, now thrown backwards to the light, now bent nearly to the ground with untiring rapidity; the occasional wild yells of a few, shrieked forth in their frenzy,—combined to produce what one might imagine to be the effect of a demoniacal revel. At length an old man and a young negro leant for a moment against each other for support, and fell together clear of the circle, whose ranks at once closed to fill the vacancy. The old man lay in a state of stupor. The negro quickly sprang up, and raising his right hand in the air, whirled round in rapid gyrations, but speedily came again to the ground.

Shortly after this episode, which in no way interfered with the general progress of the *zikr*, the shekh retired to a seat near the wall, and thither, embracing him as they passed, and ranging themselves on his right hand, the rest followed,— save one, who, dead to external impressions and rooted to his original place, persisted in all the fervour of ejaculation and in all the fierce violence of motion. Immediately one of his brethren, wrestling with him gently, laid him prostrate on the floor, where with heaving chest, rolling eyes, clenched hands and gnashing teeth, he slowly expended the terrible frenzied mania which possessed him. A cloak was thrown over him; and the others, having finished the concluding portion of their service—a short hymn or prayer—proceeded to leave the mosk, the shekh motioning imperiously to us, the spectators, to depart before him.

By an unbroken series of exhibitions somewhat of this kind, the birth of the Prophet is commemorated. And day and night the peculiar echoing croak of the derwish chant may be heard from some of the tents; while in others *fakirs* exhibit, with ingenious sleight of hand, the miraculous powers of defying both fire and sword which they pretend to have received. But a still more remarkable display is reserved for the close of the festival. On the last day, the extraordinary ceremony of the *Doseh* or Treading, is the spectacle presented to the, in many cases, obviously fervent worshippers. Having secured a very favourable position at the prescribed spot, I waited with some European friends, in the midst of many hundred expectant Muslimeen, for the arrival of the shekh of the Saadeéh derwishes, to whom is assigned the honour of being the instrument to accomplish this miracle, on his way, after mid-day prayers, from the mosk, where he has spent the night in fasting and prayer. Punctually as the hour elapsed, the mass of people on the outskirts of the crowd, swaying from side to side, told that the holy procession approached; and, acting accordingly, several men near me lay down on their faces in the dust, across the lane walled by eager spectators, but yet clearly defined, along which the shekh was to pass. Presently bands of derwishes, headed by distinguishing flags, rushed up fresh from the performance of *zikrs*, their heads still jerking upwards, their gasping throats still pouring forth the burden of their chant in harsh croaking accents. With furious ardour, almost with rivalry, they threw themselves upon the ground alongside those who had already taken up their position; and active hands quickly arranged two or three hundred men into a solid compact pavement. Two half-naked *fakirs*, one drawing the edge of a sword across the unprotected skin of his chest, the other thrusting the point of a sharp weapon loaded with a ball of lead, against every part of his person, added to the wildness of the scene. Heralded by a brilliant banner the shekh appeared, seated, motionless as an automaton, on a strong steel-grey horse, and surrounded by six attendants, two guiding the reins, two keeping him in the saddle, and two bringing up the rear. In this order the sacred phalanx advanced along the backs of the prostrate devotees. With firm and rapid, though slightly constrained step, the horse, whose motions I carefully watched, trod upon them, his foot rarely slipping between the bodies which, closely wedged together, composed the living causeway, but planting itself each time on a quivering man. Yet no cry of pain escaped the lips of those who underwent the ordeal; or if a stifled groan, which no effort of the will could control, did involuntarily find utterance, it was drowned by the shouts of *Allah* which resounded throughout the multitude. And after the shekh had passed, and those over whom he had ridden had gained their feet, or were urgently assisted to rise by their friends, even those who seemed nearly swooning, whose faces reflected the torture they endured, and who, despite their fortitude, writhed in agony, were obviously desirous to join the throng immediately and appear unhurt; because, to be injured would have been an evidence of their own unworthiness, as the miracle of the harmless treading only professes to apply to those who by prayer and devotional preparation are fit to undergo it. The ceremony over, the shekh, still on horseback, was led back by his attendants through the crowd, who eagerly pressed round him, many striving to touch his dress, and afterwards kissing devoutly the hand which had thus been in contact with his person, peculiarly sanctified by the holy mission of the day. His eyes were still closed in stupor, and his expression was supposed to be that of one rapt in spiritual unconsciousness; but although noble features are not uncommon in the East, his, unfortunately, were so essentially gross, that no amount of accidental beatitude could redeem them from repulsive coarseness, or impart to them one spark of the glow of inspiration.

Besides the *fellaheen* at Gorneeh, to whose faith such scenes as these would appeal, there are some to whom they would have been an abomination, namely the one or two families of Coptic Christians. Not, however, that the difference between the one and the other, though rigidly held by each as enormous in creed, takes, in ordinary external conditions, any very considerable practical form. In a general way, throughout the whole country, there is, of course, the marked distinction between the followers of the Cross and those of the Crescent, arising from the constant contumelious oppression to which the former were liable, not only at the hands of authority, but from every true believer. And there is reason to fear that the social disabilities and suffering thus created, while it also thinned their ranks, tended to produce a corresponding deterioration of character, by stimulating the culture of those abject qualities in which the weak can alone find defence among the lawless. Even the rudimentary education, a knowledge of reading and writing, common among them but utterly wanting to the mass around them, has led in the same direction, by giving to many, in their capacity of scribes (both public and private) to Mohammedans who were compelled to use, while they often despised them, a species of power which could only be tortuously exercised. Any such advantage in training, too, while calculated to impart superiority in intelligence under conditions where it could hardly fail to be ill-directed, would readily quicken their long descended heritage of mental suppleness without raising its scope. Indeed, in those despicable moral features which have been already referred to as characteristic of the Muslim *fellaheen*, the Copts are too often more prominently worthless than the Mohammedans. And, although they are generally more industrious, or at all events, judging by outward results, more acquisitive, they are also more greedy and grasping. Unfortunately they have one additional vice which is not a matter of comparison, as, with rare exceptions, it is all their own. Not restrained, like the disciples of the Koran, by a rigid textual prohibition, they abuse the freedom they possess in the matter of intoxicating liquors; and the practice of consuming large quantities, particularly of a potent spirit of indigenous production called *arraki*, would seem to be nearly universal.

Nor has their religion (I mean in their relation to it), and necessarily its teachers, escaped the deteriorating influences which have marked their history. It would be most unwarrantable without a much more extended acquaintance than I possess, or indeed after any practicable degree of acquaintance, with the remnants of the Coptic community, to lump them into one corrupt mass, all alike wanting in their practice and their faith. I contemplate no such rash injustice; and I would merely remark that the result of ordinary observation, and some more careful inquiry, lamentably shows that Christianity is in a general way degenerated, especially in the remoter districts, into a sort of superstition or almost Obi-worship, and that many of its priesthood are on a corresponding level in intellect and character. As an exemplification of this, we may look at the treatment of sickness. A sufferer afflicted by severe sleepless headaches, for example (as in a case I once knew even in Cairo), goes to his priest, and receives the advice to repeat the Lord's Prayer four times each night for a week before retiring to bed, and then to lie down with the Bible under his head. Or we may find another illustration in the not very comely spectacle of a bishop huxtering for a comfortable profit on some planks in his possession, which chanced to be suitable for the coffin of a Christian stranger who died within his diocese. And the gain in this and other matters, or this dignitary was sadly maligned, was by no means sought in the spirit of the lowly prayer of an episcopal predecessor, Synesius, in another part of the same country fifteen centuries before :—

> " Gold I only ask from heaven,
>   Enough to keep chill want and famine
>   From the cottage of my neighbour;
>   Lest wanting means to help the needy
>   Gloomy thoughts might overcome me." *

But although we may be grieved to see teachers with a Christian name wherever we find them, converting into a dead fetish spell words of living scope, regarding the Bible as a mere mystic talisman, or grovelling in ignorance, meanness, and avarice — and although we may think of unfaithful stewards, we ought to remember that *here* they do but represent the mind of the mass from which they spring, whose degradation (in the absence of those nobler vivifying sparks so rarely struck out) they could not but share. If we are startled by their baseness, we must not forget their psychical birth-

* Sharpe's *Hist. of Egypt*, vol. ii. p. 282.

right and their woes. They may, like all their race, be deeply to be pitied; he who cares to revile them must be very confident that he would himself rise superior to such adverse circumstances.

The few Copts at Goorneh, except that they appear to have gathered rather more substance together, are in outward social conditions in no marked way distinguishable from their neighbours. Of all, the mode of living is simplicity itself, their dwellings, their dress, and their food being of the most primitive kind. The outer rock-cut chambers of the tombs, in conjunction with mud erections in front, serve them as abodes; and these they share with the few cattle which the richer of them possess, the sheep, goats, dogs, fowls, and pigeons, which always go to constitute the household. A heap or two of thick *dhoora* straw, some earthen pots, and cupboards of sun-baked clay, would complete the inventory of the furnishings of an ordinary habitation. The luxury of raised beds formed of a framework of palm branches is of rare occurrence.

The dress of the men is merely a waist-cloth, or cotton trousers, and a loose sack garment, either of cotton or woollen material, the nearly universal costume of the country, which reaches to their heels, has a hole for the head to slip through, and wide pendant sleeves. This last, however, is always laid aside when the wearer has to engage in any active exertion; and the sun, whether in summer or winter, enables, or rather compels him to work in a state approaching to almost complete nudity. The head, closely shaven from time to time, except a tuft on the top, is protected by a dirty brown felt skull-cap, the red *tarboosh* not being possessed by all, and for the most part only being used, along with the turban, as holiday attire.

The clothing of the women is in essentials pretty much the same as, and not more complex than, that of the men, only the outer garment is scarcely so voluminous; and instead of a cap, the head is covered by a shawl with flowing ends, one of which is arranged to conceal the face when passing a stranger, as few possess the regular veil or *burko*. In their persons they are very uncleanly, although they are not the less fond of ornament; and long matted hair will have its greasy plaits looped up with pendants of shells or mother-of-pearl, glass beads, or bangles of silver. Nose rings of silver or brass are common, ear-rings universal; and when from poverty or illiberality on the part of the husband they cannot be procured of some more precious metal, they are worn of thin beaten brass, at a cost of not more than a farthing a-piece. Necklaces of variegated glass beads are equally popular, and to most of them are attached an amulet or two of some coloured stone, as onyx or cornelian. These are usually heir-looms, and looked upon as the most precious of possessions by their wearers, to whom they have been handed down as invaluable talismanic aids to the attainment of the dignity of maternity, without which an Eastern woman is held in contempt, and will probably be divorced. Other necklaces to be seen occasionally at Goorneh, but more frequently in Nubia, consist of cloves strung upon threads, and intermixed at intervals with one or two large beads. I once obtained a necklace of precisely the same kind, from an uncoffined mummy of a person evidently in poor circumstances, which was exhumed from a sand-heap in the course of one of my excavations near the temple of Der el-Bahrée. The presence of cloves with the ancient body was remarkable; but I mention the circumstance here as one of the instances of unbroken descent of fashion and practice in matters so simple.

An equally curious example of unvaried permanence of form in ornament is furnished by another adornment for the neck, not unfrequent here as well as elsewhere in the country. It is a hoop of brass or silver wire, in the latter case as thick in the middle as a half-inch rod, and tapering slightly towards the ends, which link together by hook and eye, thus completing the circle. I possess an almost identical object in bronze, from a mummy, and several of the same general form are preserved in various collections. Their analogy with the early torques of western Europe is striking, and some of these latter have been found which fasten in the same obvious manner; but this very simplicity in the design renders any wide-spread occurrence of it less surprising and less significant. It is, however, curious that the modern name of the ornament, as now used in Egypt, is *tó ok*.

Bracelets are greatly coveted, and few women are without several. They are of various kinds, the ruder being simply circles of horn, or of massive ivory which are much more valuable. Others consist of beads; but the most interesting, and also the most common, are those of metal, in which are preserved various beautiful archaic designs. The wealthier inhabitants of the towns have these in gold, but at Goorneh they are only to be seen of silver or of brass. Their shape is penannular, the flexibility of the metal sufficing to allow the ends to pass over the wrist, which then close. Sometimes they are plain, but for the most part they represent strands of cord entwined into various plaits and twists, expanding into square ends bristling with short blunt spikes. Others are flat hoops, an inch or more in breadth, having the surface covered with raised patterns, not inelegant in outline if rough in finish. A specimen of these is shown in the accompanying woodcut, which is copied from an example among those which I collected.

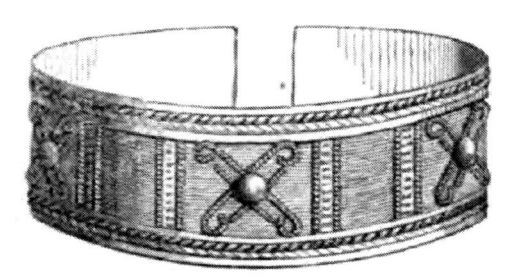

MODERN EGYPTIAN BRACELET OF SILVER.

Anklets of the same penannular character, but quite plain, except that the ends are beaten into cubes, are confined to a few. If of silver they are very heavy; if of iron, which, however, is mostly limited to children, they are little more than pieces of bent wire. And, indeed, swarms of little imps of both sexes are constantly running about perfectly naked, with nothing artificial upon their bodies except a tolerable coating of dirt, an iron anklet, and a string round the neck sustaining a ball of leather, in which a sentence from the Koran is rolled up as a safeguard against the evil eye.

Finger rings, which are almost never wanting, are coarse and clumsy, and although sometimes of silver, are rarely of more valuable material than pieces of coloured glass set roughly in brass.

It will, of course, be understood that the various ornaments which I have mentioned are those in common and constant use by a peasant population. In the towns, and particularly in Cairo, the inmates of *hareems* are adorned with far more costly objects[*]; and the wife even of a man whose means of subsistence may amount to not more than a sum equivalent to forty or fifty pounds sterling a year, will probably possess jewellery equal in value to three, four, or five times her husband's annual income, this being one of the ways of storing realized funds. Even at Goorneh, for aught that I know, the shekh's, or one or two other families may have some few richer decorations, used on the gala occasions of marriages; but the ornaments which I have described are parts of the invariable costume.

[*] In Mr. Lane's photographically accurate work several of these richer ornaments may be seen figured and described.—*Modern Egyptians*, ed. 1860, pp. 560, *et seq.*

The women never divest themselves of these in any of the occupations of their daily life; and they wear them alike when carrying water from the well or river, baking bread, or kneading the manure of cattle into cakes for fuel—an employment still more incongruous with bracelets, necklaces and rings.

Besides these duties, a little sewing, and twisting wool into thread with the hand-spindle, they have almost no other household work to perform, for the dietary is generally so simple as not to require any of the preparation of cooking. It consists almost entirely of bread, milk, and raw vegetables, chiefly onions, rarely accompanied by any sort of animal food. Although not altogether confined to festive occasions, this last is not often to be seen among them except at such times; and then also unleavened cakes sodden with butter, and coffee are added to the feast. In short they live as frugally as the peasantry of most hot climates, and many colder ones, partly, no doubt, from the dictates of nature, partly from the necessities of their condition; and what may seem wretched in their housekeeping is not now the consequence of downright misery or want. It is true that occasionally in former less prosperous times, they have been reduced to the lowest pitch, which even they could endure and live. But at present, although they have certainly no excess of this world's goods, they have enough for their humble wants, and may even be accounted as, for them, tolerably well off. Nearly all of them are the owners of such live stock as I have mentioned; and they all have a portion of land in the fruitful valley, which now yields them so good a return, in consequence of the great rise in the value of agricultural produce (amounting to fifty per cent., or even more, within ten or twelve years), that the more active are supposed to have small hoards of coin, in some cases not altogether inconsiderable, which they bury or conceal in some equally efficient manner. Some have added to their stores by the proceeds of successful finds of antiquities which they may have been so fortunate as to make.

They have usually large families of children; but except the shekhs, who can afford to have three, or the full complement of four wives, they are obliged to be content, for the most part, with one, on the score of expense. This forms the limit; for the possession of corresponding means of maintenance proportionally widens the circle of their conjugal affections, which easily become so comprehensive and elastic as to expand even beyond the prescribed boundary. Besides, in the East generally, it is a question involving dignity and social standing. I remember the old mother of the *shekh belled* at Goorneh, expressing strong dissatisfaction that her son had only three wives, — a neglect of his duty to his position which she could not endure. Eventually, ere I left, he added a fourth; but as there was trouble enough already among the three, partly, I imagine, from the limited space they had to occupy, I am afraid she can have been no addition to the harmony of the household. As they were our next door neighbours, I had occasion to know something of their movements. The house of the shekh was a square rock-area with the doorways of tombs on three sides and a brick wall on the fourth. In these inner dens each wife had her separate abode; but during the day they were all together in the court, spinning or oftener chattering childishly (as they were very young girls), amicably enough for the most part, when I chanced to see them. There were, however, from time to time sounds of grave disturbance; and we used to hear of one or other of the wives running off to her old home, of the mother-in-law unceremoniously fetching her back, and of the infinite tribulation it cost the dowager to keep them all in order. Allowing for the ruder forms, more demonstrative action, and coarser colouring applicable to the grade here represented, the same outline will probably exhibit the general realities of life in the Mohammedan *hareem*.

The social severance between the sexes, in the East, which the system of the Koran confirms, is more singularly exemplified among villagers such as these, than even in the towns. In the latter, the comparative artificiality of customs, and the privacy of domestic arrangements permitted from the nature of the case, or rather required, while tending, among other things, to maintain the strictness of the distinction, conceal considerably the evidences of its active existence. In the more unconstrained and natural life of those peasants the actual relationship is more prominently seen. It might have been supposed that with monogamy (it is true compulsorily) prevailing largely among them; that from the proximity and publicity of their simple abodes allowing ample opportunities for intercourse; that from men and women being on the same dead level of ignorance — a considerable degree of familiarity in their relations, and equalisation of their position would have arisen. But they are, nevertheless, almost like two different species of beings in this respect. Men and women, neighbours or even connexions, pass and repass without the slightest recognition of each other's existence on the part of either; and as for any merry-making in which the two sexes join, such a thing I suppose is as unknown at Goorneh, and would be held to be quite as indecorous, as in the seraglio at Constantinople.

In their gatherings they keep perfectly distinct. The women meet together, usually in small numbers, to gossip over their spinning. The men constantly assemble in the evening in larger groups with their pipes. On those occasions the passing affairs of their not very eventful days are the staple of their noisy talk; but not unfrequently they quietly and eagerly listen to one, if he happens to have learnt some new edition of any of the marvellous

> "Tales that charm away the wakeful night
> In Araby;"

or is skilful in narrating one of those of which Antar is probably the hero, and with which they may already be as familiar as playgoers in more civilized countries with the stock pieces of the stage. In some of these creations the temples are introduced, and figure as palaces; while among other constructive elements of the plot are a damsel, a warrior, a concealed treasure, *djins* (a kind of spiritual correlatives of the old Border Brownies), and lions which take part in conversation with perfect unconcern as if there were nothing singular in the proceeding.

But of all the subjects discussed in the evening conclaves, as is indeed the case I believe throughout the whole country, there is none so commonly recurred to or so fruitful as the Nile. The anxieties, annually returning which its motions beget, since so much depends upon the height to which its waters will rise, make the probable prospects of the inundation a matter for the expression of never-ending hopes, fears, and guesses. Nor can the matchless value and apparently mysterious operations of the river fail to awaken a lively interest, curiosity, and awe—sentiments which they have at all times excited among the dwellers on its banks, and which in the ancient days assumed a more special development. It was a strange commingling of the actual with the ideal; it was the climax in the degradation so characteristic in one aspect of the Egyptian Mythology, which substituted visible forms for eternal attributes; it was surely the last stage of materialistic credulity, or the first of rational unbelief, which applied to the God Nile, as figured on a Temple in the island of Philœ, the transcendent title of "Father of the Fathers of the Gods."[*] Attempts to define the

---

[*] Wilkinson's *Materia Hieroglyphica* (57, 2). Diodorus has also recorded that the Egyptians gave to the Nile this first place in their theogony.—Diod. lib. i. c. 1.

minuter mental processes which have evolved certain constituents of ancient systems of religion, have not been more productive of unimpeachable results than speculative exercises of metaphysical ingenuity are wont to be. But irrespective of such suggestions, and thinking only of a palpable typology readily present to our cognizance although not necessarily in this form operative in the minds of the ancient Egyptians, it could justly be said that if they strove to typify the grand originating, controlling and beneficent power, by that which stood in the same relation to their own material existence, they chose well in selecting the Nile.* Their country, its soil being exclusively a sedimentary deposit, was itself, as Herodotus aptly termed it, a gift from the sacred river. And the presence of its fertilizing stream was the one condition on which the life of plants, of the lower animals, and, consequently, of man himself depended. To all things animate in the valley along its banks it was in truth the essence of vitality. Far from

---

* From the point of view which we necessarily occupy, it is perhaps quite impossible for us to apprehend the evolution of ideas by which the actual deification of a river could be brought about and maintained among an intelligent people. We should be apt to accept, as the explanation, that its apotheosis was merely typical or connected with the idea of its being the instrument of a god. But an existing worship in India would show that this might only be partially right, or wholly wrong. We are reminded that "in the case of the Ganges, it is the river itself to whom they [a whole community of many millions] address themselves, and not to any deity residing in it or presiding over it; the stream itself is the deity which fills their imaginations and receives their homage."—Sleeman's *Rambles and Recollections of an Indian Official*, vol. i. p. 20.

bearing the ordinary relation of a river to a country, it is the one absorbing feature; and Diodorus Siculus was so far justified in declaring that no other stream was comparable to it.*

Nor are the modern inhabitants of Egypt less keenly sensible than their precursors of the blessings which they owe to the Nile. The days, it is true, are past when their gratitude would take the form of exalting the object of their homage into a substantive divinity. But there are not wanting traces of something like a belief that their beloved river is a gift from God in a more positive sense than even the peculiar spirit and phraseology of Mohammedanism imply. Discussions as to its source are frequent, exciting as much interest as, in another form, the question would awaken in a *séance* of the Geographical Society; and while many fanciful notions are current, the most popular idea seems to be, as far as I could learn, that the secret is among the arcana never to be disclosed. On one occasion this topic was the grave subject of conversation at an evening assemblage such as I have mentioned. Various apocryphal stories and traditional opinions had been delivered, but the general belief was strong that the mystery was one which mortal man had never been, and would never be, permitted to penetrate. To this a greybeard demurred, for he said that in a distant town he had once heard it read from a book, that to one devout *shekh* it had been granted to gaze upon the glorious fountain. In fulfilment of a solemn vow he

* Lib. i. c. 8.

had undertaken the pilgrimage as a holy mission. By fasting and prayer, in all humility he prepared himself for his weary task; and trusting to the mercy of God and the countenance of the Prophet, he steadily journeyed along the banks of the stream. As the northern plains receded behind him trials and dangers thickened on his path. The sun glared by day. Wild beasts howled by night. But the hearts of the fierce *kafirs* (unbelievers), through whose countries he passed, were turned to regard him with indifference or sometimes with pitiful compassion; and so the ferocity of man was not added to the perils of the way. At length even such chance intercourse with savage tribes as served to link him with his race altogether ceased; and save his own hurried breathing, no sound of life broke the solitude, as panting and parched he toiled up the steep face of a rocky range of mountains through which the river had cloven its way. When he had gained the crest and descended once more to the channel of the stream, the hopelessly persistent windings of the crags aroused a tremulous quiver as he thought of their barren surface, and the miserable remnant of dates plucked from the last palm grove, which alone his scrip contained. His strength failed as his resolution wavered, and the sight of a gloomy gorge from which the river emerged, quickened the impulses which the instinctive love of life had awakened. He hesitated; but he struggled, and conquered his doubt. He had chosen his own goal; he had registered his vow; he must strive to accomplish its fulfilment, or, if Allah willed it, die.

With resolute step he entered the dark ravine, and toiled on steadily as before, little conceiving that he had stumbled only at the very threshold of success. For this mountain pass speedily expanded in semicircular ranges, and the gloom loomed only in the rear. But yet, the brilliant sun no longer scorched the wanderer, and the vital essence of its beams was blended with an ethereal atmosphere which bathed him like a ripple from the fountain of life, dissipating every trace of exhaustion, of hunger, and of thirst. Crags still rose before him, but grouped in forms of grandeur and harmony; and no longer presenting the dull hues of arid rock, they glowed with the brilliant lustre of polished silver. Harassed no more by fatigue, he still pressed on for many days. The rocks of silver gave place to mountains of the purest gold. The pebbles beneath his feet glistened with the ore, or flashed with the sparkling colours of emeralds, opals, and rubies. Circling and bubbling over this brilliant bed the young river flowed vigorously along, with a volume of water not yet sufficiently diminished to indicate the close proximity of its source. But the pilgrim's steadfastness was soon to be rewarded. In the distance he descried as it were a massive pillar of crystal reaching up into the clouds, enthroned amid the gleaming mountains and flashing in the sunbeams —

"Under the Ethiop line
By Nilus' head, enclosed with shining rock
A whole day's journey high."*

---

* Milton's *Paradise Lost*, iv. 283.

Ere the twilight dimmed the crests of the hills, he approached the wondrous creation; and lo! it was the object of his search. The blessed Nile, bright with the light of the divine presence, was descending from the heavens, and commencing its earthly career on a sparkling beach of diamonds.

The legend of which this is something like an outline was, perhaps, intended by the writer of the book from which it was said to have been read, as an allegory indicating the inestimable character of the river by ascribing to it a birth so sacred amid accessories which popularly, and particularly to the Eastern mind, are the types and manifestations of pre-eminent value; and in this point of view, the fable in its scope and structure was not wanting in beauty or fancy. But on the occasion I have mentioned, when it was retailed, the listeners and reciter thought only of a literal interpretation, and were disposed to embrace so satisfactory a solution of a problem so mysterious yet so interwoven with the daily current of their lives. They were more than half content to believe as the Hindoos, who also

"Draw
Their holy Ganges from a skiey fount."
Wordsworth's *Excursion*.

## CHAP. XI.

### THE PRESENT TENANTS OF THE TOMBS AND THEIR RULERS.

Though far from devoid of the natural desire of acquisition, and secretly practising it to some slight extent, as we have seen, the *fellaheen*, with the bare necessaries of existence, spend their lives in general, if fitful, contentment, or, perhaps it might be more correct to say, in unintelligent indifference. Subject to blows, insults, robbery, at the hand of every man in authority, they are depressed for the moment like the beaten hound; but let the pressure pass away, and, still like the poor beast, they are speedily again light-hearted and merry. Theirs is not now the callousness of the helpless, it is the degradation of soul produced by the lengthened pressure of serfdom. But they are not altogether insensible to their position, still less so to their wrongs; and in their evening conclaves, the shrewder among them will at times illustrate the sad topic in the favourite Oriental fashion, by some such parable as the following, which was very popular at Goorneh.

It happened once that a Sultan captured a lion, which it pleased him to keep for his royal pleasure. An officer was appointed especially to have in charge the well-being of the beast, for whose sustenance the command of his highness allotted the daily allowance of six pounds of meat. It instantly occurred to the keeper, that no one would be a bit the wiser were he to feed his dumb ward with four pounds, and dispose of the remaining two for his own benefit. And this he did, until the lion gradually lost his sleekness and vigour, so as to attract the attention of his royal master. There must be something wrong, said he; I shall appoint a superior officer to make sure that the former faithfully does his duty.

No sooner was the plan adopted, than the first goes to his new overseer; and convincing him very readily that if the proceeds of two pounds be conveyed to their pockets, the meat will be far better employed than in feeding the lion, they agree to keep their own counsel and share the profit between them. But the thirst of the new comer soon becomes pleasantly excited by the sweets of peculation. He talks the matter over with his subordinate, and they have no difficulty in discovering that the lion might very well be reduced to three pounds a day.

Drooping and emaciated, the poor beast pines in his cage, and the Sultan is more perplexed than before. A third official shall be ordered, he declares, to inspect the other two: and so it was. But they only wait for his first visit to demonstrate to him the folly of throwing away the whole of six pounds of meat upon the lion, when with so little trouble they could retain three, being one a-piece for themselves. In turn his appetite is quickened and he sees no reason why four pounds should not be abstracted from his ward's allowance. The brute, he tells his colleagues, can do very well on two, and if not, he can speak to nobody in complaint, so why need they lose the gain? And thus the lion, reduced to starvation-point, languishes on, robbed and preyed upon by the overseers set to care for him, whose multiplication has but added to his miseries.

Such is the quaint simile; but to render it intelligible to those who do not know the nature of local administration in Upper Egypt, it will be necessary to indicate the outline of the system. In each village a *Shekh-belled*, a native, as it were presides, through whom are transmitted, and in great measure executed, the various orders of superiors, connected with taxation, public labour, levies, and, in short, all the functions of government. Over every group of villages is a *Kasheff*, a Turkish officer, who, in some cases, however, has a different title. In wider districts still, a *Nazer* perambulates, to inspect the Kasheffs, as the name signifies. And above the Nazers a *Moodir* sits in each of what may be termed three provinces, which are in turn under the control of a Pasha residing at Osioot, who rules over the whole of Upper Egypt. With the *Moodirs* the ordinary fellaheen do not come much in contact, except on special occasions connected with criminal or military business; but they shrewdly suppose that these, having generally to secure their own official position by presents, require similar reminders from the functionaries beneath, who can only wring the means from one source. As for the Nazers and Kasheffs, their periodical visits afford very palpable reason for ascertaining the extent and nature of their capacity for *backsheesh*. But the cormorant whose greed they know best, and whom the *fellaheen* most peculiarly hate, although in secret, is their own fellow, often their own kinsman, the *Shekh-belled*. It is of course impossible to tell whether all of this class, as of any class, deserve unconditional reprobation, but whenever it has happened to me to know anything of them they are universally detested and detestable. Nor is this difficult to understand, for their extortions, although they may not always be very great in amount, come peculiarly home to the sufferers. Is government labour to be allotted? bribes to the Shekh may relieve those who are able or willing to pay. Does the Kasheff come for the taxes before they are ready? delay is perhaps purchased by a present of three or four hundred piastres to that official, and in raising this from his people the Shekh will lay on another hundred for his own use. Is a certain amount of provisions ordered from the village for military stores, or any other public purpose? the Shekh in collecting it will take care to have a considerable picking for himself.

Neither is this sliding scale of rulers the only leech with which the *fellaheen* are familiar. The military police, the *askar*, of whose operations we shall presently have a specimen, will, when in their neighbourhood, come and live upon them at free quarters, afterwards seizing their horses or donkeys, in the midst of work, to ride on to the next village, there turning them adrift, and so compelling the owners to follow at their heels. The surveyor, who marks out the line of canals which, for the general good, have annually to be cut, has also a palm to be crossed to secure a favourable or equitable apportionment of labour to the given village. And so it goes on, wherever there is public duty to be performed or authority to be perverted. In fact, the one feature of the system of corruption appears to be its consistent completeness; and it is not to be wondered at that the *fellah* should perceive in the multiplicity of his guardians only so many craving mouths to be fed. Thus too, when all are supposed to be recipients, who is to listen to the complaint of the spoiled? And hence in the apologue of the lion, deafness on the part of those who should hear, is transmuted into the correlative equivalent of dumbness on the part of those who might speak.

The circumstances and conditions of life, some of which I have sketched in this and the previous chapter, as characterising the dwellers in the Theban tombs, are in certain respects a state of affairs altogether of the present generation. Fifty or sixty years ago the controlling power of a central government was hardly felt at all in those and other portions of the Upper country. Local hereditary jurisdictions, yielding then a fitful and uncertain allegiance, but now abolished, thwarted uniformity of action, or in conjunction with incursions from the Desert, even nourished turbulence;

and among the villages of the Thebäis, including those of Goorneh, violence, robbery, and murder, arising from their respective blood feuds, which even yet are not entirely unproductive of such fruits, were not uncommon features in their career. The stern vigour of Mohammed Ali reduced this lawlessness wherever it had cropped out, into something like order. And there followed, even in remote districts, security to person and property, at least from open rapine, if unfortunately the same guarantee to either failed to hold against executive venality.

And so external disturbing causes having assumed a kind of routine course, the tenor of existence does not much diverge from the ordinary outline which I have indicated. The Theban troglodites, born in the gloom of their sepulchral retreats, spend their childhood as nude, dirty little imps; and almost as soon as a scrap of clothing is given to them, there is from time to time some kind of field-work for them to do. The girls, who as women are usually well-formed, but not even comely in face, are wives at twelve or fourteen. At seventeen or eighteen the men, who, although not large, are generally strong in frame, and quick in expression, are also married. Then their years are passed in agricultural, or such other occupations as have been mentioned, or in the search for relics, varied by occasional attempts to evade the payment of their taxes, constantly met, but not always defeated, by ready application of the stick. And so, with marked immunity from the more trivial bodily ailments, they play their inglorious parts, until (not very frequently at an advanced age) the end comes. When it approaches, the prospect is commonly accepted both by the dying, and by those among whom they lived, with a demeanour so stoical that it might be supposed to be indifference, did it not spring from resignation trained by a constant dwelling on the irreversible nature of the decrees of a predetermined fate.

But in the comparatively vegetative quietude, which characterises the life of the *fellaheen*, there are from time to time breaks so absorbing and exciting to young and old, as to form a chapter rather than an episode in their story. These periodical disturbances of the balance are produced by that which is to them most abhorrent and alarming, — the conscription for the viceregal army. Until the ambitious career was checked on which Mohammed Ali entered, after having won the position of viceroy of Egypt, the draughts which he relentlessly made on the population, to procure soldiers for the prosecution of his schemes, were such as to cripple the resources of the country, and are still remembered by the people with dismay. It is natural under any circumstances, that a conquered race long governed by a military rule without the slightest approach to kindness or conciliation, if they are too heavily burdened, or too deeply degraded to think of systematic resistance, should only with many a pang allow the flower of their sons to be dragged from them by force, and added like so many cattle or chattels to the possessions of those they looked upon as oppressors. If this be a natural phase of such a system in its ordinary application, how much the more as referring to the time, of which I speak, when the lot of the Egyptian soldier was bitter indeed once. For, torn from his friends, he was from that moment lost to them for ever, without a chance of their learning aught of his fate, beyond the miserable certainty that he would perish in those Syrian wars, where life was so prodigally thrown away, in which they could have no interest, and the very object of which they knew not. It is not surprising therefore that the *fellaheen* should have regarded being included in a levy as the greatest possible curse: and so inveterate was then their repugnance to be impressed, that young men and boys by hundreds had the forefinger of the right hand cut off, or an eye deprived of sight, so as to render them unfit for military service,—practices not yet altogether disused.

The government of the present Pasha, whose strongly manifested desire to increase the number and efficiency of the troops, and the lavish expenditure upon them, have partly tended to embarrass the finances of the country, has greatly ameliorated the condition of the soldiery. They are now well paid, well fed, well clothed, bound to serve only for a fixed term, and I am assured, well treated. Still, the people are hardly less reluctant than before, to be obliged to furnish men for the ranks; and although those who are taken, are said to become reconciled after a short time to their new life, and to enjoy its superior comforts, every effort of ingenuity is made by bribery, where practicable, or otherwise, to be saved from the dreaded *nizam* (conscription). This, no doubt, is in a great measure, owing to the existence of those natural feelings adverted to already, to the sad recollection of the past, and to the complete isolation for life from home and friends, which impressment is still, although not necessarily, held to imply. But it is very clear that another very sufficient reason presents itself in the harsh preliminaries for procuring recruits constantly enacted before the whole country, which are calculated to arouse hatred and distrust. It is not likely to be enticing to successors, that the conscripts when chosen, are chained together like galley-slaves to prevent their escape, and so sent down the river in crowded boat-loads. Nor is the step which immediately precedes this more alluring; for the clumsy arrangement of assembling for the purpose of selection, all the men within certain ages, at (to many) the distant capital of the *moodireéh* in which they live, often requires compulsion, which, although in one sense necessary, is unfortunately put forth in a most ignominious not to say cruel manner. As an illustration of this feature in the life at Goorneh, I may describe what occurred during my residence there.

It happened that the Pasha's government, which had lately disbanded a considerable force, ordered a small number to be raised, to consist of the best men procurable from the districts in which the levy was to be made. The *moodireéh* of Esneh, a large tract of country, had to furnish, it was stated, two hundred; and of these the proportion that fell upon the village immediately surrounding the house I lived in, was one.

In order, however, that this one man might be selected, all between the ages of sixteen and twenty, amounting to something like thirty or forty, were commanded to repair to the town of Esneh, a distance of thirty miles. When the proper time for their departure arrived, a small party of *askar*, whom I have already mentioned as a sort of military-police, if indeed the name be not considerably degraded by applying it to them, came to see that the eligible *fellaheen* were duly sent off. These *askar* are chiefly Arnauts from Albania and Roumelia, or Turks, or half-breeds in which the blood of either of those races is the preponderating element — and search where you will, more fierce-looking ruffians will not be easily found. Nor is their appearance belied by their deeds and character. They are unhappily allowed an amount of license in their treatment of the peasantry which a conquering army in a hostile territory might well be reprobated for exercising; and the cowardly manner in which they bully the helpless people, defying simple rights of property, cannot but excite indignation. An onlooker longs to hope that the government would determine, in the interests of bare justice and for the common benefit of rulers and ruled, firmly to restrain their excesses, or, better still, to sweep them from the country, substituting in their place a more creditable constabulary. When the party of these *askar*, or soldiers, five in number, approached the village, the majority of the fellaheen who had sons of the prescribed age, fled with them quietly to the mountains, or concealed themselves in the inmost recesses of the larger tombs, arranging that their wives or other relatives should bring them food and water by night.

As soon as the soldiers arrived, the *Shekh-belled*, by name Lasum, was required to set about his duty of collecting the young men and boys specified in the list drawn up by the authorities from classified, but apparently inaccurate, enumerations of the population, which they possess. By the end of the day he had gathered together nearly twenty, and four or five women, the mothers or wives of others who had fled; and they were all placed in a sort of mud-built guard-house for the night, under charge of the soldiers. About eight o'clock, when it was quite dark, the moon not having yet risen, and light clouds obscuring the usually brilliant stars, a fierce *mêlée* suddenly arose immediately outside our court-yard. Guns were fired, men were yelling defiantly, women screeching, and dogs baying. In an instant the gate of the yard became the scene of a struggle; one party, as the noise seemed to indicate — for it was impossible to see from the window — having rushed inside, shutting the door in the face of the others, and holding it fast against their thrusts and blows. Conceiving the cause of the whole to be that some of my workmen, whom the soldiers wished to seize, had thus taken refuge, we hurried out to insist on a more pacific arrangement. The assailants, however, had already retired, and the assailed were making off with the greatest alacrity.

But I then and subsequently learned that the fight was of an entirely different nature from what I had supposed. It appeared that about sunset, the *Shekh-belled* had gone to the house of a man named Baroor in his absence, and brought away two of his sons. Baroor, who probably intended fleeing with them to the desert, was indignant on his return to find them gone, and thought himself peculiarly injured and insulted by the Shekh having kept them in his *own* house, instead of placing them in the regular manner with the others who were similarly circumstanced. Accordingly, he collected his brothers and cousins to the number of twelve or fifteen, and came to attack Shekh Lasum, who lived in a range of tombs close to the wall of our court-yard, and who, chancing to be passing at the time with some of his friends, was driven inside the gate in the way I have mentioned. The guns, which belonged to the Baroor party, were fired more perhaps to strike terror than to do actual mischief, and only one charge, as I ascertained, contained a bullet, which was fired in the air. But there can be little doubt, as in fact the leader avowed to me, that Lasum, against whom he had an old enmity, or who in any case was hated as most *Sheiekh-belled* are, on the very sufficient grounds I have formerly stated, would have been killed, had opportunity offered in the moment of anger, if indeed this result or something like it, had not formed part of the original intention.

But, although the expedition happily failed to

accomplish any revengeful object, it had another effect, which probably was not contemplated. The soldiers who were established at the guard-house about fifty yards off, no sooner heard the shots and the struggle than, doubtful of what this rising in the dark might bode, they shouldered their muskets and decamped, leaving their prisoners to take care of themselves, which they did by instantly making for the hills.

Next morning the discreet goalers returned, accompanied by the Kasheff, who sent a messenger to inform the fugitives, that if those who were ordered to go to Esneh, did not come back within eight and forty hours, their cattle and sheep, if they or their families possessed any, would be seized, and their houses given up to be spoiled and pillaged by the soldiers. With hardly an exception this brought them all down from the mountains, and the threat was not put in execution, as it had been in several instances in an adjoining village. Wishing to see in what manner it had been carried out there, I went next day to one of the houses, as if for another purpose; and, although the whole place was not by any means reduced to ruin, there was every evidence of rapine in a small hoard of corn strewn upon the ground, a handmill broken in fragments, water and other jars, almost the only furniture, if the word is applicable in a *fellah's* dwelling, smashed in pieces, and every little mud-built keeping place rifled, and its door burst open, or torn from its fastenings. A sight like this was rather a melancholy exposition of the crude directness with which determination on the one side dealt with contumacy on the other; but what could be thought of the sore and swollen hands of the wife and sister of the owner of the house, who, in consequence of his having concealed himself with his sons were beaten with a stick, not simply in the cowardly anger of the soldiers, but in the presence of the Kasheff, on the principle that they were implicated, and that the punishment would be repeated until the men should give themselves up. With regard to the feelings which proceedings of this kind were likely to excite, while reason and humanity might be equally shocked, it was necessary to remember that, although entirely indefensible, much must be allowed for the characteristic unconciliatory spirit of Eastern rule, accustomed to forms happily now, if not of old time, or even yet universally, abhorrent to European conceptions; and that it may be said with some truth of the people of Egypt, that long centuries of serfdom have deadened their sensibilities and produced a degraded nature which renders them difficult to manage without strong compulsion. But with whatever justice it might be urged that it is necessary to deal with them resolutely, it is impossible to witness without pain and disappointment the methods employed by an ignorant and often brutal executive.

On the day the young men set out for Esneh, the village was left nearly empty, for their fathers and others of their male relations went with them, while numbers of the women followed for some distance.

It had been promised by the Kasheff that the disobedience which they at first contemplated should be overlooked in the event of their departure within the given time; and it had even been arranged that the night attack of the Baroors was not to be mentioned to the *Moodir*. But, when they came before him, one of that party incautiously accused Shekh Lasum of bribery, who recriminated by telling what they had done, which opened up the whole story, and secured a severe application of the bastinado for nearly every one of them, except the leader. When the controversy began, he adroitly saw to what it might lead, quietly withdrew from the divan, and got fairly away ere his name was called for punishment. Nor, having escaped at the time, did it appear that measures were taken to call him to account again, extraordinary as that may seem, after the others had suffered so severely for an act undertaken at his instigation.

The order for the conscription had reached the Kasheff, and so had been made known to the people some days before the occurrence which I have described. In the interval I had earnest prayers from some of my workmen, beseeching me to do what I could to save their sons from being taken; but I could only make one reply — that I would not interfere in the matter at all. It was evident that I could not do so with justice, as between one and another, and I also felt that even if I had desired to, or could, exert any influence in individual cases by requesting the local officials to spare certain men for my service, it would have been improper for me to attempt to obstruct in their ordinary course the operations of subordinates of the government, as I could only have done so in consequence of possessing any authority derived in virtue of a *firman* obtained for me from the government itself.

And in thus alluding to the Egyptian government, it will not be out of place to observe that, whatever may be its desire with regard to the general internal polity of the country, it can never do itself justice with such a system and such an executive as now exist. From this remark, it will not be understood that the actual state of things is of the nature of a retrogression, and that the present government as such is on this particular account deserving of special reprobation. On the contrary, from its being more amenable to external influences, even if these do sometimes percolate through dubious channels, and from the progressive tendencies which it has in various directions exhibited, we should probably be correct in saying that, while the local administration may in, and within range of, the two cities, Alexandria and Cairo, have been in some respects considerably improved, it is certainly nowhere worse now, and generally it may be better, than at any period since Mohammed Ali consolidated the pashalik. In fact it is not a question of individual or dynastic demerit, but of traditional continuity. To the people therefore the existing condition of the executive is no new burden or unaccustomed degradation. Happily for them, too, in one sense, lamentably in another, the terrorism, the venality, above all the indignity with which they are treated, which we as onlookers, did we judge only according to our own sensations, might think would harrow their very souls, glance much more lightly off the indurated natures of those who with generations of predecessors, have known no lighter fate. The simple words of the old Scottish chronicler, are true alike in defining our incapacity to estimate their feelings, as in affirming our inexperience of suffering:—

> " He that ay has livit fre
> May nocht knaw wele the propirte,
> The angir, na the wrechit dom,
> That is couplit to foul thrildom." *

But although we may thus believe that the pressure is more endurable to them, it is impossible for any one familiar with a better state of things not to regret that so considerable a portion of mankind, under a settled government, with a place almost or altogether within the circle of European states, should remain fettered with circumstances so entirely ill-calculated to raise them in the scale of reasonable beings, or contribute to their material prosperity. There can be no doubt that to accomplish those ends, they, like other races in similar

* Barbour's *Bruce*, Bk. iv. 55, Spalding Club edition.

conditions, would need to be ruled by a strong and determined hand, if not less with due recognition of equity and some enlightenment of purpose. That their Turkish masters have meted out to them amply the first of these requirements will readily be admitted, but how much of the others it would be difficult to add. In the wide tract over which the Osmanlis became dominant, they have followed, and practically, in any real sense, have hardly advanced beyond the first simple canon of the spoiler. Relentless as conquerors, ruthlessly exacting as governors, they have ever dealt with subject territory and peoples as fierce natures might treat useful animals of the lower creation, without the slightest regard to their welfare, arising either from justice or sentiment, or even from the foresight of self-interest. Exceedingly selfish, and oppressive not merely as collective masters, but also, there is reason to believe, in large proportion among the governing class, as individual men, they have ruled only to triumph or to plunder, and have therefore administered only to degrade. Wherever they established a footing, any languishing germs of the drooping Byzantine, or rootless Saracenic civilization with which they came in contact, withered; and barbarism, if sometimes restrained in its more violent developments, was virtually deepened or confirmed. Looking to the present, even that capacity for command which of old distinguished them, coupled with a certain nobility (of expression, however, rather than of character), is clouded in the dominant or official class by the pervading corruption and venal decrepitude, which naturally overtook those who grew up within a system that knew not how to make adequate advances from rule to government, under the changed conditions of fixed possesion.

It is this on the one hand, coupled on the other with the complete political inaptitude of the lower stratum of the Turkish population proper, which is calculated to beget hopelessness as to what is termed the "regeneration" of Turkey itself under *that* race. If, however, there be one part of the Turkish dominions as such where rational reforms might take root, with some prospect of getting beyond a barren unreality, and reaching a self-sustaining, productive growth, it is Egypt. The comparatively homogeneous character of the mass of the population removes various sources of difficulty. The geographical position of the country, as the highway between the West and the East, is another favourable circumstance; for whatever government it may have will thus not merely be, like the Porte, familiarised with admonitions to improvement, but must, as an inevitable participitant, become so far interwoven with certain of the practical results of European progress. Then again, supposing some energy for internal reform infused thus, or otherwise begotten in the central power, the direct and speedy communication with all parts of the country, possible from its physical characteristics, would render local administration easily amenable to determined inspection and control.

And it is only by endeavouring to secure such favourable conditions for the welfare of the great body of its subject population, as fall within the province of a government to provide, that the existing supremacy in Egypt would have some prospect of prosperity and stability. More ambitious manifestations of an advancing tendency may be very well; but the improvement of the state of the people is the real test as well as the fruit of progress. The Suez canal scheme, for instance, full of peril to the present rule, as it may eventually be, whether as a success or a failure, might, from a different point of view, which it is not difficult to conceive, commend itself to the Egyptian government, on diplomatic and other grounds. And it would, in certain relations, be creditable to the spirit of that government to countenance in various ways within prudent limits such an undertaking. But, as well as considering the risks of pecuniary responsibility and territorial concession, the influence of the enterprise on the general resources of the country and the well-being of the people, were the true points to be kept in view, at once as a matter of policy and duty. The accomplishing of a given end, might, if possible of achievement, be desirable or advantageous; but the attainment of it may be entirely beyond the means of the expectant beneficiary, or be too dearly purchased. It is, therefore, strongly to be hoped, that if the bold project in question be seriously persevered in, any definitively sanctioned undertaking on the part of the Egyptian government to supply workmen, should be of the most modified character. The carrying out of an engagement to furnish "enforced labour" in large draughts, would be to rivet all the evils of the past and the present, to deepen the springs of internal weakness, and to thrust aside hopes of future improvement. Did we judge also by the experience of the former use of this prerogative, in the construction of the Mahmodcëh canal between Alexandria and the Nile some forty years ago, embanked, as the local phrase is, with the bones of the labourers, then we might indeed echo, even more sadly, the old lamentation of Ezekiel, and "wail for the multitudes of Egypt." But there would be every reason to expect that operations carried on now, under different auspices, and under such circumstances as to attract the eye of the whole civilised world, would not be characterised by the inhumanity of older days; and that any amount of suffering and death beyond that inevitable in the employment of large bodies of men, under very difficult conditions as to sustenance and shelter, would not be tolerated. In fact the evils to be counted upon are not so much of this nature, as those that would affect the internal economy of the country; and they are prominently two. First, the reduced agricultural population is even at present insufficient to cultivate all the available soil, and any considerable abstraction of field labour, which must of course come from this class, would so far sap the most important productive capabilities of the country. And second, to procure large masses of labourers for a distant work, and the constantly necessary recruits, would require the unceasing exercise of strong compulsion,— thus encouraging the worst characteristics of the present local administration; increasing among the people that sense of personal insecurity and oppression so fatal to their improvement; and fixing with firmer root throughout the land the very causes of retardation and misery which chiefly overshadow it.

It is the eradication of these which ought, even for its own sake, to be the first consideration of any Egyptian government. It could not indeed hope, even if it had the enlightenment to wish, to remove by a single sweep one chief obstacle to good government — the antipathy of blood, or rather the contumely with which a dominant race visit an inferior people whom they may have subjugated. Even nations as advanced in intelligence as the modern English and the French, professing to act according to different lights, and at least avowing a policy of beneficence (often, however, it must be admitted, but feebly developed), have by no means mastered individual and galling manifestations of this Nemesis of lost liberty, for example in India and Algeria*; and the less have they been able to do so from the wide divergence in civilization, habits, and creed between the rulers and the ruled. But while no government can subvert

---

* The recent rebellion has brought into prominence facts which show with only too great clearness this phase of English rule in India; and in Algeria I have had occasion to observe that a similar state of matters is not less, but probably more, distinctly marked.

this as yet invariable psychical phenomenon, by mere edictal power, it can do much to prevent the permanence of its operation by adjusting the balance of its own corporate procedure, by rigidly restraining excesses on the part of its officials, by infusing into administrative acts a spirit of unbiassed equity, diminishing within the limits of strong government both privilege and disability, and so removing, along with many causes of hatred on the one side and contempt on the other, the most serious barriers in the way of a thriving internal polity.

And, independently of the well-being of the people, or of any abstract theories, the interest of Turkish rule in Egypt as a mere selfish question would be to direct its efforts to the improvement of its relations with its people. With a fixed tenure and a perfectly subdued population, its interest is altogether opposed to the perpetuation of a system in which ferocity, ignorance, and corruption in the local administration prey upon the vitals of the nation. The evils springing from the pervading rottenness of the executive, rebound upon the government with a weight second only to that with which it falls upon the people. For the productive resources of the country are tapped at their very fountain, are drained off hither and thither as they filter through the filthy banks along which they must flow; and who need be surprised if, notwithstanding the blessings of climate, fertility and position, they should attain only the dimensions of a languid and uncertain stream.

Can it, then, be expected that under the existing supremacy in Egypt, a progressive course will be consistently followed conducive to its own continuance? It is the general interest of Europe, politically, that this portion especially of the Turkish dominions should, under present circumstances, remain in the established order, and awaken no necessity or pretence for the struggle that must arise from any attempted change in possession. But it is not less the interest of humanity that the tide of civilization should advance along the valley of the Nile. That it should find its way gently through existing channels would be a process to be desired, and every approach to it should be encouraged. But if not thus, then it must be hoped that in the course of events a new race of masters may develop the useful career to which Egypt would seem to be capable of being made largely to contribute. Her greatness in the past was of one kind; her post in the future would be of another. The subject of her early influence was the plastic youth of nearly a whole untutored world; the influence of which she may yet be the medium, though comparatively local in its sphere of operation, would not be less beneficent. Centres of dominion have no phœnix germ. Power, once dead, springs on the same soil, it would seem, no more. Nor instinct with generative activity as Aristotle declared the Nile Valley to be, is this, in its former sense, likely to be among the products. But the position of the country, with its magnificent river forming the great and, in fact, the only highway for intercourse with a vast tract of the African continent, points to the humbler, if hardly less noble, office which Egypt may be expected one day to fulfil under whatever foreign tutelage. Respectably good government, a thriving people, agricultural activity, some commercial enterprise, are surely not beyond the possibilities in store for the future of a land so blessed by nature. And the seeds of social amelioration once fructifying there would diffuse, as it were, sporadic influences into the dense barbarism beyond, opening the way for humanising, if we dare not say civilising, some of the most degraded races of mankind.

LONDON
PRINTED BY SPOTTISWOODE AND CO.
NEW-STREET SQUARE

913.32
R473

Wilkinson's Thebes
Stanley's Sinai & Palestine
Champollion
Hay
Birch
Lepsius (Prussian)
Salt
Rosini

**STANFORD UNIVERSITY
LIBRARY
Stanford, California**

Lightning Source UK Ltd.
Milton Keynes UK
UKOW042045220212

187765UK00008B/141/P